MY PU

MY PUBLIC RELATIONSHIPS

Autobiography

Lyndon Harris

© Lyndon Harris 2008

Published by
Marylyn Publishers
17 Pantglas Park, Llandeilo
Carmarthenshire, SA19 7HN

A CIP catalogue record for this book is
available from the British Library.

ISBN 978-0-9560836-0-9

Cover photograph:
'SCAMP' my true faithful friend
surveying the Herefords

Printed and bound in Wales by
Dinefwr Press Ltd.
Rawlings Road, Llandybie
Carmarthenshire, SA18 3YD

Contents

Introduction

FROM AN EARLY AGE I have always been interested in the past and particularly in what my forebears did for a living, their thoughts and what kind of people they were. I always felt how sad it was that individuals who were so full of life should have to die and that nobody would know who or what they were, or even whether they ever existed.

After a great deal of family cajoling I have succumbed to attempt to jot some of the highlights of my brief occupation of this planet and to try and describe the many interesting characters who have crossed my path over the years.

In particular, my message is aimed at my grandchildren who have been, and are, a source of great pleasure and pride to me and at least they will have some idea of what made their old grandpa tick! None of this would have been possible without the backing and support of Mary, my wife, whose culinary and intellectual attributes have never ceased to be a source of inspiration to me.

Lyndon Harris

The Early Years

MY JOURNEY STARTS ON Sunday, June 7th, 1931, at St. Tydfil's Hospital, Merthyr Tydfil, in what was then the County of Glamorgan, South Wales. My father, Richard Harris, my mother Ann Jane Harris, always called 'Nancy,' together with my brother Arthur, were living at 14, Well Street, The Quar, Merthyr Tydfil, in the same house that my mother, brother and grandfather had been born and where my great-grandfather had lived, just a stone throw away from his workshop, where he conducted business as a builder and undertaker, a business which my grandfather, William Thomas, ran successfully until his death in 1947.

Well Street, the site of my first home was on a steep hill in a quiet part of the town. At the lower end, in my grandfather's workshop, was St. Tydfil's Well from which Merthyr derived its name. My mother's brother Uncle Lyndon and his wife Gladys had lived in the house just before us and we moved in on the death of Aunt Gladys who died during childbirth. Lyndon has been a name associated with my family for several generations and originated when my mother's great aunt married a John Lyndon in the nineteenth century. My only other forename – Eric, was conjured up by my father who was friendly with Eric Warrilow who kept a music shop with his wife Alice and who later became a media photographer around Merthyr. I remember going to Port Talbot in 1937 with my father to visit Eric and was fascinated by the shiny saxophones and trumpets in his shop.

My earliest recollections are associated with No. 14. We had a rocking horse, 'Dobbin,' who featured in one of the first photographs taken of me in the front garden, with me perched on it sitting in front of Arthur. This was taken in 1934 by Maisie Richards, a neighbour living next door down. Shortly after this photo session, we moved from Merthyr. My father had obtained a job in Porthcawl as a commercial traveller which necessitated the move. I remember vividly the removal van loading up and seeing my beloved 'Dobbin' being carried into the van. This was the first move from Merthyr for my family since my birth. My parents and Arthur had lived in Aberavon before I was born for a brief period and it was there that they were to meet lifelong friends 'Uncle Wyndham,' 'Aunty Muriel' and their daughter, Joan. Both my father and mother were born and bred in Merthyr as were many generations of our family before them.

My father came from a line of farmers, blacksmiths and poets. His father, also Richard Harris, was born at Heolgerrig Farm, Penyrheol, and later farmed Coed Meurig Farm before moving to the Cefn Hotel where he died in 1931 when I was six months old. My mother came from a line of builders, accountants, ironfounders and ministers of religion.

I will delve in more detail into the pedigree aspects of the family later suffice to say that the move to Porthcawl was quite an upheaval for them leaving friends and relatives in Merthyr. So, in 1934 my mother and father together with my brother Arthur aged ten and me aged three, embarked for the sunny shores of Porthcawl to a house which would be for the next five years our new home.

Happy times

Settling down in Porthcawl was quite a contrast to life in Merthyr Tydfil. Sitting on the shores of the Bristol Channel the town had an open fresh aspect which was a complete contrast to industrialised Merthyr in 1934. The house we moved into . . . 86, Suffolk Place, was a short walking distance from the promenade and was at the end of a cul-de-sac with a wide lane at the rear adjacent to Lewis Place. At the end of the lane were fields and a small woods where countless hours were spent playing makeshift golf and football. The undulating footpath at the end of the lane served as a track for dirt cycling and I recall many a happy hour riding on the crossbar of Arthur's friend Tony Lee's bicycle as we sped up and down the path. Nowadays, these fields and the woods have gone to be replaced by housing and a school.

To supplement my father's income as a commercial traveller, my mother undertook bed and breakfast for visitors to this popular seaside resort. The house was not overlarge and in order to accommodate them in the house my father built a large garage in the rear garden with accommodation upstairs for Arthur and me when space was needed on rare occasions. Porthcawl proved to be a magnet for our relatives and a steady stream of them descended on Suffolk Place in the summertime. In slack periods I used to utilise the upper garage as a 'den' to play with my pals. My immediate circle of friends included Alan Danter who lived in Lewis Place. His father was a painter and decorator with a shop in town. He too lived in a cul-de-sac, in the end house, and their front garden was always occupied by paint carts and tins of paint. Alan's seventh birthday party was the first I had ever attended.

Other close friends included Trevor Ball, also living in Lewis Place near the back of our house, with whom I played a lot. His mother was a nice homely lady and though not well off always had a warm welcome for me. It was Trevor's mother who first gave me bread and butter pudding to try and boy did I enjoy it! Opposite Trevor lived the Lee family. Mrs Lee was a district nurse and her husband a baker. Beside their son Tony, who was Arthur's best friend, they had two daughters, Sheila and Honor. Honor was the same age as me and was a pretty blond little girl who I thought was very cool. Lower down Suffolk Place lived a boy named Michael Griffiths whose claim to fame was that he once threw an empty tin can at me while I was riding on the crossbar of Tony Lee's bike and caught me on the middle of my forehead causing a bloody mess. I bore the slight mark it left for many years before it finally disappeared.

Next door lived a young lady by the name of Molly Taylor. She was engaged to be married and I thought the world of her. Her bathroom was opposite ours and I used to sing popular songs which she enjoyed listening to. I had a reasonable singing voice and would sit on the wall at the bottom of the rear garden singing my heart out. Mrs Ball, Trevor's mother, was particularly keen on my rendering of 'Play To Me Gypsy' and would shout over the wall for me to sing it again and again.

It was in Porthcawl that I had my first proper haircut. The barber's was in the main street in the centre of town and it fell to Arthur to take me for this historic event. We arrived at the barber's okay and I was seated in the chair alright, but then things began to deteriorate and I didn't think it was such a good idea, promptly bolting out of the shop running as fast as I could all the way home with Arthur in hot pursuit. The same thing happened when I attended Sunday School for the first time. Again, I was seated in the class and again I decided I'd had enough and in order too calm things down, the teacher had to fetch Arthur out of the older children's class to take me home.

My first introduction to formal education took place in Porthcawl. This commenced in my case at the age of five in 1936. It's an under statement to say that I loathed it from day one. I had to be dragged kicking and screaming to school and Arthur had to be roped in once more to sit with me in class for the first day or two. My memory of my time in the National School there is one of a mixture of emotions. I was in awe of the headmaster Mr Skinner who appeared to me to be seven feet tall (he was in fact over six feet) and looked ominous when he carried his cane. The teachers were great and I learned to read and write to an advanced level quickly. I recall fondly the roaring coal fires with their huge fenders and the rows of bottles of milk warming in front.

Playtime was the best part of the school day and I looked forward to seeing my grandmother 'Mam' appearing over the school wall and throwing down toffees to me. Mam, my father's mother, was a real pal in every sense of the word and I loved her absolutely. She stayed with us for lengthy periods and was an immense help to my parents. It was during this period that my great aunt Mary Jane and great uncle Tom Harris came over on the original *Queen Mary* from the USA, celebrating their Golden Wedding en route (1936). They lived in Youngstown, Ohio and did not have any children, their only son having being killed during the 1914/18 Great War. They visited us in Porthcawl and being a good step dancer, I had to tap dance for them. Tom Harris had worked for my great-great-grandfather Matthew John in Vulcan Foundry, Merthyr, before emigrating to the USA. He was also a prominent Freemason over there and had prospered. It was while we were in Porthcawl that King George V died and was succeeded by his son Edward, Prince of Wales, who then became King Edward VIII and abdicated after a reign of 325 days. Another significant happening at this time was the issuing of gas masks. I can still smell the strong smell of rubber when the mask was placed over one's face and the noise of heavy breathing through the filter. All the children were issued with their masks each mask snug in its square cardboard box.

Another very welcome visitor to our house was Aunty Annie Mary who was my grandmother's first cousin. When Annie Mary's own mother died. She was brought up as my grandmother's sister. She was a very elegant woman who had lost her architect husband some time ago. I always loved to see her coming to stay with us as she drove the latest Rover cars with their polished wood interiors and leather upholstery. Her cars were the first I had ever been in which boasted a radio. She also had one of the most intelligent Fox Terriers one would wish for, named *Billy*. He was to me then a wonder dog and I would not go to sleep at night unless he slept at the foot of the bed. However, as soon as I was asleep he would jump down and go back downstairs. The drives with her up to Rest Bay were great and I can still hear the purr of the Rover engine. If the house was full of visitors she would sleep in the same room as Mam. They got on famously together and we would hear them in the early hours of the morning helpless with laughter at some private joke they never revealed.

Annie Mary's only son – Charles Lyndon Livsey Davies – was a keen yachtsman and Commodore of the Barry Yacht Club. He used to sail the Bristol Channel regularly and in 1937 sailed into Porthcawl harbour and was joined by Arthur and Tony Lee who acted as crew on a trip round to Ferryside in Carmarthenshire. I well remember my father driving my mother and me along the coastal roads from Porthcawl to Ferryside, trying to keep the yacht in sight and the excitement when we saw them sail over the sandbar and enter the Towy Estuary opposite the lifeboat house. Charles entered banking and became captain of a naval frigate *HMS Nigela* during the 1939/45 War. Aunt Annie Mary was related to Richard Livsey, MP for Brecon for many years as a Liberal Democrat and who was later elevated to the House of Lords.

A harrowing experience befell me whilst trying to see the boats in Porthcawl harbour. My father and Uncle Rupert (my mother's youngest brother), and myself went for a walk past the harbour which had a concrete balustrade type wall with holes in it. Me, of course, curious to see the boats about ten feet below must shove my head through one of the holes and could not get it out again. My father and Rupert tugged and pulled to no avail. My ears prevented withdrawal and my cheeks began to swell. Eventually they managed to get me out without having to break the wall, but it taught me a lesson not to attempt anything like that again. My ears were sore for days!

To a child of my age Porthcawl was a magical place to live during the 'thirties. The funfair at Coney Beach was at its peak with its awesome 'figure of eight' sky ride and 'water splash,' both pace setters in their time in South Wales and which brought out the 'wow' factor. In complete contrast I rode my first donkey on the beach there and I went on the miniature steam railway which travelled between the harbour and the funfair along the edge of the original harbour which had been filled in some time previously.

Adjacent to the harbour was the roller skating rink and I can still hear the strains of 'The Skater's Waltz' echoing over the harbour as the couples glided along. Further up the promenade were the two 'top' hotels – The Esplanade and the Seabank. These used to fascinate me especially the Seabank which had 'class' written all over it. Peering through the sea facing windows of this hotel was like looking into a world of glitz ad glamour. My cousin Crecy used to spend some time there with her friends when she visited us from her 'Bohemian' life in London.

My mother and Mam often took me down to sit below the sea wall on the 'Front' and we spent many an hour drinking in the sunshine and fresh air. Some times the ventriloquist put on a show for the children by the paddling pool with his dummy 'Tommy.' This always went down well and held the children in rapture. While on the beach, which at this point was pretty rocky, one would often see the paddle steamers cruising up the Bristol Channel to far away places like Weston-super-Mare or Minehead! Another great thrill at the time was the visit to Porthcawl of the naval destroyer *HMS Echo*. It was quite dramatic to see the ship appear over the horizon and anchor off the town. Campbell paddle steamers were never quite the same to me again after that visit.

The seaside and ice-cream are inseparable and this was when I first encountered the 'stop me and buy one' tricycles that tinkled their routes around town. Names like 'Eldorado' and 'Walls' were pedalled literally. Tubs and wafers came into their own and I was very partial to the triangular iced fruity bar which you pushed up from the base as it was devoured. Nestles chocolate was all the rage too and machines, very similar in function to today's cash dispensers, were to be seen everywhere. On a trip to Rest Bay my father parked the car in the large car park there and at the exit a Nestles chocolate machine was sited next to the car park attendant's box. My father put the coin in to get a bar for me and pulled the slot to pick out the bar. To our astonishment instead of one bar appearing a whole deluge of chocolate bars came out. Needless to say, we didn't have to buy any more chocolate for a very long time.

Walking from our house in Suffolk Place for a distance of some six hundred yards or so across the fields, you came to the edge of what was then a gorse common. A large field bordered the adjacent lane and it was here that a miniature airfield was established. At the top end of the field was an aircraft hangar complete with wind sock and at the bottom of the field which had an appreciable slope, was a low stone wall ideal for preventing sheep from straying. The airfield was occupied by the Pyne family who operated pleasure flights around Porthcawl using De Havilland Gypsy Moth aircraft specially adapted to carry extra passengers. An enclosed cabin was incorporated under the cockpit, with large windows and side doors. On several occasions when roaring down the field to take off, the planes failed to clear the wall and I vividly remember seeing such an incident with the nose of the aircraft in the ground. I never heard of anyone being seriously injured though. The King's Cup Air Race took place at this time and it was exciting to see the aircraft swoop over Porthcawl and Pyne's airfield, dipping their wings in salute to the blue and silver planes on the ground as they flew overhead. The same thrill was experienced when an airship flew over the town during that period.

Motoring has always played a big part in my family life. My father had motor bikes and cars from the time of the Great War. His tales of his exploits on his Rudge Multi motor cycle used to fascinate me. He was very keen on Jowett cars and in 1937, he went to the Jowett factory in Idle, Bradford, to collect a brand new car. I can see it now as it chugged up Suffolk Place on his return home. I say 'chugged' because Jowett cars had twin cylinder, horizontally opposed engines and they literally 'chugged' along. They had big bodywork in relation to the size of engine and were individually hand built. As soon as I had the opportunity I sneaked into the garage to sit in it. I can smell the leather now and see the polished wooden fascia with its large round black instruments with white numbers. The ticking of its clockwork clock was memorable. It had a dark navy blue body and black mudguards and its registration number was – BTX 626.

Not far from Porthcawl on the way to Bridgend, was a stretch of perfectly straight road called 'The Golden Mile.' Locals used to use this as a testing track for their vehicles and motorbikes. My father and Arthur were travelling along it one day and Arthur was surprised when our Jowett reached a flat-out speed of 75 mph. This was exceptional for an eight horsepower car to attain pre-war. Jowett vehicles became very popular in our family. My Uncle, Jack Harris (my father's elder brother), had a series of Jowett vans for his dairy rounds in Cefn Coed, Merthyr. He ran these until his untimely death in 1947.

I must have walked miles when living in Porthcawl, either with my mother or grandparents. My grandmother Thomas loved to tell the tale of when she, Mam, my mother and me, went for a walk up to Rest Bay and I became separated from them. A man passer-by was asked if he had seen me, to which he replied, "Yes." A little boy (me) had asked him, "Have you seen two grandmothers and a girl looking for me?" About the same time, I decided to write to my grandfather in Merthyr and did so with a vague address written on a postcard. He received it alright much to his astonishment and amusement and he kept it until he died. I still have it in my possession.

Arthur was well settled in Bridgend County Secondary School and with friends like Tony Lee and Eric Cattanach was getting along fine. He was there at the same time as Jack Matthews who was to become a famous Welsh rugby international centre. He was dubbed 'Iron Man Matthews' by the New Zealand All Blacks and in later life became a GP. He always had a chat with Arthur whenever their paths crossed. I too, had come to terms with having to go to school but this period of relative peace and tranquillity was about to be brought to a close. My father had secured a better job in England with a paper manufacturers named Cheverton & Laidler based in Bucks. We went to stay with Uncle Wyndham and Aunt Muriel in their new home in High Wycombe. While there, we had a good reconnoitre of the surrounding area and came to the conclusion that St. Albans in Hertfordshire would be a nice and convenient place to live.

My grandmother 'Mam'
(Margaret Harris).

Arthur and me on 'Dobbin' (1934).

Arthur and me on Porthcawl Promenade (1936).

Aunt Mary Jane and Uncle Tom Harris celebrating their Golden Wedding on board the Queen Mary *in 1936.*

Aunt Mary Jane and Uncle Tom Harris (USA).

17

Me on my 'bike. St. Albans, 1938.

My earliest recorded literary work!

Moving Experience

I N LATE 1938, WE SADLY UPPED sticks from Porthcawl and moved to a rented house in Stanley Avenue, St. Albans, Hertfordshire, while our new house was being built. I watched the house going up brick by brick on land which once formed part of the estate of the famous old time music hall artiste, Harry Champion, whose theme song for which he was noted was, 'Any Old Iron.' His nearby mansion called 'Ragged Hall,' had been abandoned by him, it was said, when house building began to encroach upon his privacy. Our site was at that time in the heart of the country just a couple of miles from the centre of St. Albans. The builders were one of the largest in Hertfordshire by the name of H. C. Janes of Luton. When ours was completed we moved in and No. 34, The Mount, Watford Road, St. Albans, Herts., became 'Vaynor' named by my parents after the historic beauty spot near Merthyr where my paternal grandparents got married, pretty Vaynor Church.

Compared to now, prices were ridiculously low in 1938. A three-bed roomed semi-detached could be bought for £500 and a larger detached for around £900 to £1,000! One of the first things we did after moving in was to erect a garage for our beloved Jowett. Arthur designed it and he and my father built it. The house was surrounded by fields and our neighbour was a Mrs Ensor who had been a housekeeper to Leslie Henson another noted artiste. On our other side was a vacant plot and next to that lived the Bird family. I used to play with their two children John and Audrey. I caused a bit of a stir when, in a fit of generosity and gallantry, I cut off all the tulips in Mrs Ensor' front garden and gave them to Audrey.

Time arrived for me to start another new school, this time Mount Pleasant Junior School in Mount Pleasant Lane, Brickett Wood, between St. Albans and Watford. A boy who attended the school and who was to become one of my best friends, was Morris Chalkley.

Morris lived opposite us on Watford Road, his father managed a motor dealership in the town. Not far from Morris lived 'Ginger' Roberts who was Welsh and a breath of home.

Both Morris and Ginger had bicycles and I didn't, which meant my mother and father came under a barrage of persuasive propaganda to buy me a bike. Eventually, they succumbed and I was given a secondhand cycle purchased off some local people for the princely some of £1. I had never ridden a two-wheeled bike before and it took me a couple of days to master it. So, after about the third day, I set off down Ragged Hall Lane to join the main Watford Road and was going down the slope of the lane, when I lost control and went smack into the side of a car travelling along Watford Road. I was thrown off the bike, but luckily, sustained no injuries except to my pride. The front wheel was buckled out of all proportion and I went home to face the music. Had I been a second or so sooner hitting that car, I doubt whether I would be writing this now. I was not allowed to ride it again after it had been repaired, for several months. I never fell off a bicycle again!

I travelled to school by London Transport bus service 321, which covered the route from Uxbridge/Watford to Luton. I got on and off at the *Black Boy* pub at Brickett Wood and vice versa at *The Three Hammers* public house near home. *The Three Hammers* was a picturesque olde world establishment and I don't think it had a vertical wall in the building. Taking everything into consideration, St. Albans was a very pleasant place to live. Events soon took a turn for the worse however, I was playing on the grass verge between the service road and the main Watford road, when my father called me in to listen to the wireless. The prime minister, Neville Chamberlaine, was about to address the nation. My parents sat huddled around our Murphy radio and in a few minutes we heard the prime minister say that Poland had been invaded by the Germans and that we were from that moment declaring war on Germany. It was September 3rd, 1939. I realised this was pretty serious when, within minutes of the broadcast, a siren placed on the end house opposite ours adjacent to Laburnum Grove, wailed into action. A sound which sets the nerves tingling even today whenever I hear it on television or radio.

For a while after the declaration, things appeared to be pretty normal, with no signs of major happenings on the home front. So much so, that my parents took Arthur and me to see 'Bandwagon,' a show running at the London Palladium, starring Liverpool-born Arthur Askey and Richard (Dickie) Murdoch. This was a true break from reality and the first West End production to which I had ever been. The glitz, the lights, the music from a live orchestra was magical. My cousin Crecy and her husband Vic were then living on Broadwalk, Winchmore Hill, London. Vic, who was old enough to be Crecy's father, owned an upmarket shoe factory in Edmonton. They travelled a lot abroad on business and when visiting the USA would often bring back a new Buick car. They had no children but Vic did have a son, Roy, by his previous marriage, he was killed on a motor cycle when he was seventeen. They took Roy and myself to shows in London to see stars like Fred Emney and Dickie Henderson. I loved going in the Buick which just floated over bumps and with its massive straight eight engine, was so smooth and quiet you could not hear it. The Packard was the nearest competitor it had at the time.

In the meantime, Arthur was attending St. Albans County School, which was at the other side of the town. He sat his matriculation examinations there and when the results were announced he was told he had failed. This really put the cat among the pigeons and it seemed any chance of him going to university had been scuppered. After a family conference it was decided that he would try and get in to the De Havilland aircraft factory at nearby Hatfield as an engineering draughtsman. Vic knew people there and he was able to secure an opening for Arthur. Then, like a bolt out of the blue, Hertfordshire Education Department wrote saying that they had made a dreadful mistake and that Arthur had matriculated with flying colours. This put a new complexion on things and it meant that he could now go to university. Vic and Crecy were not very enthusiastic about the turn of events and never quite adopted the same attitude as hitherto to Arthur ever again.

Matters on the war front were beginning to hot up. Children were being evacuated to 'safe' areas of Britain and abroad. Great Aunt Mary Jane and Uncle Tom Harris in the USA had written to my father and uncle Tom Jones, asking them to send Arthur, cousin Pat and myself to them in Youngstown, Ohio, for the duration of the war. They agreed that this was the best course and the requisite forms were filled. However, just before matters were finalised, a ship carrying evacuee children to the US was sunk by German U-boats, so that put the lid on any thoughts of us crossing the Atlantic. In any case, as Arthur was approaching military age it was doubtful whether he would have been allowed to go. Eventually, Arthur was accepted in Bristol University where he went to do an engineering degree course. This was the university Uncle Gilbert, my mother's second oldest brother, had obtained his Bachelor of Science degree in chemistry in the twenties before emigrating to Jamaica.

In 1941, my father obtained a job with Thomas Hedley Ltd, manufacturers of soap products which included brand names such as 'Fairy' and 'Oxydol.' His territory was to cover the south and west of Wales which meant we would again have to move. Hostilities in London were getting worse so it was decided that we would temporarily move in with my grandfather and grandmother in Lancaster Villas, Merthyr and my father's eldest sister Aunty Kate (Crecy's mother) would look after our house in St. Albans, together with Crecy and Vic who would use it as a 'bolt hole' from Winchmore Hill. Aunty Kate had been a housekeeper close to Buckingham Palace, so it was a sensible move on her part.

Once more I bid farewell to my new friends and arrived back at my birthplace. At least I would be assured of a good supply of 'Nipper' books from my grandfather! The school I was now to attend was Penydarren Junior School. Luckily for me the headmaster was my Uncle Tom Jones. This gave me a sense of 'power' over the other pupils who were watchful of their attitude towards me. I used to walk to school each day passing my maternal grandmother's cousin's house 'Rhoscolyn' in The Grove. This house attracted me being large and set in well kept gardens. I used to call there for a cup of tea en route to school just to see what it looked like inside. The Hopkins branch of our family lived here. They were old established hay and corn merchants in Merthyr.

I had never liked arithmetic or any kind of mathematics, so it was no surprise that the powers that be thought I should receive extra tuition if I was to get anywhere in life. My parents were friendly with a teacher named Tom John Williams, known to us as 'Twm John.' he was a funny little man barely five feet and thought a great deal of himself and gave me the impression of being devious. Twm John was given the task of coaching me in maths which he did for a couple of months to no avail. I had not improved a jot. His wife, Gladys (also a teacher), used to visit Aunty Narsa (my father's youngest sister) and Uncle Tom at their home in Awelfryn Terrace, Penydarren. Mam, who was living with Aunty Narsa, would tell me not to stare at Gladys or say anything untoward as she invariably turned up with big holes in her stockings. Twm and Gladys' son, Gwyn Alf Williams, became a noted professor and historian in later life but a that time I remember he had a bad stammer and was of a quiet disposition. My coaching continued with another teacher, Emrys Thomas who was also an official in the ILP (Independent Labour Party) in Merthyr. He was a nice man and I got on alright with him except for the fact that I still couldn't do maths. If only they had invented pocket calculators then!

A highlight of this period in Merthyr were my trips with Uncle Jack on his milk rounds. He had a dairy in Cefn Coed from which he and Aunty Reenie (his wife) operated and I jumped at the chance to join him in his Jowett van to deliver the milk. We would cover the whole of Merthyr and I went to places I had never seen before.

I proudly placed the milk bottles on doorsteps and watched Uncle jack ladle milk out of churns into jugs brought out by his customers. He collected milk from farms on Aberdare Mountain and took it to his dairy where he placed the churns in a tank of boiling water to pasteurise the milk. When cooled, the milk would be bottled and capped by Aunty Reenie and placed in crates ready for distribution. After our return to base they would give me a half crown and all the milk I could drink. They had no children of their own and sadly, Uncle Jack died in 1947 at the age of 49. He was, like my father, physically strong. He was in Merthyr High Street one day, when a horse and cart bolted, Uncle Jack ran alongside the runaway horse caught hold of its bridle and forced it to a halt. A frequent visitor there was Aunty Reenie's niece Shirley who lived in Barry. Shirley was a vivacious youngster and a terrible flirt with a heart of gold.

Not a block away from Lancaster Villas was a private house set in its own grounds called Harrap's Park. This was a perfect 'hunting' ground for us youngsters. My friend Vernon Lewis who lived next door but one and Leonard Goodwin, David Jenkins, Eric Fine and many others, had our secret 'gang' den there in the mass of bushes and trees which grew in profusion. So well organised were we that we even had our own newsletter the *Daily Gang* for which I was responsible. A keen but friendly rivalry existed between us and a similar setup on The Quar, which was led by my cousin Ronnie Thomas, who lived in our family home in Well Street. We were all more akin to Robin Hood than those yobs associated with the term 'gang' nowadays.

Living next door in Lancaster Villas was the Richards family. Dick Richards owned and ran the largest departmental/fashion type store in Merthyr named 'Theophilus.' He also had similar stores in Pontypridd and elsewhere in South Wales. The Richards family had come to Merthyr with their Uncle and founder of the business whose family surname was Theophilus, from the wilds of Rhandirmwyn in the uplands of Carmarthenshire. Dick's brother Tim managed the Pontypridd branch and the remaining brother Will stayed on the family farm in Carmarthenshire. Dick was a handsome lively character and the brains behind the outfit. He married a woman a lot older than himself who came from Pontardulais. They had two sons and two daughters. The elder daughter Marion was pretty and soon attracted the attentions of the opposite sex. One of these suitors was a young man named Geraint Evans who worked as a window dresser in the Theophilus store. Marion did not like him and would complain to her father about him pestering her. He finally got the message but continued working in the Pontypridd branch. I remember him coming to Lancaster Villas to see Marion, little knowing then, that in later years he was to become Sir Geraint Evans the world famous baritone singer whose voice was one of the most distinctive in international opera. Marion became Aunt Marion after marrying my mother's youngest brother Rupert during the early years of the war. Betty, her younger sister became a vet, went to America and disappeared off the face of the earth never to be seen again.

My father's work was keeping him busy and he was asked to concentrate on the West Wales territory. This meant that another move was in the offing and so it proved to be. We duly moved to Ammanford in Carmarthenshire. A house was rented in College Street right opposite the Ford Main Dealer (David Jones & Sons) and once more my parents had to seek another new school for me to attend. This turned out to be Ammanford Junior School which was right in the heart of the town but within a short walking distance. When I went to school for the first time, it was like going into a foreign country. Everything was taught in Welsh and I couldn't understand a word. The class teacher a Miss Rees was unsmiling and unsympathetic and I simply loathed the school. I made friends with a boy who also lived in College Street and whose grandfather David Jones owned the Ford dealership. Arwyn Jones was his name and he and I became good buddies. We used to play in his grandfather's showroom and in the spares loft above. My father had a firm's Ford car at the time and so he had it serviced there as well.

Arwyn was a very good violinist and later played in the first Youth Orchestra of Wales. He was also very enthusiastic about pet birds and kept and bred canary's and budgerigars at his home. Arwyn and I cycled to Glynhir Mansion in Llandybie to see another friend and was told that the pigeon house there was historic. The news that Wellington was victorious at the Battle of Waterloo, was first known in Britain when a message conveyed by a homing pigeon from Glynhir arrived at their loft.

Another long cycle ride I did was when cousin Pat visited us and she, Betty a friend from Ammanford and me, cycled to Llandeilo. This was the longest ride I had done and I thought it was never ending. We stopped at a milk bar in Llandeilo for refreshments before returning home to Ammanford. Betty's uncle and aunt kept a shop in Wind Street and they became very friendly with my parents. The husband, Jack Richards, travelled around the country for a butter merchant collecting butter from farms and delivering to shops. Needless to say we never went short of butter which was strictly rationed then. Mrs Richards' father was a butcher and I often heard the 'grown-ups' talk of illicit pig killings being conducted at the rear of his house near Ammanford. Betty worked for Angus James who ran the local bus service and married Danny Davies of Llansawel Quarries, settling down in Llandovery.

Jack Richards became increasingly fed up with his butter job and he asked my father if he could get him a job with Thomas Hedley. This he did and so Jack became a salesman. My father was one of the best sales representatives his firm had, having won many awards for achieving bumper sales and exceeding targets. It was not long after that the firm's management asked my father to take over the Bristol area having appointed Jack Richards to take on the West Wales territory. When I was told we would be moving to Bristol I felt very relieved. I hated the school in Ammanford and wasn't very keen on the town either finding it depressing and lacklustre. Incidentally, Jack didn't last long in the job due to friction between him and the area management. He ultimately told them what they could do with it and resigned. He and his family moved to the Edgware Road in London where he took over a dairy business and flourished.

The move to Bristol took place in 1942 just after the city had sustained a pounding from German bombers. The Bristol aircraft works at Filton had been a prime target. My parents again rented a house at 46, Luckington Avenue, Horfield, Bristol. This was very near the northern Southmead Hospital complex. With Arthur in Bristol University this worked out quite well. I was placed temporarily in Horfield School which once more proved to be a harrowing experience. Schooling was regularly interrupted with air raid warnings and I think we must have spent hours in our Anderson air raid shelter at the bottom of the garden. There was a large field to the rear of the house and on the edge of it was sited an RAF barrage balloon unit. Each evening as dusk approached the balloon would rise stealthily into the darkening sky without a sound. It was to me very dramatic. Filton airport and factory was within a mile or two and was ringed by a large number of these balloons providing a deterrent to any enemy plane likely to attack. The Bristol Aeroplane Company's factory was where the famous *Blenheim* and *Beaufighter* aircraft were made.

I was not getting anywhere in Horfield school and it was decided that I should try the entrance examination to get in to the private day/boarding school St. Brendan's College which was in the city centre off Whiteladies Road and opposite Bristol University. To my and everyone else's surprise . . . I passed! So, a daily bus ride to the centre of Bristol became the norm. The school was a Catholic establishment and all the masters were Roman Catholic priests dressed in ankle length robes. They were dedicated and strict and were feared by the pupils. I learned more when I was in St. Brendan's than I did in all the other schools I had been to put together. Underneath their robes the teachers carried a short leather strap which they produced when necessary and whacked the hand of the unfortunate recipient with considerable force. When in class all the boys (it was a strictly boys school), rose to their feet and crossed themselves every time the clock struck the hour. Non-Catholic pupils were excused this performance much to my relief.

There were no meals provided in the school so I had to walk down to what was known in the war as 'The British Restaurant.' In Bristol, this was a large building under construction as a council office but not completed. It was adapted to serve nutritional meals for the public and was very popular. It was in St. Brendan's that I first played rugby. We used to play on the University playing field and I took to the sport like a duck to water. During breaks in the day we boys used to congregate around Cabot Tower which was adjacent to the school. Here, in its park-like surroundings we watched, with considerable interest, the anthropological antics of the American GI soldiers with their British girl friends.

The war was in full flow by now and people were being called up for the armed services on a massive scale. You can imagine then the shock my father had when he received his calling up papers and asked to report for his medical examination. Uncle Rupert had also received his at the same time the difference being that my father was 42! They both went and it resulted in my father failing the test on the grounds of 'flat feet' and Rupert passing. Rupert was a chemist (MPS) and became a sergeant dispenser in the RAMC (Royal Army Medical Corps).

I was now becoming interested in the boy scout movement. I had devoured Lord Baden Powell's *Scouting for Boys* and became eager to join the scout movement. The nearest troop was in Horfield so my friend Bernard Back and me went along and joined the 248th Troop of Horfield Boy Scouts. Bernard was a great lad, very tall and had a good sense of humour. He had a nasty experience at the beginning of the war when he was standing overlooking Filton airfield. He saw a squadron of German bombers sweeping in to drop their bombs. As a result he was so frightened that he lost all his hair and it took some time before it grew back again. His sister, Doris, was like him in temperament and she joined the girl guides at the same time.

The Horfield scout troop was quite large and was in the charge of a scoutmaster who was known as Skipper Brewer. He was unmarried and had a pronounced limp in one leg. Bernard and me settled in quite well and we enjoyed our scouting. I progressed rapidly through the 'ranks' and became an assistant patrol leader and then full blown patrol leader. When Lord Somers the Chief Scout came to Bristol, I was chosen to represent northern Bristol scouts involving carrying the flag at the Colston Hall and meeting Lord Somers.

A dramatic turn of events was about to take place in my scouting life. In the summertime the troop went camping to Cadbury Camp (Blaze Woods), near Clevedon, Somerset. This was a pleasant country site with plenty of trees and bridle paths. We could light fires and have sing songs and generally a good time was had by all. However, one night after we had pitched camp and set up our bell tents with about ten scouts in each tent, I noticed that Skipper Brewer was getting a bit too friendly with some of the boys in the tent he slept in. The next day on our return home I told my parents what had occurred and although I was not directly involved, the matter was reported to the police. In due course it was taken to the local magistrates court where I appeared as a witness. After my testimony, the chairman of the magistrate complimented me on my action. The case was taken to Winchester Assizes where Skipper Brewer was given a seven years prison sentence for child abuse.

I was still doing a fair bit of cycling and one of my 'long distance' efforts was when a friend of mine and myself rode to the small village of Winford which was not far from the present Bristol International Airport. I thought we would never get there but get there we did and spent the night in my companion's relative's pub which was in the centre of the village opposite the tiny cattle market. They had a skittle alley on the premises and this was my first introduction to the 'sport.' The daughter of the pub owners was home on leave from the WRNS at the time and she looked after us well.

Prior to going in to the army, Rupert had been managing a chemist shop in Horfield and had chummed up with the proprietor of a cycle shop by the name of Bill Fairman. Bill and Rupert used to play snooker and tennis together and had became firm friends. My parents got to know Bill and Doris Fairman and also became the best of friends. Bill was a very unusual man. In his younger days he was given months to live due to a severe heart condition. He was determined that he was not going to accept this and so embarked upon a regime of extreme exercise and healthy organic eating. His wife Doris, backed him to the hilt and became an expert in cooking and preserving naturally healthy home grown food. This was the first time I had tasted steamed vegetables when we visited their home which was some miles out of Bristol on the Gloucester road. They had a spacious detached house set in its own grounds complete with tennis court. Nearby, they had a motor garage and petrol pumps called 'Abadan Garage.'

This way of healthy living made a big impression on my family and was the catalyst for our interest in organic eating for the years to come. We spent many a weekend at the Fairman's and it was a relief to get out of Bristol and the risk of being bombed. I used to see the lights of the South Wales coast across the Severn on our drive out and wished that I was over there. There can be no doubt that Bill gained himself many more productive years by the lifestyle he adopted some twenty-odd years previously.

It was in Bristol that I was introduced to the magic of live orchestra music. Both Arthur and I loved music of all sorts but particularly jazz and the swing music of the big bands. During the war a lot of musicians were called up for military service so that a great deal of the music heard on radio was played by older instrumentalists. I had been 'weaned' on Henry Hall and his theme tune, 'Here's To The Next Time.' So you can imagine how thrilled I was to be able to go with Arthur to the Colston Hall in Bristol to see and hear live, the RAF dance bands 'The Squadronairs' and the 'Skyrockets.' The gleam of the lights on the brass and silver instruments in contrast to the air force blue of their RAF uniforms and the hair bristling shiver when they break into the rhythm of their signature tunes is an experience that will live with me for ever. To see instrumentalists like George Chisholm, Tommy McQator and the best trumpeter ever to come out of Britain – Kenny Baker . . . with vocalists such as Ann Lennor during wartime, was a privilege. I was truly hooked on big band swing.

On another occasion, Arthur and I were passing near the Colston Hall when we spotted Harry Parry another contemporary musician passing by. Welshman Harry Parry and his Sextet were all the rage in the early forties. The same applied to Nat Gonnella who Arthur also saw in Bristol. He was a trumpet player who, because of a 'funny' lip, used to blow into the mouthpiece from the corner of his mouth. Nevertheless, a good trumpet player.

Besides Bernard Back, I had made many friends and there were ample opportunities to get up to mischief. The fields that had not yet been built upon in the area were cultivated and grew potatoes and wheat. At the top end of Luckington Avenue the farmer had built a large corn stack in which we kids loved to play. I was playing there with John Murphy and his sister Mary, when a 'whisker' from an ear of wheat went in my ear and frightened the life out of me. I ran home and Mam, who was staying with us, pulled it out, happily with no lasting after effects. Other pals that come to mind were Eddie and Gloria Warren and Derek Goddard.

Apart from the hostilities, Bristol was quite a pleasant place in which to live. It was here I went to my first zoo. The star turn then at Bristol Zoo was 'Alfred' a giant of a gorilla He used to sit impassively staring at all the idiots looking at him. Not far away was Brunel's masterpiece, the Clifton Suspension Bridge, spanning Clifton Gorge. I didn't like stepping off the cliff on to the bridge, it sent cold shivers up my spine and it took some time before I could pluck up enough courage to walk across. The Downs were very popular and there were always lots of service personnel making the most of any fine weather to be seen sunbathing. Horse rides were obtainable and it was here that had my first and last ride on a horse.

Another bolt out of the blue hit the family in 1942. Arthur, as part of the University's programme, was doing OTC (Officer's Training Course) in readiness of his impending call up to the army when he was told that as a result of a ballot, he was to be sent to work underground in the coal mines. There was no choice in the matter and these conscripts who were to be known as 'Bevin Boys,' named after Ernest Bevin, the government minister who thought up this daft scheme, were sent underground. Young men from all walks of life were roped in with the only concession being that they could choose the region to which they would be posted. So Arthur, fresh from officer training on Salisbury Plain, opted for South Wales. After a period of training at Oakdale Colliery in Monmouthshire, he was sent to Merthyr Vale Colliery, Aberfan, Merthyr. This meant he could 'lodge' with Aunt Narsa in Penydarren and travel to work daily from there. The job he was allocated was to drive an underground stationary engine which hauled drams of coal from the coal face to the pit shaft bottom, deep underground.

Our periodic trips home to Wales from Bristol via the unpredictable Aust to Beachley car ferry was about to come to an end. My father who was superb at his job, had created some jealousies with certain people in a managerial capacity. He was experiencing some of the same frustrations as Jack Richards had in Ammanford and so he too packed in his lot with Thomas Hadley Ltd., and obtained a similar appointment with Messrs. Caperns Ltd., the Bristol bird, pet and animal foods manufacturers. The only snag was that he was given the London and Home Counties to cover and that meant only one thing . . . we would be on the move again!

The Teenage Years

URING THE TIME WE HAD left our house in St. Albans, things had progressed on the Aunt Kate/Crecy front. Vic and Crecy took over a very large Georgian house The Limes, Upper Marlborough Road, in St. Albans. This left our house on Watford Road vacant for us to move back into and this we did in late 1943. Aunty Kate moving in with Crecy and Vic at The Limes.

It seemed unreal to be back in our old house as such a lot seemed to have happened in the interim period. My old friends had become that much older and our former neighbour Mrs Ensor had been replaced by Mr and Mrs Cross and their two children, Philip and Joan. In the vacant plot next door on the other side was now a huge static water tank holding an emergency water supply in case the area got bombed. The Bird family were still living in the same house on the other side of the tank. Morris Chalkley and Ginger Roberts were also still living opposite. The building of new houses had stopped after the Declaration, so the surrounding area was very much the same as when we left. Blackout restrictions were rigorously enforced and there was a much more wartime atmosphere than before.

Once again, the question of my schooling came up once more and after sitting another entrance test, I started in Arthur's old school, St. Albans County Grammar School. The Headmaster was still Mr Bradshaw and his secretary, Miss Eagle, was quite a character; they both remembered Arthur well. I started in Form One and began to make friends again. To this day I can recite the names of my fellow form pupils in this all boys school, as they were read out at morning roll call and registration. They were:

Alexander	(A quiet studious boy no good at sport)
Barnett	(Extrovert, Jewish and good rugby player, very small)
Bishop	(Pleasant, from London Colony)
Butler	(Strong minded type, good at sport)
Chalkley	(Morris' cousin)
Chapman	(Another quiet boy, academic)
Clarke	(Big boy, a bit on the introvert side)
Cox	(Unobtrusive, didn't bother much with him)
Deal	(A bit of a 'raw' individual, simple)
Dollimore	(Studious, quiet and pleasant type)
Firzhugh	(A swot, and no good at sport)
Fox	(Quiet, a run of the mill type)
Glaister	(An objectionable type, didn't like him)
Gordon	(Jewish, wouldn't say boo to a goose)
Halpern	(Also Jewish, one of my best friends, excellent at rugby and sport)
Harris	(Me)
Havingdon	(Not much to say for himself, a bit 'slow')
Hunt	(Good in class, assured, good at sport)
Ison	(Terrifically tall and thin, butt for jokes)
Javelau	(Studious, strong personality)
Kingsmill	(Another best friend, usually top of the class, good at sport)
Lello	(A big boy, unobtrusive and good in class)
Longland	(Also good in class, bright nature always pleasant).
Magee	(A small boy from Redbourne, happy and good pal).
Minter	(A prankster from Harpenden, good rugby player)
Orme	(Owlish appearance, quiet)
Posner	(Jewish. Run with the hare, hunt with the hounds type)

Saunders	(Tony. Another best friend from Harpenden, good at sport)
Shepherd	(From a poor background, left on his own to a large extent)
Simpson	(A strong type, academic and good at sport)
Udell	(Also a good friend and prankster, from Harpenden)
Ward	(A bit of a 'selfish' type, not a mixer)
Wilmot	(Salt of the earth, heart of gold and a good pal, good at sport)

Even now, I can picture all these boys vividly in my mind. I can hear their voices and see their faces and even though over sixty years have passed, I can still recall things that happened at the time. Like the time Minter and Udell took me to woods in Harpenden to 'meet' the American singing star Dinah Shore, who, they said was camping in the woods. Of course, she wasn't, but they were very convincing at the time.

My first year in the County Grammar School was not too bad. I was elected form rugby captain and I came top of the class in General Science much to the amazement of my classmates. I think my St. Brendan's schooling was still having an effect. Even in this new school, we still spent some time in the air raid shelters every time the air raid sirens sounded. I travelled to school by bus and each bus had its windows taped up with just a small 'diamond' to look out to see where you were going. This anti-shatter bomb precaution was repeated on shop windows and public buildings. All car and motor cycle headlights were fitted with special masks to keep the light down so that German planes would not see them. I had to carry my gas mask everywhere. Though food was rationed, we had very good meals in school in the assembly hall and I really enjoyed them, prunes and all!

Our house was right on the main Watford Road which was the main route from north to the south-west through St. Albans from

Luton in Bedfordshire. The huge Vauxhall factory in Luton was producing army vehicles in their thousands. A constant stream of new army Bedford lorries and Bren Gun Carriers (tracked vehicles) drove past our house every day from the factory in Luton to their military destinations. We boys used to sit on the grass counting them to see how many would pass in a continuous convoy. Far more exciting however, was what was passing overhead. Not far away was the Handley Page aircraft factory at Radlett. Here, was one of the most important bomber production lines in the British war effort. The famous 'Halifax' bomber was manufactured there and every day we would see these beautiful aircraft pass right over our house as they took off after leaving the production lines for delivery to the RAF. I personally always thought that the Handley Page Halifax was a better looking plane than its more illustrious and more publicised contemporary, the Avro Lancaster. The purr of the Halifax's four Rolls Royce engines was unmistakable and to me was one of the great sounds of the war.

Morris Chalkley, me and another new friend I had made living opposite as well and living nearer the 'Three Hammers,' named Roger White, used to cycle down the lanes to Park Street which was near the Handley Page factory, to watch the planes take off the runway. On our way we would come across soldiers camping in orchards and fields with their camouflage netting draped over the apple trees hiding their tanks and guns. They used to wave to us as we cycled by. Roger White was slightly younger than me and was in a lower form in school when he came to the grammar school. His father was a water engineer and Roger had a sister, Barbara, they all lived together with their mother in Eastbourne, Watford Road. Barbara was a big strapping girl and nobody took liberties with her! Barbara and her friends, like Christine Clark, went to the girls grammar school which was near the boy's school. The girls got on the buses at separate stops to the boys and needless to say, some fooling around went on!

Roger tended to be 'spoilt' by his father especially. His parents organised a birthday party for him and invited all his friends, including me, to the party. Remember, this was wartime with food rationing, no bananas, ice-cream, limited chocolate, and what there was came in grease proof paper. So imagine our surprise and delight when we were given as much ice-cream as we could eat when we sat down for the birthday tea. It turned out that Roger's father had a black market source on Hollywell Hill in town where it was made illicitly. It was a party hard to forget. Unfortunately, Roger's father had a 'roving' eye and he caused his mother a lot of heartache at the time. She used to visit my mother and pour out her feelings to her. I don't think Roger or Barbara knew at the time. The fact that Roger had a near escape when he contracted Peritonitis and had to be taken to St. Albans Hospital, helped to put things in perspective for them. I visited Roger in hospital several times and on each occasion his father was by his bed.

A favourite place where we used to congregate was the deserted Ragged Hall I mentioned previously. One wing of the house had been taken over by the ambulance service and was used to house ambulances which may be needed in cases of emergency. We played for hours in this mansion, climbing over the roof and exploring all the rooms. The gardens around the Hall contained a lot of fruit trees which gave us an endless supply of apples, pears and cherries, these would otherwise been left to rot on the trees. It was a real getaway in every sense from the realities of the time. Another favourite haunt was the woods at the end of Laburnum Grove. These woods were at the top of a steep sloping field and when it was covered with snow in the wintertime we used to toboggan down at breakneck speed. I made my own toboggan out of wood and I went to have steel runners made by the blacksmith in St. Albans, to my own design. There was a bit of jealousy by John Bird regarding my toboggan and one day he picked a fight with me on the top of the slope. I gave him a good hiding and we were the best of friends from that day on.

In St. Brendan's, we used to have to attend school every Saturday morning. Here, we did not except on the occasion that we played rugby at the school playing fields sited in Sandpit Lane. Sport was regarded as important in my school. We played rugby in the winter and cricket and athletics during the summer. I was very good at rugby and played at scrum half and captain of the form team. I was okay at athletics running for my 'house' which was Park the 'houses' being named after the streets bordering the school. The others being Brompton, Hamilton and Jennings. I preferred the short distances such as the 100 yards and 220 yards and invariably came first or second in my year. I was never very keen on cricket regarding it as a dangerous sport. I remember taking part in a school match in which I was bowling to the best batman in the school. I thought I would give him a really fast bouncer of a ball, so I ran up at top speed and bowled a ball which was so wide that it nearly decapitated square leg! I had a heated telling off by the master in charge, Mr H. R. Neal, and told to take it again and to be more careful. This I did by bowling a full toss which flattened the wicket. I don't know who was most surprised, me, the batsman or Mr. Neal.

My mother was an accomplished piano player and she was keen that I learned too. She arranged for me to have private tuition at home and so I started piano lessons. Alas, what a pantomime this turned out to be. The teacher was a nice enough chap, but gullible. He would give me pieces to practise and would then test me on his next visit. I have a good ear for music and would learn the music off by heart by listening to it. However, when the theory came up I was absolutely stumped. I would not practise and it was like being in prison for me to have to miss playing with my pals and having to stay in. This went on for some time until in the end my mother gave in and I was 'free' once more. I wish now, looking back, that I had stuck to it and learned to play.

We did not go short of anything during the war. My father always had enough petrol, due to his job, for the car. He was allocated extra because he was authorised to locate any metal which could be used to manufacture munitions or aircraft he might come across while doing his work. We were not big tea drinkers, so my mother used to swap tea coupons for equivalent sugar instead. Crecy and Vic were friendly with an American army captain named Nelson Carmen who they used to do business with in the USA. He was stationed in the UK and came to St. Albans to stay with them when on leave. He always brought a load of sweets sent to him from America, and a lot of these found their way in my direction. I think Nelson was rather keen on Crecy!

By now, I was outgrowing my bicycle and it was sold to a youngster living near us. This meant that I was now without a bike! Luckily Crecy had a girl's Raleigh cycle which she said I could borrow now and again. New cycles were unattainable then. I did many a mile on that Raleigh and we even used to hold races in Stanley Avenue which were quite hairy. We used to belt round the bends so fast that the pedals would hit the road and bounce the bikes back up again sometimes with disastrous consequences for grazed knees and elbows.

The Cross family next door were the type that kept themselves to themselves. Mr Cross was a lot older than his wife and had come from a wealthy middle-class family whereas Mrs Cross had been in service to the same family and so was not quite so gentile. Her husband had converted to Catholicism some years ago and was a strong practicing Catholic. He sent both their children Joan and Philip to the Convent School in St. Albans. By profession he was owner and editor of a magazine covering the wine trade. Every month just before publication neither Mrs Cross or the children dare go near him while he was checking the proofs. Apart from that, he was a very quiet man. Hardly ever talked and would spend hours in the garden wearing a long overcoat even in summer while he mowed the lawn or weeded the garden. He would even keep his trilby hat on while working. As soon as he saw a neighbour appearing he would disappear indoors. Joan was a nice little girl and had two Welsh friends living in Stanley Avenue, by the name of Diane and Jaqueline Fowles. Their father was an Air Commodore in the RAF on a 'hush hush' intelligence mission. Philip looked like his father and did not have an ounce of surplus flesh on him. In later years he became a Roman Catholic priest in Harrow.

June 6th, 1944, will always be a special date for me. It was a boiling hot day with clear blue sky. My grandma Thomas from Merthyr was staying with us and we were all sitting enjoying the sun in the garden, when all of a sudden, the sky became filled with rows and rows of Stirling and Dakota aircraft all towing gliders heading south. They all had the distinctive striped bands round their wings and fuselages and it was a sight to behold. They seemed to be flying past for hours. Afterwards, we discovered that this was 'D-Day' – the invasion of France had begun. This will always be etched in my memory because this historic event took place the day before my birthday, June 7th.

Other relatives visiting us at this time were Uncle Gilbert and Aunty Cecille. Uncle Gilbert had met Cecille while he was teaching at Wolmers College, Kingston, Jamaica. She was the daughter of a plantation owner whose surname was Urquart. The name of their property had a strong Welsh connection being named 'Glan Rhymney.' They grew bananas and sugar cane and Gilbert and Cecille were married there. Captain Morgan had a strong Welsh influence in that part of the world in days gone by. They never had any children and spent most of their lives travelling and living in far away places like Trinidad and Nigeria, where Uncle Gilbert held government lecturing posts. On a visit to Crecy's she gave them some parsnip flavoured with banana flavouring to taste. Cecille, who was an expert on the growing of bananas, tasted it and was convinced that it was real banana. She could not believe it when Crecy told her the truth. During the war lots of food substitutions were made a good example being dried egg. I made many a scrambled egg using dried egg and it was delicious.

A common occurrence was the 'pea soup' fogs that plagued the London area. We had them in St. Albans too. Rupert was stationed nearby and came to see us in an army ambulance complete with Scottish lady ATS driver. He had to walk in front of the ambulance on Watford Road to guide her to our house. I often saw bus conductors walking in front of buses and coming home from school could be quite exciting if you could not see the bus stop to get off. Not only could you not see, but you could taste it too and white shirts or clothing became dirty very quickly.

While Rupert was in the area, Marion (his wife) came to visit us bringing their baby daughter cousin Jacky with her. I was into experimentation with chemistry sets and kept my equipment in my bedroom on the dressing table. Marion took Jacky up to my bedroom for her to have a sleep and you can imagine the rumpus when she went to get her to find Jacky's face covered in a green tinge. She had got hold of a bottle containing copper sulphate and had put the crystals on her face. Thankfully, she had not swallowed any but it taught both Marion and me to be more vigilant. Rupert, being a chemist, was not amused! They had two further daughters (all my first cousins), Lesley and Ann.

We had a Murphy radio which had a wonderful tone and countless hours were spent listening to programmes, news bulletins and for me especially, music. Arthur was busy in the mines and used to write home to ask my mother to buy the latest Harry James releases, which were then recorded on vinyl 78s. She would trek to the records shop near the Chequers Cinema to buy these for him at least once a month. Music played a major role in keeping up morale during the war. BBC programmes like 'Music While You Work,' 'In Town Tonight,' and the singing of Vera Lynn, Ann Shelton and others were listened in to by huge audiences.

1945 proved to be a momentous year. The war with Germany came to an end and a whole new era of freedom and normality beckoned. Sirens sounded the 'all clear' right around the country and street parties and festivities were organised on a grand scale. All my friends and our parents went to Verulamium Park where a huge fireworks display and various events took place alongside the lake.

The atmosphere was jubilant and was something that had not been seen since 1939. We simply could not believe that the war was over, it seemed it had been going on for ever. We spoke on the 'phone to Arthur and all the family back in Wales and they were feeling the same emotions. It wasn't long before the blackout curtains were torn off the windows and the gas masks banished for ever.

I was now well into my teens and things were getting harder and harder for me in school. I still hated maths and felt an increasing feeling of being in prison. I dreaded going to school and with the exception of French, I was losing ground on most subjects. I spent more and more time with my local friends instead of studying and doing my homework. Morris was a year older than me and he bought a second-hand 1928 BSA motorbike which looked as if it had come out of the Ark! It was a 350cc, side valve model complete with hand pump on the tank which circulated the oil Morris wasn't old enough to have a licence or the appropriate insurance, but this didn't stop him riding about the country lanes near us and so I had my first ride on a motorcycle albeit a pillion passenger. I say 'pillion,' it was more a luggage type grid behind the saddle! Riding on that motorbike was like nothing I had ever experienced, the noise of the engine, the surge as the hand throttle was opened and the rush of wind through the hair, it was intoxicating.

Morris was fast becoming regarded as a superman by the boys and he could do no wrong. I spent hours in Morris' garage helping him to tinker with that 'bike. While the war was on, my father's Jowett had been garaged for the duration at 14, Well Street, Merthyr. He didn't need it as the firms he worked for always supplied him with a car. So, when Arthur's twenty-first birthday came up in August, he was presented with the Jowett as a present. It was not long before Arthur had it on the road and it was a great day when he drove it from Merthyr to St. Albans for the first time. I was becoming very interested in motor cycling and started taking the magazine *Motor Cycling* which was the number one publication in the motorbike world. It was hard to obtain copies just after the war and they were sold on a first come first served basis. The nearest newsagent was in London Road, near the cinema, and each week either my mother or myself would trudge down to get hold of a copy. I was itching to have a go myself at riding a motorbike solo and thought that there should be some sort of organisation which could teach youngsters to ride. I therefore put pen to paper and wrote on the subject to the editor of *Motor Cycling*, Graham Walker, himself a noted racing motor cyclist and revered in the motor cycling fraternity. He published my letter and so at the age of fourteen I had my first published writing. This letter caused quite a stir in the St. Albans Motor Cycle Club and led to them and other clubs to think about tuition courses. Graham Walker's son is Murray Walker the famous television motoring commentator of today.

John Bird, next door, bought an old Austin Seven saloon, he too was not old enough to drive it and had it parked at the front of the house. We both used to drive it up and down for about twenty yards and this was my initiation into driving a car. His father drove a large Lanchester saloon and worked in the De Havilland factory where he obtained aviation petrol during the rationing and sold it for £1 per gallon to his friends.

The BSA was by now beginning to show its age, so Morris bought a 250cc OK Supreme which was a big improvement. His father was manager of Coupers in St. Albans who were dealers for Bentley and Austin cars and Triumph motor cycles. The post-war Austin cars were now appearing in the showroom. Mr Chalkley would bring a new one home every day and Morris and me would scrutinise them from top to bottom. It was at this time that Roger White had a new bicycle, the first to be manufactured post-war. These bikes were all black with no chromium whatsoever.

Morris had a friend who kept the Hummingbird Garage on the near bypass. He had a 500cc Gold Star BSA which he let Morris borrow. This was a really powerful machine and a thrill to ride. Morris and I would go for runs to Tring and Berkhamstead and without our parents knowing, we even went to Wembley Stadium to see the speedway match between Bill Kitchen with the Wembley Lions and Jack Parker and his Bell Vue, Manchester team. It was a memorable sight with 100,000 fans cheering their teams amid the roar of the dirt track 'bikes grappling round the open track. I can smell the Castrol R now! That was the one and only time I ever visited the old Wembley Stadium.

There was an old disused sand pit near Watford Road on which local motorcyclists practised dirt riding. It was owned by the two Pearson brothers, builders by trade, who had bought two brand new Matchless motor cycles. These were a big advancement on previous models as they featured hydraulic front forks patented as 'Tele-draulic.' These had been fitted to army despatch riders machines during the war and were the first of their type to be a standard fitting. The Matchless and AJS motor cycles were made in Plumstead, London. Morris decided he would have a go on his OK Supreme in the sand pit, but came a cropper when he failed to take a bend and came off damaging his arm, which kept him out of action for a while. He eventually recovered and was as keen as ever.

I was beginning to influence Arthur with my enthusiasm for motor cycling and the inevitable occurred. He decided to sell the Jowett and buy a motorbike! By now, the car had knocked up a good 110,000 miles without a hitch, so perhaps the timing was about right. It was decided that the BSA range looked great and the new models were outstanding. Once again, there was a waiting list but he did see a 1946, BSA, B31 model for sale in Comerfords of Thames Ditton in London. So, off my father, Arthur and me drove down to Comerfords showrooms. We saw the 'bike and fell in love with it and Arthur bought it. Its price new was £125. The snag was how were we to get it back to St. Albans? Arthur had never been on one, I wasn't old enough to drive and my father had not been on a motorbike for over quarter of a century! It was decided that 'poor old Dad' would have to draw the short straw. He got on the BSA as if he had never been off one and drove it all the way home to St.

Albans without batting an eyelid, with Arthur and me driving behind in the car marvelling at his expertise and pluck.

The B31 was a 350cc, ohv, machine with telescopic front forks and the speedometer set in the top of the silver petrol tank. The standard of finish was high and it was quite nippy. The BSA's registration number was KPC 108. When we did arrive home, one of the first people Arthur allowed to ride it was Morris, who tried it out round the block. He thought it was a 'smashing' 'bike and was able to give Arthur a few tips on riding it. By the time Arthur was ready to return to Merthyr after his 'leave,' he was very proficient. One of the first things he bought for it was a pillion seat. Unfortunately, the supply of accessories was still slow and pillion footrests had a waiting list. Arthur rode it back to Merthyr along the A40 with me on the pillion with my legs dangling for the whole journey. Our parents followed in the Jowett which was to be delivered to a cousin of my father's living in Cefn Coed. His name was Will Thomas.

School was now becoming more intolerable. One of the favourite pastimes of my friends and me was to 'spot' train numbers. This was the age of steam and Morris, Roger and me used to catch the train at Abbey Station at the bottom of Hollywell Hill and go to Watford Junction to see the express trains travelling north and to Scotland. A publication was sold which listed all the locomotive numbers for the GWR, LMS, LNER and SR lines. When a loco was spotted the number was underlined in the little 'ABC' publication. Imagine the thrill standing on Watford Junction platform and seeing the streamlined 'Scot' class trains coming towards us round the curve from the direction of London and then thundering through the station with everything shaking and steam everywhere. What a sight!

So, I made the 'decision' that I wouldn't go to school any more and started playing truant. I would get on the bus in the morning as usual to go to school, but instead of getting off in town, I would stay on until it reached Harpenden Common. I got off there and walked the short distance to the main King's Cross to Scotland LNER railway line and spent the day train spotting. The engine drivers used to wave to me sitting on the embankment and on a sunny day it was a very enjoyable experience. I would return home at the appropriate time, with my parents none the wiser. I would vary the process some days by going to Watford Junction instead. This went on for some time before the powers that be twigged what I was doing and my parents became aware of the situation. I was hauled before the headmaster, Mr Bradshaw, who proceeded to give me six of the best with his cane, which I didn't feel but which certainly hurt my dignity!

The new Triumph motor cycles were making their appearance. The police were being issued with the Triumph Speed Twin and this was a beautiful machine. finished a dark red it had telescopic front forks and boasted a twin cylinder 500cc engine, it was perfection, I thought. I used to go to Couper's showroom just to look at them and later its more powerful version, the Triumph Tiger 100, which was finished in aluminium silver and had a large bulbous petrol tank, even more perfection. Mr Chalkley would see me looking in and would invite me in to have a closer look. I could not wait to be old enough to ride one of these dream 'bikes.

Later, in 1946, my mother had bad news from Merthyr. Her father, Grandpa Thomas, was ill and my grandmother could not cope as he became bedridden. The decision was made that my father would apply for a transfer to Merthyr and we would sell up in St. Albans and move in with my grandparents. We sold most of our furniture before moving and I was pleased that a Welsh dresser which had belonged once to Mam, was bought by Morris' mother. I was very sorry to leave my friends, we had many happy times over an eventful period, but I wasn't sorry to see the back of the school!

We moved back in to 24, Lancaster Villas and one of the first things to happen was for Arthur to move in from Aunty Narsa's. We were complete once more. My grandfather was really ill and had his bed moved downstairs to the middle room. My mother was kept busy, my grandmother could not have managed without her. The topic of school reared its ugly head once again and I was sent to

Quakers Yard Grammar School on the outskirts of the Merthyr Borough in the direction of Cardiff. This was the eighth school I had attended in just on ten years! One consolation, Arthur kept the BSA in a shed he and my father constructed in the rear garden of No. 24.

The Richards family were still living next door and we used to see Marion and the children from time to time. The Theophilus shop was prospering and Dick Richards was living life to the full. He spent money lavishly and bought Marion's eldest brother Cliff, new car after new car including hand-built expensive cars like the Armstrong Siddeley Hurricane. Rupert, Marion and family were now living in Weston-super-Mare, where Rupert owned a chemist shop. This rich living eventually caught up with Dick and he died resulting in the demise of the Theophilus empire. Glyn, Marion's youngest brother, took over the Aberdare branch until he too died in tragic circumstances.

Quakers Yard Grammar School was a peculiar school. The buildings looked as if they had been prefabricated in the first world war, as I believe they had. To get there I had to walk from Lancaster Villas across town to Merthyr's main railway station and catch the train to Quakers Yard station. This was the best part of the exercise. The train was pulled by the old 0-6-0 GWR Pannier Type Tank Engine. These were wonderful steam locomotives and real workhorses. Merthyr station was influenced by Brunel and was a terminus for the Cardiff to Merthyr line. It ran alongside the River Taff for most of the way to Cardiff which was also the route of the old canal. My mother's cousin, Idwal Thomas, drove one of these engines and it was great to see him on the footplate with his oily rag and steam spurting out of everywhere from this distinctive iron horse.

Life in school was even worse than in St. Albans. The curriculum was foreign to me the Welsh system being based on different values. This was the first secondary mixed school I had been to and I found sitting with girls very off-putting. They were always top of the class.

One thing I was thankful for was meeting a boy who was to become my lifelong friend, Ted Martin, from Troedyrhiw. Ted and me became bosom pals and remain so today. His father, Bert Martin, worked in the lamp room at Merthyr Vale Colliery where Arthur worked, and he knew Arthur well. Ted also shared my enthusiasm for motor bikes and his father was the proud owner of a Douglas Twin sidecar outfit. Ted and I travelled on the train every day together with classmate Norman Lloyd Edwards who in later years became Lord Lieutenant of Glamorgan. One of the masters at Quakers Yard by the name of Ron Gethin, used to come to school on his Triumph Speed Twin, the sound of it outside when I was in class was like music to my ears. Ted and I played rugby in the same team and the school pitch had to be seen to be believed. It was a long walk from the school and was scraped out of the side of a rocky hill still retaining an appreciable slope. The posts were not vertical and the lines non existent. Nevertheless, I did score a try on it!

I became reunited with some of my old Merthyr friends notably Vernon Bowen from Dane Street. His parents had been friends with mine since both Vernon and I were born. They used to visit us in Porthcawl and were also friendly with Uncle Tom and Aunty Narsa. Vernon had not been in robust health when very young and had to be careful and look after himself. He had two younger sisters, Marion and Betty. Vernon's father, Ernie Bowen, was an odd man and gave Vernon's mother a hard life. He spent a lot of time in Cardiff and was unfaithful to her, spending long periods away from the family.

He had an illegitimate son with a woman he lived with during the week and had the nerve to come 'home' to Dane Street at weekends as if everything was normal. Vernon told me that his father had a cousin, Jeremy Bowen, who is now the BBC Middle East correspondent and editor. Vernon couldn't tolerate his father and did his best to ignore him. He rarely talked about him and how his mother put up with her husband nobody could understand. Ernie had big ideas and often claimed he was descended from the noble Norman Mortimer family which was going strong at the time of Owain Glyndŵr. Vernon's full name was Vernon Mortimer Bowen. When Ted and I used to visit Vernon we used to see Ernie occasionally, he would be slumped in an armchair by the fireside and would try to sell us wrist watches, several of which he would have strapped to each wrist and right up his both arms.

Vernon had very similar musical tastes to mine and after first learning to play the violin, progressed to the clarinet. I used to borrow Glyn Richards' clarinet and Vernon and I would play for hours in his front room in Dane Street. We used to listen to Artie Shaw and Benny Goodman records and dreamed of playing like them. At least there was no harm in dreaming! Arthur, had bought a trumpet and became quite a competent player. As a result of spending a lot of time with me, Vernon became a motor cycle enthusiast too. He bought a very old Douglas twin which he restored. He was one of the best friends I ever had and I can see him now in resplendent bright green hacking jacket, hair greased down, wearing his leather gloves whatever the weather was like. Ted, Vernon and me joined the Merthyr Motor Cycle Club and we followed all the trials they organised in the area. We were great buddies!

Working with Ted's father in the Merthyr Vale Colliery lamp room was Tommy James who was secretary of the club. He rode an AJS sidecar combination and both he and his wife were the mainstays of the club, thoroughly nice people who had a lot of time for we young enthusiasts. They also lived in Troedyrhiw not far from Ted's. Vernon and me were treated royally by Ted's mother and father whenever we visited their house in Pembroke Street. Ted's mother was a marvellous cook and the teas she prepared were out of this world.

1947 turned out to be the most significant year of my life to that point. Winter was diabolical easily one of the worst in living memory and one I have not experienced like it since. It snowed in March as if it would never end. Waking up we found drifts so deep that the whole area of Merthyr was impassable. Life came to a stand-still. Schools were shut and it was impossible for most people to go to work. Walking from Lancaster Villas to see Mam in Penydarren was like trekking to the North Pole with snow drifts at least eight feet on the road with tunnels and narrow paths cut through them to enable people to get anywhere. The dead could not be buried, water pipes were bursting all over the place and it kept snowing and snowing. When it did eventually finish and the thaw set in, it cause floods on a terrific scale throughout England and Wales. Arthur and I went up to the Storey Arms in the Brecon Beacons on the BSA when the snow melted and saw mountain ponies frozen stiff and still standing on the side of the road. This was in April!

Grandpa Thomas had deteriorated steadily after we returned to Merthyr from St. Albans. He died in 1947 and was cremated at Taffs Well Crematorium near Pontypridd. His life was spent in the building trade, a staunch Conservative, Freemason and expert bowling green exponent. He was a man with a seemingly stern posture though a good sense of humour, ruddy complexion, of middle height and a pipe and cigar smoker. He always walked with his two hands locked behind him in the small of his back. After he died, my Uncle Lyndon carried on the business until he too died at the early age of 57.

My beloved Mam was the next to go and she too died shortly after in Penydarren and she also was cremated at Taffs Well. I was so dejected by her death that I refused to go to her funeral. Mam was to me the embodiment of everything that was good and safe in this world. She nursed me when I was not up to scratch and was my mentor. I could not associate her with death. I thought formal funerals were irrelevant then and I have not changed my mind to this day. Mam was short, well rounded, had a lovely smile and a terrific sense of humour. On her mother's side she was related to Dr Joseph Parry the well-known Welsh composer.

Uncle Jack was the next to go, followed by Grandma Thomas, both cremated at Taffs Well. Grandma suffered for most of her adult life from asthma and was a slim, small lady with whom I had many conversations regarding family trees. Our trips to Cefn cemetery on the trams I always enjoyed. Her tales of her visits to her grandfather, the Chartist leader, Matthew John, in his home in Vulcan House, Bethesda Street, used to fascinate me and I could not get enough of them. I used to drive her to distraction with my questions on religion and politics.

However, life must go on and so my sixteenth birthday was fast approaching, this was when I could obtain a license to ride a motor cycle. Months before this historic milestone I used to mitch from school (yes, again!), slip over to the garage in Well Street where Arthur kept his motor bike, pinched it, then rode it on my own up to Cwm Taff and the Storey Arms. Once up at the top reservoir, I would unbolt the silencer and then go flat out along the straight revelling in the roar of the engine which was similar to that of the racing 'bikes. The AA man used to turn a blind eye and just warned me to look out for the law. I did this many times and the only person to see me take the 'bike was my cousin Christine, then a small girl, who used to sit on the steps of No. 14 and watch me disappear down Well Street in a cloud of dust.

While working in Merthyr Vale, Arthur became friendly with Gordon Fitzgerald, also a Bevin Boy. He had been seconded from the RAF because he was prone to air sickness. Gordon too came under the influence and was persuaded to buy a new 500cc BSA motor cycle. Gordon has never ridden a motor bike before and so it was left to Arthur and myself to go to the John Lewis showroom on Pontmorlais to collect his brand new BSA. After putting petrol in the tank we tried to kickstart it, with no success. We took it in turns to try and get it running until at last at the point of exhaustion, it sprang in to life. What a relief! The next few days were spent in teaching him to ride and eventually he went solo and never looked back (figuratively speaking). Gordon frequently came to Lancaster Villas to see Arthur and if they happened to go out anywhere together leaving Gordon's BSA outside, I used to take it for a spin without either of them knowing. Once I rode it through town to Abercanaid and on the way back I was passing Conway's Dairies near the Parish Church, when I saw that the road was covered with a film of milk. Too late, the 'bike went from under me and I was left on my back in the middle of the road with the BSA spinning round and round pivoting on its footrest. I got up like a flash, picked up the bike and rode back home without a scratch and no damage to the BSA. The 500cc version was a great deal heavier than the 350cc B31, I discovered!

Arthur and Gordon, with me as pillion passenger, covered many miles on the two BSAs. A regular trip was to the motor bike races on Pendine Sands which took place on Bank Holidays. The road to Pendine on these occasions would be packed with motor cycles and combinations all heading for the races. Laugharne was crammed with 'bikers filling the restaurants and open spaces. Riding a motor cycle on sand was a queer feeling as it felt as if there was a wobble in the steering. The races themselves were simple affairs the track being a straight up and down course with a bend on either end. Skill wasn't a major factor as the winner invariably had the fastest machine. Many 'local' riders made up the entries with stalwarts like Eddie Stephens of Carmarthen, with the added interest of seeing more well known riders like Dennis Parkinson on his Manx Norton sweeping the board.

We were riding to Pendine races on one occasion and came towards Milo just on the outskirts of Pendine, when we came across a 'pile up' in the road. A motor cycle combination had been involved in a collision on a nasty bend, one of a series of bends on that stretch of road. We were shocked to see that it was Ted's father's Triumph Speed Twin and sidecar with both Ted, his father and mother involved. Luckily, they were not too badly hurt but certainly shaken. Every time I pass that bend right up to the present time, I think of Ted's father and the accident. Another place we used to go to see sand racing was Aberavon Beach near Port Talbot, but this was not as popular as Pendine.

Morris Chalkley on his Scott at St. Albans.

Ted Martin on his Matchless in Merthyr.

Me speeding on the Douglas near Cwmtaff Reservoir, Merthyr.

Ted and me on our mounts (1948).

My sports Douglas and me in 1948 at Cwmtaff, Merthyr.

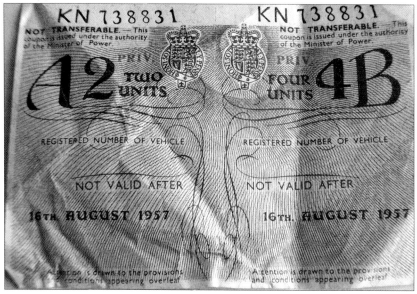

Petrol rationing coupons for the motorbikes, post-war.

Ted and me taken at the Storey Arms,
Brecon Beacons, 1948.

My two buddies, Ted Martin
and Vernon Bowen.

Arthur's first motorcycle, the BSA 'B31' (1946).

A more interesting race venue was the Eppynt circuit set on the army firing ranges near Sennybridge. This was a road race on a narrow tarmac road with loose gravel on the edges. The riders took their lives in their hands here as it was dangerous banking on the bends on loose gravel. There were many hairy moments. Even the great Les Graham on the revolutionary works AJS went gingerly. The races there did not last long and were ultimately abandoned. It was great while it lasted! Only the sound of gunfire reverberate around the hills of this beautiful part of Breconshire, Powys, nowadays.

June 1947 was a great month for me. My sixteenth birthday was on the 7th and a trip to the Isle of Man to see the Motor Cycle Tourist Trophy Races (the TT), was on the cards. My application for a motor cycle driving license had been lodged and I was due to take my driving test on returning from the Isle of Man. Arthur had booked our holiday in Howstrake Holiday Camp which was just outside Douglas. He had booked for himself, me, Gordon and another Bevin Boy, Ken Hooper from Merthyr Vale. I polished the B31 until it was gleaming and we all set off for Liverpool for embarkation on *The Manx Maid* to the mecca of motor cycling. I had dreamed of going to see the TT since I had read an article by Graham Walker entitled 'Mist on the Mountain,' in which he described the rider's view of the course and personalities who had ridden in this famous race, including himself.

The crossing from Liverpool was lengthy and rough. The boat was crammed with motor bikes and I was very excited. Gordon was a sight to behold. He was as sick as a parrot all the way. They say people go green when they are sea sick and this proved to be the case with Gordon. He was literally green and just wanted to die there and then. We reached Douglas and the sun came out and everything was lovely with the world. The camp we stayed at was not far from the race circuit and it was not long before we set off for a complete lap of the course. The thrill of plunging down Bray Hill, circum-navigating the Mountain and rounding Kate's Cottage, was sheer heaven for me. The roar of the exhaust coming from the silencer under my feet while sitting on the pillion behind Arthur was unforgettable as we completed the circuit.

Before the actual races started we toured right around the island, Port Erin, Ramsey and Douglas itself. I was impressed by the scenery which ranges from the cultivated to the high land reminiscent of the Brecon Beacons. The camp we stayed at was small and friendly and full of motor cycle enthusiasts. I made friends with a girl of my age whose father was a director of Pacey Plugs Ltd, manufacturers of sparking plugs. They were trying to compete with KLG and Champion plug makers. Her name was Eileen Long and she lived in Bletchley, Bucks. She sent me some plugs when she returned home and we corresponded for a while until it eventually fizzled out. While in the confines of the camp I took the opportunity to give Gordon's 'bike an airing when he went off with the others!

The actual race days were memorable. We placed ourselves in good vantage points and the first sight of a rider appearing crouched over the tank and the glorious sound from the megaphone exhaust of a racing camshaft Norton or Velocette, was bliss as the machine roared past and disappeared down the road. I could actually see my 'gods' like Harold Daniell, in the flesh at close quarters. No Japanese motor cycles to be seen then. Whereas the German BMW dominated the immediate pre-war TT races, the single cylinder 500cc Norton dominated the first post-war Senior TT, the single cylinder 350cc Velocette similarly won the majority of the post-war Junior TT races.

Our journey back to Liverpool after the TT was equally gruesome for Gordon who had a repeat performance of the outward crossing. We arrived at The Pierhead late evening and rather than ride through the night we slept alongside the 'bikes on benches until daybreak. Most uncomfortable! Gordon and Ken Hooper parted company from us on leaving Liverpool, they headed back to Merthyr and Arthur and I made our way to Sale in Cheshire which was near Manchester. Uncle Wyndham, Aunty Muriel and Joan were living there, Wyndham having secured a job with *The News*

Chronicle newspaper. We stayed with them for a couple of nights and made the most of it by going to see a rugby match at the Sale Club ground before we too returned to Merthyr.

Since my grandmother's death, my mother had been complaining of backache in the kidney region. She was diagnosed with a stone in the kidney and advised that it could not be dispersed which meant that she would have to have an operation to remove it. My father had her admitted to St. Winifred's private nursing home in Cardiff and there she underwent an operation by the surgeon Mr Rees Mogg. The operation was successful but afterwards, Mr Rees Mogg told my father that they could not remove the stone because it was too large which necessitated the removal of the entire kidney, leaving her with just one functioning kidney. The stone was very jagged and was called a 'stag' kidney stone. This left us very worried as the surgeon only gave my mother a maximum of ten years to live. My mother was 46 years of age at the time and she went on to live into her 100th year, long after Mr Rees Mogg had pegged out! She suffered no after ill effects and was extremely healthy, taking care she did not eat any rubbish and religiously drank her honey and cider vinegar every day.

At last the day for my driving test arrived and I set off on the BSA down to Merthyr High Street to meet the examiner. The test consisted then of a solo circular drive through the streets of the town with the examiner observing from various undisclosed points en route. Off I went down the tramroad and as I drew adjacent to a row of houses, a front door flew open and a dog shot out into the road like a rocket from outer space, right into my path. There was nothing I could do about it and I ran over it, coming to a shuddering stop. People came pouring out of the house ready to put the blame on me but luckily the examiner was in the proximity had seen what happened and soon put them straight. The dog was perfectly alright which was more than could be said for me in the circumstances. The examiner asked me if I could continue and I did so and completed the test. When I hoisted the 'bike on its stand and went in to the examiner's office, I thought I didn't stand a dog's chance (forgive the pun) of passing, but pass I did and the relief and joy of achieving my goal was stupendous. At last I was free to ride my beloved motorbikes without fear of breaking the law. I often wondered if the examiner was curious as to how I was so competent a rider so soon after my sixteenth birthday. Little did he know!

Shortly after I passed my test, Arthur decided he would buy a new motorbike. We had seen in *Motor Cycling* that the Douglas Motor Cycle factory had brought out a revolutionary flat horizontal twin cylinder, 350cc machine, This had special radius arm front forks and torsion bar rear suspension and was called the T35. It had a unit construction gearbox but unlike the BMW had a chain final drive to the rear wheel. We went to see the 'bike at the nearest dealer, which was Cyril Morgan in Caerphilly. Of course, we fell in love with it and bought it straight away, putting in the faithful BSA in part exchange. Compared to the single cylinder BSA, the Douglas just purred along and the springing was superb. Thus, 1948 saw a new chapter opening in our motor cycle story.

Peacetime conditions were still stringent with rationing and scarcity of some commodities. The armed forces were being de-mobilised and likewise Arthur and the other Bevin Boys were discharged from the mines. No longer would I have to wait for him to come out of the pit head baths at Merthyr Vale to take him home on the 'bike. He now had to decide what he was going to do in the future. He was a talented artist and could draw anything, people, buildings, landscapes anything one could name. He decided to go in for architecture as opposed to engineering which he formerly studied at Bristol University. He applied for entry to The Welsh School of Architecture at Cathays Park, Cardiff and was invited to attend for an interview with the Principal, Lewis John. I went with Arthur for company and the result was that he was accepted for the six years course.

The question now was what was to become of me? I still detested Quakers Yard School and did everything I could to avoid attending.

Instead of catching the train to go to school I used to catch a bus to Cardiff and spend the day walking around the shops or sitting on a seat opposite City Hall waiting for a bus to return to Merthyr to coincide with the end of school time. Again I was summoned to the headmaster's study and given a dressing down, but it was hopeless. We all came to the conclusion that I had better start thinking of what the alternatives were. I always wanted to be a farmer but Mam did everything she could to put me off that course saying it was a hard life with little reward. I looked very much like Grandpa Harris, who died when I was six months old and who was a farmer. He was my boyhood hero and I longed to emulate his farming prowess.

I decided that journalism sounded pretty attractive and that a job as a reporter on our local weekly *The Merthyr Express* would fill the bill. Uncle Tom knew one of the directors of the newspaper, named Illtyd Rees. He lived in a large rambling house at the top of The Grove near the Cyfarthfa Park gates. He asked me to come and see him at the house and I duly met him and Mrs Rees and had some tea with them. Mrs Rees was related to the Berry family who practically controlled Fleet Street. A further meeting was then arranged for me to have an interview with Mr Longville Bowen who was the editor of *The Merthyr Express*. I went along to the *Express* offices in Glebeland Street and met the editor who was a large portly man constantly smoking a cigar. I knew his daughter, who lived with her father and mother just around the corner from us, in Dane Terrace. The long and short of the interview was that providing I learned shorthand, I had a job with *The Merthyr Express*. Classes in shorthand were being held in Dowlais School and I duly enrolled to attend. Imagine my discomfort when I turned up for the first lesson to find that I was the only male in a class of some fifteen girls! I stuck it for a while and picked up a reasonable speed but the novelty wore off and it became a repeat performance of my erstwhile piano lessons, so I finished. As a point of interest, the editor was having an affair with a cousin of my father's at the time, Katie Harris, and that intrigued me.

Arthur on his Triumph Tiger 100 and me on Douglas.

My first 'bike and me, the Douglas Twin.

Me posing on Arthur's Triumph Tiger 100.

'The Three Musketeers,' Ted, Vernon and me.

63

Meanwhile, the new Douglas was going great and I attended many motor bike trials held in the area including the leading Mitchell Trial. Ted, Vernon and I covered the lot and we followed the leading riders such as Bill Nicholson (BSA), Fred Rist (BSA), Phil Alves (Triumph) and Harold Tozer (BSA Combination). It was during this time that I went to my first rugby international. Ted, Vernon and me went by train from Merthyr to Swansea to see Wales play France in St. Helen's. This was early 1948 and it was a privilege to see the great Welsh international scrum-half Haydn Tanner play. This was one of the first rugby international matches to be played since the war ended. We three went to many more club matches including visits to Cardiff Arms Park to see Cardiff play on a pitch which used to resemble a mud bath at times. Players took part then for the enjoyment and the honour of participating rather than the megabuck philosophy of professional players nowadays. You had to have the ball before you could be tackled then and three points for a try! Rugger becomes more like American football as time passes.

A frequent visitor to Lancaster Villas was Arthur's friend from Cefn, Elwyn Bowen. Elwyn had been appointed headmaster of a school in Beulah, Breconshire, the youngest person to hold such a post in the county. This was a very rural location and its pupils were drawn from the local farming community. He used to travel week-ends from Beulah to Cefn Coed on his AJS motor cycle. Dewi, his younger brother who was also a Bevin Boy, years later became an arts master in Cyfarthfa Castle Grammar School. Elwyn's mother was a half sister to one of my father's cousins. Elwyn used to come out with elaborate tales of life in the country and how well farmers were doing financially, plenty of unrationed food and a healthy way of life. This fired my already susceptible imagination regarding farm-ing and the more I thought about it, the more I wanted to become a farmer.

Another family pow wow followed and it was thought that I had better find out the hard way what farming was really like. I started taking *The Farmer & Stock Breeder* trade magazine and avidly read it from cover to cover. In it was advertised a 'situation vacant' for a farm pupil to work on a farm in Devonshire. So, with a light heart and not a backward glance at school, I applied and was accepted. I caught the train at Cardiff and arrived in Exeter station where I changed trains for the final leg to Barnstaple in North Devon. Here I was met by my to be tutor/employer, Mrs Marshall. We drove to her farm which was called Darracott Farm, Georgeham, Braunton, North Devon. This was a typical Devonshire thatched farmhouse with about 30 acres of land. It was right alongside the road off a short entrance drive. It looked exactly how one imagined a farm should look and the peace was shattering! I discovered that I was not the only pupil, there was another who's name I cannot recall. We were given a nice roomy bedroom, tastefully furnished and the accommodation could not be faulted. Mrs Marshall was not the typical farming type as I expected, but more of a 'hobby' farmer. She was quite a well off, middle-class woman, who always wore riding breeches and tweeds.

The farm carried a herd of pedigree Guernsey cows, a bull and a small amount of arable for growing kale and other root crops. Grass and hay were the mainstay of the farm and the milk was sold as Channel Island milk. All the cows were hand milked and it was here that I first experienced catching hold of a cow's teat and feeling its rubbery texture. It was here too that I first saw a cow being serviced by a bull and that too made a deep impression! It beats the 'birds and the bees' hands down.

As well as dairying, Mrs Marshall bred pedigree Dalmatian dogs. I can't say I took to this breed. They have a nice disposition but put on the spot, I would say they are not pretty. By the time I had been there a few weeks, I was beginning to look like a Cornish pasty. She served these up meal after meal and while they are very tasty, there is a limit. She was quite kind and took us out for the odd visit to places like Croyde Bay and Saunton Sands. At night, from my bedroom, I could see the light on Lundy Island winking off and on at regular intervals. The actual day to day work was undertaken by her manager cum cowman who was employed full-time. he was loathe to delegate any 'tricky' work to us youngsters so that it was a bit of a job to learn anything.

I did feel homesick at times. I wrote regularly home and the theme was mainly when can I have a motor bike? Mrs Marshall had an interesting experience of motor cycles. Prior to her coming to Devon, she lived near T. E. Lawrence in southern England. Better known as 'Lawrence of Arabia,' Mrs Marshall often heard him ride past her house on his Brough Superior motor cycle and she actually heard him crash when he got killed in 1935. The tasks we were given were jobs like chaffing straw and chopping up kale and swedes for cattle feed. After giving it a good trial it didn't take me long to realise that I was going nowhere fast and that I would have to find a more workmanlike and efficient farm if I was to progress. I caught the train back to Merthyr via Exeter and Bristol and decided to take stock before my next step.

Reunited with Arthur and the Douglas I was again in my element. I kept up the pressure for a motor bike of my own and so Arthur decided to buy a new Triumph Tiger 100. This was a 500cc twin cylinder machine capable of over 100 mph and was a beautiful motor bike to look at. I could now have the Douglas! Arthur and I went down to Alex Thom Motors in Cardiff and collected the brand new Tiger 100. It had a novel rear suspension with the coil springs enclosed in a large hub in the rear wheel. In 1948 this was unique. Having a motor bike of my own was a feeling like nothing else I had experienced. I could go anywhere I wanted within the confines of petrol rationing which was still in being. With Ted on the pillion we travelled the countryside far and wide and when Ted had his own machine, Vernon became my rear 'gunner.' Ted's father bought him an ex-army Matchless motor cycle. Together, we went to the Merthyr Motor Club and rode to club outings. We really were 'kings of the road.'

Later in the year, the Douglas company brought out a sports version of the T35 with improved cylinder heads, a new exhaust system, new colour scheme and improved various bits and pieces. I wrote to Douglas and asked them if it would be possible for them to update my T35 to full 'Sports' specification. They replied they could and asked me to bring my 'bike to their factory in Kingswood, Bristol, for them to do the necessary modifications. This I did via the Aust ferry which proved to be a nasty crossing with a high wind and the ferry rolling so much that the motor bikes on board were in danger of falling off their stands. The factory loaned me a T35 machine for me to get home and this turned out to be the very 'bike that had been tested by *Motor Cycling* when the model was first introduced on the market. It took two weeks for the modifications to be completed and I returned to Kingswood to collect my gleaming 'new' motor cycle. It was a big improvement on the previous version, much smoother and with a bit more poke. I was very pleased and floating on air.

As time went on it became imperative that I had to decide what my next stage career wise was to be. A Miss Griffiths who farmed Rhydycar Farm in Merthyr, used to bring fresh farm eggs regularly to Mrs Richards next-door in Lancaster Villas. When she heard I was keen on farming, she suggested I got in touch with her niece and husband who farmed in Pembrokeshire. I jumped on the Douglas and went to see them. Mr and Mrs Mansel Cole farmed a holding named Whitlow Hill, Landshipping, Martletwy, near Narberth. Mr Cole was born and bred locally and his wife was, of course, from Merthyr. They were a very nice couple, very countrified and the complete opposite to Mrs Marshall in Devon. They were prepared to take me on as a pupil and so the deal was struck.

A Decade of Farming

IN LATE 1948, I FILLED THE DOUGLAS with petrol having packed my wellies and went west to Landshipping. I soon fitted in to the routine. The farm was about 80 acres and the land ran down to the River Cleddau where it branched off to Haverfordwest on one arm and to Canaston Bridge on the other. Picton Castle could be seen plainly on the opposite bank. The land was mainly grassed with a little crop growing mainly roots and carried a few milking cows of Shorthorn extraction plus some geese and chickens. The cows were milked by hand by Mrs Cole. The 'mechanical' power was supplied by horses and there was little in the shape of modern farm machinery. It did not take me long to convince Mansel that a tractor would make life a lot easier for him (and me!) The lorry duly turned up on the yard carrying a nice new Fordson Major tractor. Looking back now the design of this model looked really antiquated and was the next model to follow the old standard 'stand up' Fordson. It needed a stepladder to get on and off it and an oxygen mask would not have been amiss! Mansel could not drive a car so it was left to me to drive the tractor and to later teach him how to drive. Having the Douglas with me was a great help to the Coles. When Mansel had a dental appointment in Tenby he would ride on the pillion and enjoyed every minute of his first ever trip on a state-of-the-art motor bike.

My father too was becoming more bitten by the farming bug and started to seriously consider packing his job in and buying a farm providing a suitable place could be found in the right location. At weekends, I travelled back home to Merthyr and we would visit farms that my parents had short listed as eligible for inspection. We saw a variety of places but none filled the bill. What they gained in one respect they failed in another. Joan came with us on one occasion when we went to Caerphilly to see a possible candidate. The house was magnificent but the land was too near a built-up housing area, so that too bit the dust. That particular venue is now a housing estate.

Landshipping was a quiet little hamlet which had once seen more prosperous days when it was used to ship coal during the birth of the industrial era. The Cole family had farmed in the vicinity for generations but could not be described as wealthy farmers. It was in early 1949 that Mrs Cole called me in from the fields to tell me my father was on the 'phone and wanted to talk to me. Imagine my shock and delight when he said that they had found a farm and had decided to buy it and that I had better come home straight away. I broke the news to Mansel and Mrs Cole and set off back to Merthyr the next day. They were very sorry to see me leave and we parted on the best of terms. On my arrival home I was told that the farm they had selected was called Green Meadow Farm and was situated in Taliaris, five miles north of Llandeilo in Carmarthenshire. It was an eighty-eight acres holding laid down to permanent and temporary grass leys. I couldn't wait to see it and the next day we all drove down to Llandeilo. The approach road to the farm was through the yard of Troedyrhiw yr Esgair and was about half a mile in length to Green Meadow Farm.

I fell in love with Green Meadow as soon as I clapped eyes on it. The farmhouse was a solid stone constructed building with sloping walls three feet thick, dating back 250 years. The rooms were low with lovely oak beams and an inglenook fireplace in which you could hold a concert. The land was in a ring fence around the house and buildings, mainly level with some slopes to the north side. A good range of stone buildings around a large square yard was separated from the house by a big orchard. It had been well farmed by the previous occupiers, the Thomas family, who were tenants of the owner Miss Evans, a spinster, who lived with her niece and husband, Mr and Mrs Gwyn Walters in Troedyrhiw yr Esgair Farm, which she also owned. The Thomas family had applied for and was granted the tenancy of a Cawdor Estate Farm at Broad Oak. They were successful because of the high standard of husbandry they had achieved at Green Meadow. Miss Evans was an elderly lady who had never married but stayed at home to look after her late brother who never married either. However, she did have an ongoing courtship with Ivor Evans who lived on the neighbouring farm, Pyllau-cochion, and who also never married. Ivor lived with his older brother, Tom, who had parted from his wife. I think Ivor and Miss Evans used to meet by appointment. Who said romance was dead?

Prior to us moving from Merthyr and until the purchase was completed and the house in Lancaster Villas sold, I stayed with Mr and Mrs Walters and their only son Howell, while I kept an eye on Green Meadow. Howell was a couple of years older than me and we shared a bedroom in the back slope of their farmhouse. It got quite crowded on occasions when Howell's cousin Lyn Walters who was younger than us came to help out on the farm. Back in Merthyr the house was sold and Arthur secured lodgings in Cardiff while he studied at the college. The next task was to move our belongings. Lynn's father, Lloyd Walters who was Gwyn's brother, ran a livestock haulage business in Llandeilo and he offered to move our furniture etc, in his cattle lorry, an offer which we accepted.

Looking back, it must have been a terrific upheaval for my mother who had lived in towns all her life, for her to bury herself in the heart of the country without any conveniences such as electric light, no telephone, no flush toilets, no piped water and the nearest neighbour not within shouting distance. On top of that, there were no shops within five miles and no buses passing the door. She must have felt it was akin to trekking west to California! I never heard her complain. Happily, she had made a remarkable recovery from her kidney operation.

One of the first things my father did after packing in his job was to buy a car. It was a Vauxhall Twelve saloon, this enabled us to get out from the farm and I still had my precious Douglas. The next thing was to have the telephone installed so that at least it felt that we were not being cut off from civilisation. All the water for drinking and washing had to be carried in containers from a well situated 250 yards from the house. For light we relied on paraffin lamps and candles and a primus stove for cooking. What a life! The first priority was to get the water supply sorted. During the war, a lot of Poles came to Britain to fight the Germans and when the war ended a large number stayed on in this country and settled. They needed work and we were fortunate to find two Polish men who had worked on farms and who were prepared to look for water and dig a well for us. They divined a source between Green Meadow and Penybank Farm and proceeded to dig, using just iron bars and picks and shovels. I had never seen men work so hard. Stripped to the waist they dug nonstop until they came across an excellent source about ten feet down, eureka!

After lining the well with concrete pipes the water was piped down to the house and buildings and taps were installed. What a joyous event it was when my mother turned on the tap in the kitchen and the water came gushing out spitting and spluttering before it steadied into a smooth flow. A bathroom followed in due course when the small middle bedroom was converted and life became a little easier. Cooking and hot water problems were solved by installing a Rayburn cooker but we still had to put up with oil lamps for lighting for some time to come.

Having sorted out the domestic situation to our satisfaction, it was now time to turn to the serious business of farming. All the farms in the area were milk producing. They had very little modern machinery, relying on horses or old pre-war tractors for power. Milking was done by hand with the exception of the two old boys in Pyllaucochion who had the latest type of milking machine which took the milk straight from the cows along a pipeline to the farm dairy. Their herds consisted of Shorthorn-type cattle and their income was supplemented by keeping pigs, poultry and sheep. Farming was still under the supervision of the War Agricultural

Executive Committees and they laid down what farmers could grow and imposed quotas. In Green Meadow we had to grow a specified acreage of potatoes, for example.

A tractor was to us a necessity and there was only one make that we would consider buying and that was the Ferguson tractor. The brainchild of genius Harry Ferguson, this tractor revolutionised agriculture with its unique hydraulic system and design. The 'Fergie' was the pace setter and with its distinctive grey paintwork was a 'must have.' We bought our first brand new Ferguson TE20 tractor from the dealership Morris Isaac in Llandovery, for the princely sum of £325. It was a petrol driven tractor for which the government issued petrol ration coupons for it to run on 'red' agricultural petrol. The engine was the same basic design as the popular Standard Vanguard car which was introduced at a later date. We bought a second TE20 later, which ran on TVO (tractor vaporizing oil, paraffin). This had to be started on petrol and when hot, switched to TVO.

It could be tricky and was not as good or as efficient as the pure petrol model. With a transport box mounted on the rear hydraulic arms and top link, the Fergie became a multi-purpose machine enabling us to carry milk churns, sacks and tools without having to hitch a trailer. Other implements designed for the system included, ploughs, sub-soilers, harrows, trailers and many more useful items, and the backup service provided by the dealer was second to none. In 1949, I passed my driving test on the TE20; this was conducted at the 'Square and Compass' junction at Llangadog.

The obvious farming course for us to pursue was to produce milk. We installed the latest Alfa Laval bucket system milking machine in the cowsheds, were granted a license to produce milk, which at that time had to be sold to the Milk Marketing Board, so all that was then needed were . . . cows!

Having studied many agricultural journals and literature on livestock and talked to many farmers, I was increasingly drawn to keeping pure bred animals. By so doing. The market for their products would be the same as nondescript animals with the added advantage that stock for breeding purposes would also have an additional specialised outlet. The breed to go for was the British Friesian. This breed of mainly Dutch origin was noted for its high milk production and yet had a useful carcase for the meat market. Where to get them was the next problem to tackle. We had met a noted local breeder, Mr D. R. Thomas of Crymlyn Manor, near Llandeilo. His Crymlyn herd was first-class and contained some of the best bloodlines. Unfortunately, his stock was well out of our price range and he suggested we go to see his brother who was farming Fenton Home Farm in Pembrokeshire. His brother, a retired engineer, had bought the farm and was breeding Friesians and now had some surplus stock. My father and I went to see him and we bought our very first cow off him. She was an all black cow with white socks by the name of 'Pansy.' She turned out to be a prolific milker and a very good buy.

For the next few months we visited farms and markets including the special pedigree sales at Reading and Carmarthen. We bought cows with the herd prefixes of 'Hallfarm,' 'Dulais,' and 'Rodmel,' ending with a herd of some twenty-five cows. We were in business! All the milk we produced was taken in churns to a stand we had built jointly with Gwyn Walters at the entrance to Troedyrhiw yr Esgair. The milk was collected daily by lorry and taken to the CWS Milk Factory at Ffairfach, Llandeilo. I did all the milking myself with Arthur helping out when he came home at weekends from Cardiff. The cows grazed grass during summertime and were fed hay during the winter. Concentrates were purchased to boost milk production. Haymaking was a pure gamble in Carmarthenshire as the heavy rainfall made the job very difficult to gauge. The process was still very antiquated with the grass being cut, allowed to cure on the ground after numerous turnings by horse and rake, and then hand pitched loose on to carts and taken to the rick yard. There, it would be pitched off again in to the shed or lifted off the carts by a large fork pulled through pulleys by a horse. 'Blossom,' Gwyn Walters' horse, did her fair share of that work.

My father and mother with our Rover 90 at Green Meadow Farm.

Mother and Ford Zodiac.

My father and Arthur baling hay at Green Meadow.

The Ovaltine Jersey cows at Green Meadow Farm.

Several times we loaded the cart only to tip the lot when going through a bumpy gateway and having to load it by hand again. It was hot work with the hay seeds going down a sticky shirt neck. We certainly got through a fair drop of cider during the season with no ill effects. Other times it would rain and as soon as it became dry it would be a mad dash to harvest the hay. I've seen us making hay in September before we could even get in the fields without sinking in the ground. The decision was taken that we would minimise the risk of a bad harvesting season and go in for that new fangled stuff called 'silage.'

Nobody around us was in to silage making in 1949/50. We looked at the various options open to us and decided that the pit method of conserving the grass was our best bet. The only snag was we didn't have a pit! So, out comes the executive pick and shovel and Arthur and I dug by hand a silage pit at the rear of the barn in Green Meadow which took a lot of blood, sweat and tears! We were pleased with the finished job and so the next thing was to fill it. I ploughed a field and we planted a crop of oats, vetches and ryegrass and looked around for the best way of harvesting the crop. The hitherto conventional method of haymaking using 'slave labour,' was being superseded by hay crop loaders towed behind a tractor. The International Harvester Company brought out a green crop version of this which would pick up green fodder and place it on a trailer. We asked their local dealer, Evans Motors in Carmarthen, to come and demonstrate one on the farm. The salesman turned up and took it to a field next to Aberdeunant towing it to the top of the slope. The chap unhitched it from his pick-up truck and before he could fix it to the trailer it started rolling down the slope with the salesman hanging on trying to stop it. Luckily, as it gathered momentum it started to zigzag and eventually came to a halt on its own. I'll never forget the look on that salesman's face, the whole episode became folklore at Evans Motors.

We bought the green crop loader and proceeded to make silage. After mowing the grass we moved in with the tractor and trailer with the loader at the rear. My father drove the Ferguson while Arthur and me stood on the trailer placing the crop with our pitchforks like a pair of dervishes faced by a sea of endless green grass swamping us. Fred Astaire had nothing on us, it was as much as we could do to stop ourselves being overwhelmed. When we got back with a full load at the pit it was tipped out and spread by hand to consolidate the grass and exclude any trapped air pockets and then rolled by the tractor. A sprinkling of molasses followed which aided fermentation essential for high quality silage.

Enough was enough, if we wanted a full and long life a better and easier means of making silage must be in existence somewhere. So it came to pass that a visit to the Pullman factory in Ammanford ensued. Here they manufactured the 'Silorator' forage harvester which cut the grass, chopped it up and blew it up a pipe in to the trailer. This it seemed was the answer to our prayers. We were the first to operate this type of machine in Carmarthenshire and when it was in use on our top fields it could be heard in Llandeilo, so loud was the whine of the Silorator when operating.

The Milk Marketing Board had a scheme whereby for those farmers who did not own a bull they supplied an artificial insemination service (AI) from their bull stud. These bulls of all breeds were from the best breeding stock. As we did not have a bull at that stage, we utilised this service quite a lot. Mr Walters had a Friesian bull named 'Sawel Air Romance,' but he was of dubious origin. I remember riding on the Douglas down to Llwyndrissi Farm, St. Clears, in order to obtain his pedigree from Mr Davies the bull's breeder. Mr Davies originally came from Llansawel, hence the name of the bull.

The Milk Marketing Board bought the best bulls available and as I have mentioned, in the initial stages we utilised their services although I was not convinced that artificial insemination was a satisfactory way of getting cows in calf as it was a completely 'unnatural' process. In 1950, a large number of pedigree Friesian cattle were imported from Holland. Similar importations had taken place pre-war in 1914, 1922, 1936 and now 1950. Of these imports the most famous bull was 'Terling (Imp. 22) Marthus.' The latest importation cost the earth when purchased by British breeders among whom were the Williams family who owned the 'Grove' herd at St. Clears, Carmarthenshire. The Grove herd was probably the best Friesian herd in the entire UK. They purchased a heifer which had a dodgy udder and cost thousands. One of the Williams sons, a veterinary surgeon, operated on her and got her firing on all cylinders, enabling them to recoup their outlay many times from the sale of her progeny.

Several of these Dutch bulls went for stud to the MMB and we used them quite a lot. We named our herd 'Vaynor' and were able to sell young bulls and calves over a wide area of the UK, from Yorkshire to Devon. We showed bulls in the 1951 Llandeilo Show then held in Dinefwr Park (Cae William) and the BFCS Show and Sale in Reading. It was not long before a 'proper' bull was bought for our herd. In the shape of 'Pitsea Met Rooske.' The Pitsea herd was based in the village of Pitsea in Essex and was a very large pedigree herd which was kept to supply milk to a big dairy company operated by its owner/farmer, Mr Howard.

In order to ensure safety and ease of handling, Arthur designed a model bull pen which we built ourselves at the rear of the cowshed in Green Meadow. There was not one like it in West Wales and it attracted a lot of interested cattle breeders who came to see it, including Messrs Evans, breeders of the noted 'Deri' herd from Derimoelion, Dryslwyn, who were favourably impressed. This pen enabled one man to handle the most ferocious bull and have the females served without the handler coming in contact with the bull.

Taking an animal to Reading Sales was quite an adventure. When I took a young bull there in 1951, the best way was by train. We were taken by cattle truck to Llandeilo station, transferred to a special rail truck complete with passenger compartment for me. This had been shunted into the sidings at the station by an engine sent from Carmarthen. It was then hitched to the passenger train going to Llanelli and there added to the train bound for London via Swansea. On reaching Reading, we were again shunted in to a siding and from there I led the bull through Reading streets to the cattle market which was not too far from the station.

Maximum milk production from cows was the driving force in those days. I was a fan of George Odlum who bred the noted 'Manningford' herd in England. He wrote a book in which he described his breeding technique and views. I devoured this intensely and agreed with most of what he wrote. His cow, 'Manningford Faith Jan Graceful,' broke world records for production and gave a lifetime milk yield of over 50 tons. Three times a day milking was advocated for high yielding cows as this emulated a calf's natural way of feeding 'on a little and often basis.' Thrice daily milking meant less strain on the udder resulting in less chance of the cow contracting mastitis which is the scourge of the dairy farming industry. So, I decided to milk our cows three times daily. The first milking I did was at 6.30 a.m., the next 2.30 p.m. and the last 10.30 p.m. I kept this up for six years and the results were outstanding. The yields went up, disease down . . . and me tired out at the end!

One of our heifers, 'Dulais Popularity,' gave over 2,000 gallons on her first year's lactation, proving to be one of the highest yielding heifers in the MMB's National Milk Recording Scheme. The butterfat content increased dramatically and this was important as the Friesian breed at that time had difficulty in meeting the minimum legal butterfat and solids not fat content of their milk. Many herds had the odd Jersey or Guernsey cow to boost the quality of the milk. Thrice milking certainly helped in this aspect.

All this milking and farm work left me with very little leisure time, and so it was with a very heavy heart that I decided to call it a day as far as motor cycling was concerned, and so I sold my pride and joy, my Douglas! The storeman/mechanic in the Ferguson dealer's had fancied the T35 for a while and often saw it when working on our Fergusons. He bought it so at least I knew it was going to a good home and to an enthusiast. I still had access to Arthur's Tiger 100 when he came home on visits, so things were not all bad.

Milk production was going fairly smoothly but was still not generating enough income, so 'thinking hats' went on and it was decided that retailing our own milk in Llandeilo would be one way of doing this. I was becoming very keen on the Jersey breed and thought it would be a good move to sell Channel Island Jersey milk in Llandeilo. We had enough surplus cowshed capacity to accommodate another fifteen cows, so we set out to buy the best pedigree Jersey cows we could afford. Upon joining the English Jersey Cattle Society, we were given a list of appropriate breeders. The first my father and I went to see was Captain Hext-Lewes of Talsarn. We were entertained royally by him and his wife (he was a friend of the Duke of Edinburgh), and was a former captain of the aircraft carrier *Ark Royal*. We had a look at his herd but decided they were not the type we were looking for. The next port of call was to Mr C. B. Crocker at Paviland Manor on the Gower coast. Here was a very large pedigree herd run on commercial lines. Mr Crocker was a real enthusiast and it was he who introduced me to the 'Guenon Theory' whereby the potential milking ability of any breed of cow could be accurately diagnosed by the pattern of the hair forming the escutcheon on its rear flanks. I tested this theory on many cows and and it proved to be so. Guenon was a Frenchman who wrote an illustrated book expounding his theory, which is now out of print. Mr Crocker did not have any surplus stock to sell so we continued the search widening the net.

I was always partial to a cup of Ovaltine and had been an enthusiastic collector when a boy of labels off the Ovaltine tins in order to get their badges. The firm had a model farm in King's Langley, Herts., where they had a pedigree herd of Jersey cattle which had won prizes throughout the Jersey world. They also advertised the fact that their Jersey milk was an ingredient in their Ovaltine product implying that the quality was second to none.

'Ovaltine Brampton Baby.'

'Pitsea Met Rooske' and me when both young! 1949.

'Hallfarm Akke Innocent,' one of our best milkers.

'Pansy' the first cow we ever bought (1949).

My father and I were met at their farm by the manager and shown around. I had never seen a farm like it. It was magnificent, not an ounce of muck or dirt to be seen and the cowshed would have put a hospital to shame. It had white ceramic tiles from floor to ceiling and the tubular standings were immaculate. Every cow in the building wore a top blanket embroidered with the Ovaltine logo and the whole place breathed opulence.

Their herd had been founded on the best bloodlines from both Jersey and Canada. The Brampton herd in Canada had supplied much of their foundation stock. We liked what we saw and did a deal with the firm by buying ten Ovaltine cows and heifers. Gwyn Walters had the shock of his life when, a few days later, two large purpose built livestock lorries passed through his yard emblazoned with 'Ovaltine Dairy Farm' all over them. We had our first Jerseys.

Having had enough of AI, we felt we should purchase our own Jersey bull. Where was the best place to get one? . . . Jersey of course! I could not leave the milking to go there so Arthur and my father went. They caught the boat across and it was a pretty rough crossing it seems. My father was ill all the way and swore he would never go on a boat again, after the return trip. They met the Jersey cattle export agent in St. Helier and he took them around the farms. All the cows were tethered by the horns in the fields and they had no difficulty in choosing five in calf heifers and a bull. The bull was an Island Champion by the name of 'Peter Pan's Jester.' They were shipped over in a week or so and arrived in Green Meadow to join their Ovaltine cousins. When I first clapped eyes on the bull I thought he was gorgeous, with large eyes and the most lovely range of colours on his head and coat. I soon found out that all that glitters is not gold. Jester was not very big but could he turn on a sixpence! You had to be very careful handling him as he would go for you as good as look at him.

The milk that the cows produced was thick with cream and a butterfat content of over 6% compared to the Friesian 3.2% to 3.5%. They were little devils to milk and temperamental. They would keep their back legs together to make it difficult to put the teat cups on and if any slight thing upset them they would not drop their milk. Compared to Friesians they were a dead loss. We pressed ahead to retail their milk and set up our hand bottling shed where we filled our own designed bottles. The cream came down to the bottom of the bottle neck and looked very attractive. Complete with gold top it looked a winning product. We loaded the Ferguson with crates of Jersey milk and set off for town. It was hard work working up a customer base but eventually a few stalwarts were enticed to try the high quality milk, but it was an up hill struggle. People in Llandeilo were not prepared to pay that little extra for Jersey milk and to put the finishing touch to the whole exercise, a local town milkman went round our customers smashing the empty bottles before we could collect them. Cow and Gate could rest assured that we would not be competing with them just yet! Eventually, we sold all the Jerseys in the pedigree sales in Crewe. I was glad to see the back of them. They are pretty animals but that's about all they are, certainly not to be compared to other dairy breeds such as the Ayrshire or Friesian or even the traditional Dairy Shorthorn.

Apart from the dairying, I was becoming interested in pig breeding. Our first encounter with pigs at Green Meadow was a pig that we had been given and which we fattened up. The time arrived for us to kill it and a farmer cum butcher named Mr Thomas from Bridge Farm, Llandeilo, came to do the necessary. We borrowed a large wooden table from Gwyn Walters and he, my father and me managed to subdue the pig and lift it on to the table then proceeded to sit on it while Mr Thomas slit its throat. I'll never forget it. Blood spurted everywhere as we tried to hold it down in its death throes. At last it gave up the ghost and peace reigned. If that didn't persuade anyone to become a vegetarian, I do not know what would. It brings home the eternal question why does one species have to kill another in order to live, who thought that one up?

One of the rooms at the back of the house was fitted with large flat stone slabs all around the room. The pig was cut up and jointed there and salted on the slabs, the salt being well rubbed in to preserve the meat. The hams and sides were then hoisted on to hooks in the ceiling and left to continue curing there. Brawn was made from the head and was like minced beef in the shape of a Christmas pudding and tasting like salty corned beef. Grand stuff for cholesterol sufferers! Keeping pigs for pedigree breeding seemed to me to be a less barbaric practice. The Welsh pig had a good reputation, it looked a bit on the heavy side but there were strains which could be worked on and improved. We bought our first three gilts from Mr M. L. James of Ysgubor Fawr, Myddfai. He was a friendly man, getting on in years, who had bred Welsh pigs all his life. We had pigsties behind the house which were of the conventional, traditional type. Pibwrlwyd College in Carmarthen also bred Welsh pigs so we called on them to see if they had a suitable boar. They did and we purchased 'Pibwr Gwron 5th' who turned out to be an excellent boar producing good progeny. He had a happy time in those sties!

Ted's mother and father came to visit us on their Speed Twin outfit and Ted on his Matchless. Ted and I were in the calf shed while I was feeding stock, when all of a sudden there was a crunch in the ceiling a hole appeared and a kitten fell out on Ted's head. It was a pretty kitten all black with a white bib and paws. It was promptly named 'Twm Shôn' after the Welsh 'Robin Hood,' and spent its entire life as part of our family.

As we did not have sheep we didn't have a sheepdog, but we did have a black cocker spaniel called 'Bobby' which we had brought with us from Merthyr. He had a marvellous nature and could catch rats with ease. Other species we kept were geese for the Christmas trade, which again we used to rely on Gwyn Walters to kill for us, and hens for egg production. The stone slabs in the house came in to their own again when it was time to dress the geese. They were lined up like soldiers with their 'icing' of goose fat slapped on top of each one.

Life in the country certainly wasn't drab or uneventful. Two former Polish servicemen farmed Cefn Hendre opposite Tŷ Coch

Farm. The bearded smaller of the two could often be seen walking into Llandeilo, and my father gave him lifts on several occasions. I too had spoken to him. He was a pleasant individual, and both of them fitted into the neighbourhood well. One day his partner suddenly disappeared and the police were called in. They failed to find him but discovered one of the farmhouse rooms spattered with blood. His partner claimed they had been killing pigs there, also stating that the KGB or similar Russian intelligence personnel had come to the farm and taken him. He was sent for trial for murder and found guilty. This was the first conviction in Britain of murder without a body. A queer twist of fate was that many years later, after he was released, and while standing on a corner in London, a car came along and knocked him down, killing him, and the driver was never caught.

Our Vauxhall car was now beginning to show its age having been used for a variety of tasks on the farm from carrying sacks of cattle food to transporting the odd calf. The Ford Motor Company was setting the pace in the motor world with the introduction of the Consul and Zephyr Zodiac models. We rather fancied the Zodiac so a trip to the main Ford dealer in Swansea, C. E. M. Day, followed. Their showrooms were sited in St. Helen's Road and were quite modest then. The owner 'Jimmy' Day was a brother Freemason to my father and was a bit of a character. He told us that the business had been financed by his father importing carpets from abroad and selling them in the UK. We bought a new Ford Zodiac and enjoyed the drive back to Green Meadow. The car was two-tone, cream on the top and blue from the waist down. It had whitewall tyres and a steering column gear lever to a three speed gearbox. With its six cylinder engine it was a lively car and a pleasure to drive. It was followed by a second replacement Zodiac from Day's in due course, this time having a colour combination of cream and fawn.

We had a mixed bag of neighbours, the Walters family were great and we got on well with them. Aberdeunant, which was on our eastern boundary, was owned and farmed by the Thomas family. Mr and Mrs Thomas were strict disciplinarians and ruled the children with a rod of iron. Old grandmother Thomas looked to me like a witch. One of our best Friesian cows gave birth to a calf in a field next to Aberdeunant, but when I went to bring them in to the buildings, the calf had disappeared in a very short space of time. We never found it, despite a thorough search. Days later, Gwyn Walters said he had a good idea that somebody had taken it but he could not prove it. We never saw the calf again!

The Williams family lived in Penybank Farm on our northern boundary. Mr Williams rented the farm and had a young family. He was a hard-working young man and strong. I've seen him carrying heavy sacks of potatoes slung on his shoulder up the steep slope to his house from Green Meadow, a distance of half a mile. He eventually went to farm in Trap. Our remaining neighbour was Mr Morgan and his family in Tŷ Coch Farm on the western boundary. Mr Morgan had been farming in Eppynt before the army took it over as a firing range during the war.

Following the Jersey episode another approach was called for to increase milk output. We were at full capacity in Green Meadow so the best way to achieve this was to buy more land. Following Mr Williams departure from Penybank to Trap, the farm came up for sale. Arthur was nearing the end of his architectural course in Cardiff and was thinking of coming on the farm to work. We bought Penybank jointly, which gave us an extra 82 acres to play with. The farm sat on the hill above Green Meadow. It had a substantial stone built house and a range of buildings which were good for dairying. The land was all grass, dry and the views from there were breathtaking looking across to the Black Mountains and the Brecon Beacons. To get to the farm by road it was necessary to drive to Halfway on the Llandeilo to Talley main road, turn right at Glanyrafonddu Isaf, drive again for a mile and a half past two farms before entering Penybank's farm road which was again a further half mile to the yard. As the crow flies it was only half a mile over the fields!

Green Meadow Farm photographed in 1950.

'Dulais Popularity,' a 2,000 gallon producing heifer.

First of our imported 1950 Dutch progeny bulls.

Me showing a bull at the 1951 Llandeilo Show.

Me ploughing with the Ferguson in 1950.

The cowshed was fitted out with concrete partitions and standings for twenty cows in one long line. The dairy was attached to one end with an open yard fronting them. We had a new Alfa Laval milking machine installed and we built a massive milk stand at the entrance of the farm road. We now needed more cows. We had come to know many breeders of British Friesian cattle and one I liked the look of was Messrs T. Adams & Sons of Penyrheol Farm, Cowbridge, in Glamorgan. Their 'Cowbridge' herd had bloodlines I was seeking which included Manningford, Elmwood and Terling and Lavenham breeding. My father, Arthur and me went to see the Adams family and had a warm welcome. We met Mr Tom Adams and his sons, Richard and Trevor. Richard was the main partner in the business and it was with him we did our negotiating. He was as straight as a ruler and a genuinely nice person. What he did not know about cattle and pig breeding was not worth knowing. The Manningford element through the bull 'Manningford Norah Ephos' was strong and we ended up buying a large number of cows off Richard.

Having their own cattle lorry, delivery to Penybank was made in the days following. However, on our way back home from Cowbridge, we were rounding the bends near Meusydd Garage on a bitterly cold day with ice forming on damp roads, when a car coming round the bend in front of us lost control on the icy surface and slid into the offside of our Zodiac making a nice big dent in our car in the process. Luckily, nobody was hurt and we managed to limp home.

Arthur successfully completed his course and became a fully qualified registered architect under his name of W. A. R. Harris (Dip. Arch.), ARIBA. Back to the farm he came and he too, like I had with my Douglas, decided that the faithful Tiger 100 would have to go. He sold it to a chap in the north of England, delivering it himself and catching a train to get back home. The cowsheds in both Green Meadow and Penybank were now a hive of activity. As soon as milking had finished in one we trudged up the hill to Penybank to do another milking, often in the dark, carrying oil lamps to see the way and to light up the cowshed when we reached there.

It didn't take us long to realise that this was pretty laborious. Large herds were using the parlour system in England, so we thought it a good idea to bring all the cows to the one point for milking, put them through in relays and then return them to their sheds after milking in the winter and straight out for grazing in the summer. This we did, and it worked! In the meantime, Mr Morgan in Tŷ Coch, had decided to move. He had bought the farm from the firm of solicitors who owned Pyllaucochion. He bought a smaller property in Taliaris known as Banc Farm. Arthur and I were tempted to go for this farm also, this time it was the 'big' stuff as Tŷ Coch was 150 acres on its own. We asked the Carmarthen auctioneer, Major John Francis, to come and value it for us. This he did and was of the opinion that it would be a good buy as well. It happened that Major Francis knew the locality from way back. As a boy he had attended his first farm auction with his father at neighbouring Glanyrafonddu Isaf, bringing back happy memories for him.

Tŷ Coch Farm in 1959.

We purchased Tŷ Coch Farm and a few days later the auction sale of Mr Morgan's stock took place in the yard between the barn and cowshed. Scores of people attended and the living room in the house was used as the sale day office. Mr Morgan had not farmed intensively so that he did not have a great deal to sell, but I do remember him putting his sheepdog up for auction, which I thought was a heartless thing to do. It was not a young dog and had worked faithfully for him. It left a bitter taste.

So now we had another cowshed to fill. Like Penybank, this one was also concrete stalled and in one line of twenty cow places. Mr Morgan had not milked there relying mainly on beef and sheep production. In fact, it was more or less dog and stick farming. The entrance to Tŷ Coch was off the main Llandeilo to Talley road near the Goitre Farm and another through the yard of Glanyrafonddu

Isaf and along the right of way to Tŷ Coch. This latter entrance was the only one passable for most of the year as the other went through the River Dulais. As there was no bridge it could be dangerous when the river was in full flow. Not the route to take walking home on a dark night!

A trip to Cowbridge to see Richard Adams was now imperative. We needed another fifteen or so cows which with our own reared heifers would bring us up to capacity. We selected our cows and Richard duly delivered them to Tŷ Coch. We still had our Welsh pigs but the breed was no match for the Danish and Swedish Landrace pigs. Richard was breeding Swedish Landrace and his pigs were outstanding, long, lean and prolific. We persuaded him to sell us an in pig gilt and we were in the Landrace business. Her progeny crossed with our Welsh, produced super pigs ideal for the lean bacon market.

A cow from this batch of Cowbridge females proved to be a winner. She was named 'Cowbridge Norephos Tea' and she gave over six gallons per day after calving. We now had three relays going through Penybank 'parlour' and a fair drop of milk was being produced. At one stage we were knocking out over twenty-two churns per day containing 220 gallons of milk. The largest producer sending milk to the CWS milk factory in the area. It was a sight to see the milk stand at the entrance to Penybank jam packed with gleaming milk churns. We still milked thrice daily at this stage which was not very popular with our NMR recorder, Cyril Rees from Llandovery. He had to travel at the dead of night to record the yields at milking time which was 10.30 p.m. for the third milking.

We were still making silage and storing it in the pit in Green Meadow. Now with our added acreage we had to find extra storage space. A fair amount of hay was made but we had mechanised the process more as the time went by and had invested in an International McCormick B45 hay baler. I discovered that by fitting a special trip mechanism, bales of half the normal size could be produced thus enabling fresh cut grass to be baled as silage. We tried this and found that you had to be Charles Atlas to lift them on to the trailer. We employed a local man named David Kirkup and his cousin to help us. David was terrific and as strong as an ox, I have seldom seen anyone working so hard. We stacked the bales in the barn at Tŷ Coch and waited to see how it would turn out. It was not a success, the centre of each bale was okay but air got to the outer surface creating mildew and rot.

Hiring powerful tractors and double chop forage harvesters was the order of the day. We used a Taarup forage harvester and tractors hired to us by Gwili Jones, Peniel, Carmarthen. He was a dealer who bought second-hand tractors and hired them out before selling them for export. This worked well for us, giving us access to the most powerful tractors on the market. The next step was to exchange our two Fergusons for two bigger tractors which we did by buying two new Fordson Major tractors. The difference in performance was marked and gave us that little extra for heavy work.

Our family in Merthyr kept an eye on our activities. Friends of my mother who had a grocery business and also a stall in Abergavenny market lived in a nice detached house in Vaynor. Estlyn and Millie Evans had been friends for many years. Millie had been in Cyfarthfa Castle School at the same time as my mother who herself started there in 1912. Estlyn had also known my mother since they were children, his brother Gomer had married Aunty Annie Mary, my grandmother's cousin. Estlyn himself once had a soft spot for my mother when they were teenagers. Gomer was a ship's engineer and was torpedoed during the war by a German submarine, he was in a lifeboat in open sea for a long time. One of his shipmates in the same lifeboat was the husband of Nancy who lived in Glandulais Uchaf on the bank of the River Dulais, next to Pyllaucochion. They both survived their ordeal (that is, Gomer and the husband!).

Estlyn's family and my mother's were staunch Unitarians, Estlyn having been named after a noted member of that following. He had some land around his house and owned about 20 acres on a nearby smallholding he had bought. He asked us to pop up to see them as he was keen on starting a small herd of milkers. Following our visit,

Estlyn, Millie and their daughter Nesta, an only child and the same age as me, came down to Green Meadow to see our herd and pay social visits. Nesta was a qualified pharmacist and was a very attractive girl, full of bounce and brimming with confidence. It was not long before she and Arthur began to see more and more of each other, culminating in them becoming engaged to be married. Everyone was pleased and the future looked rosy. However, Nesta had a track record of a trail of discarded suitors and when a chap by the name of John Kendal appeared on the scene things were never quite the same. In due course Arthur and Nesta broke off their engagement and that was that. We did sell Estlyn a few splendid heifers from our best cows, but a combination of insufficient experience and environmental factors resulted in the failure of the enterprise. John Kendal's father lived in the Pandy Farm in Merthyr and had a milk round. In his younger days he tried to court Aunty Annie Mary but she would have none of it describing him as an 'uncouth' individual.

It still felt as if we were living in the dark ages in the late fifties, and we were. We still did not have mains electricity so we lashed out on a portable generator, powered, funnily enough, by a Douglas engine. This worked alright as long as the belt to the alternator did not slip. It was quite novel reading a book at night with me trying to read quickly while the light was bright and the belt not slipping. My father decided to do something about the situation and started a petition signed by as many people possible in the neighbourhood to send to the Electricity Board requesting a service. He went round all the farms and houses locally and was surprised by the resistance to the idea on the grounds that some yokels thought it would be too expensive to operate. In the end he was successful and the day came when poles went up in the fields, a meter fixed in the house and the supply turned on . . . Sheer joy!

As soon as I was twenty-one I had become a Freemason, as did Arthur who was twenty-eight. My father was one, as was my grandfather, Uncle Tom and Uncle Davey, together with other close members of the family, such as my mother's cousin, Willie Thomas, Cefn Coed. We were both initiated into the North Glamorgan Lodge in Merthyr under the direction of Uncle Tom who was a Worshipful Master in the Masonic Lodge and who officiated at the initiation ceremony. I remained a Master Freemason, deciding not to go through the various offices which could be very time consuming. Freemasonry was of great interest to me as it was based on friendship, history, and family connections. Great Uncle Tom Harris was a prominent Freemason in the USA, as were other members of the family who had emigrated.

Events moved quickly in the latter part of the fifties. My mother's eldest brother, Uncle Lyndon, died leaving a widow Dilys, who continued to live in Dane Street, Merthyr. We sold our Ford Zodiac and bought a new Land Rover from Edwards Garage in Carmarthen. The first time I took it through the river at Tŷ Coch, I had to drive a couple of miles before the brakes worked. It was too heavy for light work and vice versa. It was noisy and draughty, not at all as I imagined a cross country vehicle would perform.

Thrice daily milking was by now beginning to take its toll and we reverted to the standard twice daily routine. It was like winning the 'pools.' It meant I could now have some social life. We had bought a Murphy television set when the mains electricity was connected and a programme which I enjoyed was 'Come Dancing.' This was followed by a competitive show to select the 'National Ballroom Queen,' which was watched by millions. After fierce competition, a young lady, Gwenllian Bowen, from Llanelli won and was crowned 'Queen.' Within weeks of her winning, she opened a dance studio in the 'Golden Lion' in Carmarthen's Lammas Street, in partnership with Martin Silva, who was also an accomplished dancer. It was called the Silva Dancing School.

I didn't waste any time in enrolling to learn to dance, braving all in the Land Rover to drive in the evening to attend dancing classes in Carmarthen. The dance studio was at the rear of The Golden Lion. It had a polished wooden floor and sophisticated audio system.

I was soon made welcome by Martin and Gwenllian and I embarked on a ballroom dancing learning curve. Martin was almost old enough to be Gwen's father. He was a forceful man who did not suffer fools gladly. The other 'pupils' attending were of all ages from sixteen to fiftyish, drawn from all walks of life. I took to dancing like a duck to water. After all, my Great-Great-Uncle Thomas Harris, had been the Dancing Master at the famous Crawshay Ball held at Cyfarthfa over 150 years ago!

Little did I know that this establishment would change my life for ever. Apart from me, there was only one other person from Llandeilo who also attended. Her name was Mary Davies, who lived in Gellideg, Ffairfach. Mary worked in the Midland Bank in Carmarthen and would come to class after work with her friend and colleague Betty who lived in Llangathen, Broad Oak. Llandeilo was an awkward place to get to by public transport so that Mary, who didn't drive, had to rely on Betty to get home. It was difficult for her when Betty could not make class, and so it came to pass that yours truly stepped into the breech and offered my services, albeit in a Land Rover. At first Mary was hesitant about accepting a lift from a comparative stranger, but as time wore on she could see that she was in the hands of a thoughtful, intelligent, charming and entertaining companion!

However, the Land Rover was not doing the job to my satisfaction, so off we went to Messrs Edwards in Carmarthen and swapped it for a brand new Rover 90. This was a marvellous car built on a superb chassis (as was Mary!), it had a six cylinder engine with an interior which smelled of wood and leather. It was really a miniature Rolls Royce. Finished in black paint it had an air of sophistication and elegance. At least, I now had a decent car to take to dancing classes (and take Mary home!).

The dancing was going great guns. In order that progress continued passed the medal stages, Gwen put me through my paces and taught me the correct technique. They selected a lady who was also coming to class, who was already a good dancer and had won competitions. Her name was Rita Harris and she lived in Carmarthen. Rita was a lot older than me but was short and very light on her feet which suited me down to the ground. I probably danced with her more than anyone else in class and together we won several competition cups in Carmarthen and the 'Thomas Arms' in Llanelli. I went on to pass the various medal examinations of the ISTD (Imperial Society of Teachers of Dancing), Martin maintaining that I was the only 'naturally gifted' dancer in the entire Carmarthen class,which, without being big headed . . . I was!

The number of lifts I was giving Mary grew steadily week by week and we were beginning to enter Mills and Boon territory. We went for long drives to the coast including Bosherton Pools, Llangrannog and St. David's. Mary and I went to Hunt Balls including one at Hafodneddyn, Llandeilo. She invited me to tea at her sister Dorothy's house in Carmarthen. This was the first time for me to meet Dorothy and she discreetly let us both have tea on our own. I remember we had fruit cocktail and it was delicious. It was not long before I met her parents and we all got along famously. On one occasion we all went for a run in the Rover to the Brecon Beacons passing the Newport reservoirs en route. Mary met my parents and Arthur at Green Meadow. It was more intimidating for her to meet my parents as she was by nature a quiet, thoughtful and sensitive girl. She survived and we never looked back.

We met in 1957 and in 1959 we went for a run to one of our favourite places, Llansteffan. The grass in front of the houses overlooking the estuary was ideal for parking and so there I parked the Rover. The scene was romantic, the sun was setting over the water, the castle was silhouetted against the evening sky, all was quiet. I looked at Mary and she looked at me and without further ado, I asked her to marry me, to which she replied she would. We were engaged to be married!

Apart from dancing, I had been a couple of times to play badminton in Llandeilo with Arthur. Arthur was more involved in tennis and badminton and played a lot with Llandeilo stalwarts like

Joe and Olga Harries. Basil Smith and Len German were regular players as also was Mike Rees of Albion Concrete Products, Llangadog. Arthur, now well over the Nesta saga, became interested in Indeg the only daughter of a Mr and Mrs Harvey of Bank Buildings. Indeg was the same age as me and a good player. Her mother's family were butchers in Llandeilo and her father had spent many years in the merchant navy. He had been torpedoed in the 2nd World War. Mrs Harvey was a nasty piece of work and tried to frighten off any suitors Indeg might attract. She had a vitriolic tongue and led her husband a merry dance. He was quiet, unassuming and tolerant. It was not long before Arthur popped the question and Indeg accepted, despite her mother!

Farming in the late fifties was financially difficult. The returns were poor compared to other types of business. I've seen us selling bull calves for thirty shillings and adult stock below production costs. The British Friesian breed was coming under fire for poor milk quality and the mastitis levels in dairy herds was high. The vets were doing a roaring trade in supplying dairy farmers with streptomycin, penicillin and even stronger antibiotics in an effort to combat this scourge of the dairy industry. There was little or no organic milk produced in Wales in 1959, anyone advocating it was regarded as a crank.

Enough was enough! I began to look round for a more lucrative way of making a living. Hugh Busher, the Agricultural Correspondent of the *Western Mail*, had died leaving a gap in that newspaper's ranks. Viscount Kemsley, the Fleet Street magnate, owner of *The Sunday Times* and Kemsley Newspapers, was former owner of the *Western Mail* before selling it to the Thomson organisation. A lifelong friend of my grandfather, Bertram Besley, was a boyhood schoolmate of Lord Kemsley in Abermorlais School in Merthyr. As boys, they both went to a concert in the Drill Hall in Merthyr to see and hear Col. John Philip Sousa from America play his music. Well into the concert, there was an almighty cracking sound and Sousa and his musicians disappeared below the collapsed stage in to a black void. Mr Besley said he had not seen anything quite so dramatic in his life.

I decided I would go to see Lord Kemsley to see if I stood a chance of getting a position with the *Western Mail*. I made an appointment to meet him in his private apartment in Mayfair, London, and off I went to see what the possibilities were. He met me, shook hands and offered me a cup of tea. I mentioned the Sousa debacle which he remembered. We then talked about Merthyr and my career to date. The outcome was that he told me to go and see David Cole the managing editor of the *Western Mail*, telling him that he (Kemsley) had sent me. I knew David Cole from when he lived in Penydarren next door to Uncle Tom and Aunty Narsa and Pat. David's father died young as a result of his fondness for alcohol. His father was a Freemason which entitled his family to certain benefits. Uncle Tom was a prominent Freemason who saw the potential in David (we always called him Claude), and engineered his entry into the Masonic School. He prospered, ultimately becoming Fleet Street's youngest editor. He went to Havard in America and had a major stake in Reuters. It is interesting that this University was founded by Havard, a Welshman, and named after him.

Off I went to Thomson House in Cardiff to see David Cole. I was ushered into his office and we had a chat about Merthyr and Lord Kemsley. David sent for the editor, D. G. H. Rowlands, and we explored the possibility of me contributing material relating to agriculture. They asked me to write articles for a trial period to see if I was up to it and this I did. In due course they informed me that they liked my work and appointed me Agricultural Columnist for the *Western Mail*.

Mary and I decided that we would get married on Saturday, 23rd April, 1960. This was the following year, so we had a bit of time to sort things out. I had by now also met Mary's only brother John and his wife Haulwen, who lived in Glyntwrch, a house in the grounds of Golden Grove mansion. They didn't have any children. John worked in the railway station at Ffairfach. I had also met Dorothy's

Mary and me, married in Llandeilo in 1960.

husband, Ieuan Gealy. He was employed by Carmarthenshire County Council and was a real motoring enthusiast.

We were still milking as usual and Mary and me still went to dancing class but visits there were getting fewer and fewer. Mary was transferred from the Midland Bank to the Forward Trust in Carmarthen, an arm of the Midland Bank which dealt with hire purchase. As 1959 neared its end we found that farming was losing a lot of its appeal. Interest rates were high, cattle and milk prices low, so that the writing was on the wall. We could not continue as we had in the past for much longer. Arthur was becoming more interested in pursuing his architectural career and began putting out feelers.

Spring 1960 soon arrived with preparations for our wedding well advanced. Our actual wedding day turned out to be glorious with

Our wedding reception at Carreg Cennen Guest House, now a private residence.

wall to wall blue sky, but with a stiff breeze blowing. Saturday, April 23rd was also St. George's Day. It was with a feeling of excitement that my parents and me parked the car on Crescent Road, Llandeilo, for the marriage which was to take place in Ebenezer Chapel, the Rev. J. J. Lewis officiating. We walked into the chapel which was packed with people. I took my place next to Arthur, who was my best man, and waited for Mary. She looking radiant walking through the congregation, escorted by her father, to join me. After the ceremony and registry formalities we were driven in the hired Vauxhall to the reception which was held at Carreg Cennen Guest House (now a private residence), in full view of Carreg Cennen Castle. This was an idyllic setting. All our families and friends were present making this day truly memorable and apart from being born, it was the most significant happening that I had or would ever experience. I had a wife in a multi-million!

After the reception we went to Swansea railway station for the honeymoon send-off on the London-bound train. We were on cloud nine! An added pleasure for me was the fact that we were travelling on my favourite railway harking back to my train spotting days. The locomotive heading our train was a GWR Castle Class engine which with the King Class were the elite of the Great Western Railway. My father's uncle had been a driver of the express locomotive 'Caerphilly Castle.' We arrived in London and had a taxi to our hotel where we had booked to spend the night . . . Hotel Montana.

The next day we set out for our honeymoon destination, Paris, catching the train to Dover where we embarked upon the cross channel ferry. Mary was not a good sea person I discovered. Before we had even left the quay at Dover, she felt queasy. Calais couldn't come quick enough for her and we eventually arrived. The train for Paris was waiting at the quayside, we boarded and a couple of hours later we reached Gar du Nord railway station in Paris where we transferred to our hotel 'Hollandais' which was in Rue de le St. Martin. The hotel was a comfortable establishment with old fashioned open cast iron lifts. It was centrally situated and within walking distance of most of the Parisian attractions.

Our great adventure has begun! During the days that followed Mary and I walked the length and breadth of Paris. We climbed the never ending steps up to the Sacre Coer. We were admiring the fantastic view of Paris from there when we met an old woman who was dressed in sombre, dark, clothes and who started to talk to us. She told us what it had been like to live there during the war, pointing out bullet holes in the walls which were still plain to see. We mustn't forget it was only fourteen or so years after the end of the war that we were there. We walked through Mont-martre admiring the artistic nature of the district. Strolled along the banks of the Seine where we ate oranges in the grounds of the Notre Dam without seeing the Hunchback! We even went to a cinema to see a film which was all in French. I had never seen a cinema like it. We were in the front of the upstairs balcony. To our amazement, there was no rail or any other safety device in front of the first row to stop anyone falling into the seats on the ground floor below.

We walked to the Eiffel Tower but couldn't sum up enough courage to go up it. Likewise at the Arc de Triomph. We walked the length and breadth of the Champs-Elysees. Standing in these spots I could conjure up the pictures of Hitler saluting his troops goose-stepping past. Taking everything into consideration, we came to the conclusion that Paris was something special and that we would come back some day if we could.

All good things come to an end and so we did our journey to Paris in reverse arriving in due time at Green Meadow. We intended setting up our own home in Tŷ Coch once we had bought some furniture. However, within a day or so of returning my father and me had to drive down to Devon to sort out a problem a buyer of some of our stock was experiencing. We set out after morning milking, drove to South Devon over Dartmoor to a farm south of Truro, sorted the problem and returned to Llandeilo in time for the evening milking.

Our first home together on our very own was Tŷ Coch. We went to Pugh Bothers of Llanelli to buy our essential furniture which was delivered to the house and we commenced our married life solo for the first time. Amenities were sparse but with an internal telephone system connected to Green Meadow and Penybank, at least we were in touch with civilisation.

I was now doing regular writing for the *Western Mail*. I travelled around Wales covering stories and doing my own back-up photography. On one occasion I ran foul with Lord Dynevor whose family had lived in Llandeilo for a thousand years. He owned a herd of White Park cattle which were quite unique and whose ancestors were equally as ancient as his. They were all white animals with black noses and ears and huge horns. I decided to write an article and illustrate it with a picture of the White Park cattle. This was published in the *Western Mail* and in no time at all, Lord Dynevor wrote to me to say I had no business taking photographs of the cattle without his permission. I pointed out to him that public rights of way existed over his land and that no permission was necessary. I didn't hear any more from the good Lord. He died shortly afterwards.

I was asked to join the organising committee of the forthcoming Royal Welsh Show in Llandeilo as *Western Mail* representative. I also became an Associate Member of the Guild of Agricultural Journalists. Overall, 1960 was becoming an eventful year. Arthur secured a post with the Ministry of Agriculture as regional architect to be based in Aberystwyth. He had asked Indeg to marry him and she agreed, the ceremony to take place in August of that year. They duly married in Taliaris Church, with me as best man. It was shortly after that Indeg's father died at the age of 59.

The Ford Motor Company in Dagenham, Essex, advertised in the *Daily Telegraph* for a Press Officer and Editor for its Special Equipment Division in Essex. I applied and was asked to attend an interview at Ford's Regent Street Suite in London. They required a journalist who could head the public relations aspect of Ford's input into the special fields of sports/racing cars, marine and agricultural and industrial activities. I was invited to a further interview at the Ford Motor Company's South Ockendon offices in Essex and after the interview was offered the post, which I accepted.

This was the final piece of the strategic jigsaw and so steps were taken to sell the three farms and all our stock. We sold them quickly. A woman from Salem bought Green Meadow and Penybank. Tŷ Coch was bought by a man named Fred Jones. The cows were all sold in the cattle market some for meat, the pigs suffering the same fate. At least we felt that they all had gone to good homes. The tractors and implements were advertised and sold to various farmers and dealers so, in a short space of time our farming operations ceased. Had the financial and economic climate been more favourable I know we would not have looked elsewhere for alternatives. I suppose it was fate stepping in.

My Motoring Era

M Y PARENTS MOVED IN WITH Arthur and Indeg into a flat they had rented above a baker's shop in Portland Street, Aberystwyth. It was a large flat on three floors just a short walking distance from the sea front. Mary, who was now pregnant, went to stay with her parents in Gellideg, Llandeilo. I had to commence my job with Ford and went to 'lodge' with cousin Pat at her home 47, Kingswood Chase, Leigh-on-Sea, Essex. Pat and her husband Glyn, had two young daughters named Vicki and Jane. I soon settled in and made the best of being separated from Mary. For transport, I brought a Ford van we had used on the farm, this was okay for travelling to Wales and back, but was really a bit basic.

My colleagues at Ford were great and very friendly. At first, I was based at the giant Ford factory at South Ockendon. Here, many of the the parts and equipment that had ever made up a British Ford vehicle were stored. Mary and I obviously needed a house of our own especially as the baby was due in September, a matter of months away. A couple of chaps at work were in a similar position to me and were also looking around. They told me that a new housing complex was being built in Hadleigh which was ideally placed. I trotted off to have a look and was impressed by the type of houses going up and the location. It was a semi-rural area mid-way between the Southend arterial road and the Leigh-on-Sea, Canvey Island, South Benfleet roads. Two fast rail links from Southend-on-Sea to London were right on the doorstep.

I selected a building site, paid a deposit, and gave the go ahead for the contractors to build us a brand new semi-detached three bedroom house for the princely sum of £3,250, which was a lot of money in 1961. Pat's house was a short distance from the building site so that I was able to keep an eagle eye on the building process.

Vic Jupp who worked in my office also booked a house right oppo-site and we became firm friends. The weekends I found to be particularly long. Uncle Gilbert and Aunty Cecille had retired from the Colonial Service after Uncle Gilbert had finished in his teaching post in King's College, Lagos, Nigeria, and had taken up a post as lecturer in chemistry in Kingston on Thames. They bought a house in Ewell, Surrey, where my aunt died shortly afterwards, Uncle Gilbert continued living there on his own. It was fairly easy for me to get to Ewell from Leigh-on-Sea, so I used to pop down to see him and have a chat.

I was on one of these visits to Ewell, September 10th, 1961, to be precise, when the 'phone went and Uncle Gilbert came in to the room and said, "congratulations you have a baby daughter." With-out more ado, I contacted my office to tell them the news and I immediately set off for Llandovery Hospital where this wondrous event had taken place. I drove down floating on air not being able to believe that I was a 'daddy.' I parked on the kerb outside and rushed in to be met by the Matron who took me in to see Mary and the bundle of joy who was to be known for ever more as . . . Ann! I thought she was gorgeous and looked a typical 'Harris.' Mary and I looked at each other, the thought going through both our minds, nothing could be more perfect than this moment. Mary looked really great, it wasn't long before she returned to Gellideg to her proud parents now also grandparents for the first time. My father and mother came down from Aberystwyth post haste to see their first grandchild also, it was not long before the cameras were out recording this joyous occasion for posterity. In due course I went to the registrar of births in Llandovery and the name, Carolyn Ann Harris, became carved in the annals of history.

It was with great reluctance that I returned to Essex being even more keen to see our house completed. In Mary's absence, I had to choose the décor which I did, selecting a nice shade of pink for the bathroom fittings and walls with black panels in the bath and Walt Disney-type figures for Ann's bedroom. The lounge would be wood block flooring and the house centrally heated by an oil fired unit.

An open fireplace in the lounge was incorporated, designed to use smokeless fuel which was becoming law at that time as a result of the smogs that used to be commonplace in the London area.

In the months following Ann's birth, Mary's father was not at all well. He had spent a great deal of his working life employed underground in a coal mine. This resulted in him not enjoying the best of health. He compensated for this by concentrating on horticulture and was a past master at growing vegetables and flowers both for family consumption and competition. He won many prizes over the years. In 1961, he was invited to an award ceremony in London by the Royal Horticultural Society. Unfortunately, this was not to be for within six months of Ann being born, he died at the age of sixty. This came as a great shock and as soon as I heard he had died I headed back to Llandeilo once more, this time with a heavy and sad heart.

He was buried in the grounds of Golden Grove Church (Gelli Aur), within a stone's throw of the little school room he had attended when a boy. The funeral was huge and a large number of mourners were present. The church itself was packed and the singing during the service was awe inspiring. After the service, I met members of Mary's family I had not had the opportunity of meeting before. Like her cousins Gwyn, Cecil and Brian. It is always the case that it is only at weddings and funerals that families ever get-together, which seems a shame. Tom Davies was a quiet, gentle man, who loved his family and just lived long enough to see and hold his first grandchild. Although not an academic, his ability to do mental arithmetic was outstanding. He would be sorely missed.

Our house in Hadleigh was at last finished and arrangements were put in hand for my little family to join me. Vic Jupp who had moved in to his house opposite, let me have his car to go and fetch Mary and the baby. A van was organised to bring the furniture. Mary, her mother and the baby and myself duly arrived at our new home ... 61, Falbro Crescent, Hadleigh, Essex. I was a bit anxious regarding Mary's likely reaction to seeing the house for the first time. I needn't have worried for she gave it the seal of approval and I breathed easily again. The estate was still in the process of being

Mary, baby Ann and me on Clacton Beach in 1961.

Mary and Ann at our new home in Hadleigh, Essex.

Wynne, Ann and me taken in 1964 at Hadleigh.

built with lots of activity. At least five senior Ford personnel had bought houses there making it quite a Ford complex. It was handy from the travelling to work aspect as we took it in turns to give each other lifts.

The Ford Motor Company was a good company to work for and its senior management were an enthusiastic bunch of motoring enthusiasts. The general manager was Sam Rees who had grown up with Mary's cousin, Cecil, in Henllan, a village between Carmarthen and Newcastle Emlyn. Sam drove around in a top of the range Ford car with the number plate EJ 1. He was number one in the overall management of the manufacturing side of the business, ruling production with a rod of iron. My brief was on the public relations, press and media aspect of Ford's special operations which gave me a marvellous insight in to the whole Ford set-up. The ghost of its founder, Henry Ford, still influenced the philosophy of the company even though his grandson, Henry Ford 2nd, headed the world-wide Ford activities.

Dagenham was 'Ford City' with practically every employable person for miles around working at one or other of the many Ford plants in the area. Most of them drove Fords taking advantage of the generous concessions employees enjoyed to assist them to purchase cars. Ford had a special department just dealing with this and it was the largest outlet for the sale of vehicles in the entire UK Ford dealer network. The first sight I had of the giant Dagenham factory was mind-boggling. Ford made all their own engines. The Foundry where they were cast reminded me of Cyfarthfa Iron Works when it was going full blast during the nineteenth century. I can still smell the hot molten metal as it was poured into the moulds, a pungent sweet smell. The heat was overpowering and it was wise to keep a safe distance. At that time the Dagenham plant was also manufacturing Fordson tractors, later, production was switched to a brand new plant at Basildon, Essex. Engines for the Swedish Volvo car firm were also manufactured at the Dagenham plant. Volvo later becoming Ford owned.

One of my tasks was to organise VIP visits to Dagenham. The sight of cars and engines being made always went down well with visitors. On one occasion I organised the visit of the senior hierarchy of the Royal National Lifeboat Institution (RNLI), headed by Earl Howe. We arranged for them to be picked up at Charing Cross Wharf, transported them by luxurious cruiser with onboard lunch, up the Thames to the Ford Jetty at Dagenham, followed by a tour of the works. This was important customer relations as the RNLI were fitting marinised twin Ford diesel engines to their latest lifeboats. These craft were the last word in sophistication as far as rescue boats went. I did a story on them for the media which involved me driving to Southampton and catching the ferry to Cowes on the Isle of Wight. It was at Cowes that the RNLI lifeboats were built. I went there to see the latest lifeboat undergoing rigorous self righting tests

Some of my Ford Motor Company publications.

Ford logo designed by a Welshman.

*Ford 'Powertalk,' which I edited and
produced (1961).*

Earl Howe and RNLI Committee and me at Ford Dagenham.

whereby it was deliberately turned upside down to test its ability to right itself automatically, which it did every time. Fitted with the Ford diesels, RNLI lifeboats were a terrific endorsement for Ford quality and reliability.

The Ford Company was keen to emphasise the diverse nature of its products, feeling that the most appropriate method of doing this was by public relations and particularly the written word. I edited and produced the first publication in this field. It was called *Power-talk*. It featured all aspects of Ford products in special articles I wrote covering – sports and racing cars, powerboats, industrial equipment and agricultural applications. This magazine had a world-wide distribution through the international Ford network. One of the first pieces I wrote dealt with the European combine harvester market which meant I had to do a great deal of travelling throughout Europe.

In 1963, I caught the train from Hadleigh to arrive at the West London Terminal for Heathrow Airport. Tickets were issued there at that time. I was transported by bus to Heathrow where I boarded a Lufthansa, Vickers Viscount turbo-prop plane, for my flight to

Cologne in Germany. History was being made! This was the first ever time I had flown in a plane and I was not quite sure of what to expect. We taxied to the end of the runway and with a thrust in the back, accelerated down the runway with every bump being felt and the wings doing their level best to leave the fuselage by popping all their rivets. Suddenly, all went quiet as the wheels left the runway and the ground fell sharply away, with cars and buildings becoming Lilliputian. A gentle swishing sound took over the cabin, I was surprised how smooth and quiet it was. I really began to enjoy it and I can honestly say that from that moment on to this present day, I have thoroughly enjoyed flying.

On arrival at Cologne airport I was met by a Ford Germany representative named Dieter Heinz, who was to accompany me on my visit to Germany. He drove me to our hotel in Cologne on the banks of the River Rhine near Cologne Cathedral. Looking out of my hotel window at night, I could see the 'eau de cologne' advertisement flashing at the top of the tall building opposite. The next day we drove over the bridge crossing the river, I could not help thinking of what went on there during the war as this part of Cologne was absolutely plastered with bombs. We were aiming for Harsewinkel, a town in Bavaria where the Claas combine harvester factory was situated. We duly arrived at Frankfurt for an overnight stop in a hotel right opposite the main railway station. Heading south the following day we stopped on the banks of the Danube. I expected to see a lovely blue river and was quite disappointed to find it a dirty brown colour. Another myth out of the window! We stayed the night in a hotel on the Danube's bank in the town of Ulm which was the birthplace of Albert Einstein.

Harsewinkel in Bavaria was the home of the Claas Company, manufacturers of agricultural machinery and particularly combine harvesters. I was greeted on arrival by their public relations officer and various managers. This was followed by a tour of the establishment which covered a large acreage. I was able to see many combines powered by Ford engines. On completion of my visit, Dieter drove me to Munich where I was to board a plane to take me to Brussels in Belgium. While in Munich, I visited a toy shop to buy model cars for a colleague back home, apparently it was the only shop in Germany that these specific models could be bought. I did my good deed before setting off for the airport. I found my trip to Germany to be very interesting. I had the feeling that there was still an undercurrent of resentment towards the British as a result of the war. Most of the people I met were adults or teenagers during the war and still had a bit of a chip on their shoulders, so I thought.

The flight from Munich to Brussels was by a smaller Fokker piston engined plane which landed at Frankfurt en route. The door to the pilot's cabin was always open so that I could see exactly what was going on. This didn't worry me as it was all part of the magic of flying for only the second time. We finally landed at Brussels airport. The airport impressed me at the time as it was the first I had been in one which had glass doors opening automatically when approached. This time, I was met by a chap from Ford Belgium who ushered me to his Ford Lotus Cortina to take me to my hotel in Antwerp. To say that trip was hairy is an understatement. I don't think we travelled at less than 90 mph all the way on the dead straight Belgium roads. I don't think Colin Chapman ever intended his Ford/Lotus combination to perform in quite such a heart-stopping manner.

The object of my trip to Belgium was to visit the Claeys factory at Zedelgem. Founded by the late Leon Claeys, this factory turned out combine harvesters again powered by Ford engines and was still a family-run firm. I was invited to lunch at the Claeys family home where I met several members of the family. My fact gleaning tour of the factory followed and I returned to the hotel in Antwerp equally as swiftly as the outward bound journey. I liked Antwerp, it had character, the square where my hotel was, had cobbles and mock half timbered buildings, very picturesque. While driving along the roads, it was quite normal to see a funnel and masts of a ship gliding along in the middle of the country on one of the many shipping canals to be found there.

Brussels Airport, even in the sixties, was a busy place. I checked in for the next stage of my European tour which was to my next destination, Italy. This time I travelled on my first jet powered flight, on a French Caravelle operated by the Belgium airline Sabena. This was a totally new experience. With its jet engines placed on either side of the tail plane, they could hardly be heard in the cabin. We flew over the Alps en route, the view out of the porthole type window was spectacular. The mountains with their razor sharp looking ridges, some speckled with snow, looked very inhospitable and I prayed the pilot had put enough fuel in before taking off. Approaching Milan the plane flew for what seemed ages up the Po Valley at a very low height. I could see into farm yards and houses as we sped along.

With the usual high efficiency of Ford, I was met at the airport by Bruno Civillotti of Ford Italy. He was a pleasant individual who knew northern Italy like the back of his hand. My journey to Italy was to visit the Arbos factory at Piacenza which, like Claas and Claeys, manufactured combine harvesters fitted with Ford diesel engines. We arrived in Piacenza after driving down from Milan on the autostrada, where I booked in to my hotel. It was a reasonable sized town with the River Po flowing through it. Sometimes it flooded and in the centre they had placed a pole which showed the various heights the water had reached over the years. The hospitality I received from the Italians was overwhelming. They insisted on taking me to a hostelry near Verona where Verdi was alleged to have frequented. This necessitated another high-speed car ride along the autostrada. This was the first time I had come across the 'Agip' petrol filling stations which seemed to be all over this part of Italy.

Italian architecture is very distinctive and reflects the climate. When at the Arbos works, I was surprised to see that they were also producing combines which could also harvest rice. It grows in profusion in the Po Valley and there was a strong market for these machines. This was useful information for me to incorporate in my write up on the visit. All good things come to an end, and so Bruno bade me farewell at Piacenza railway station and I caught the train to Milan. It was funny boarding an Italian train; there was virtually no platform, so I had to climb up to get in the carriage. Milan Station was huge and looked more like an opera house from the outside. I had a good look at Milan which was very crowded and caught a taxi to the airport for my return flight to Heathrow. This time it was a Caravelle belonging to the Italian airline 'Alitalia.'

It was great to be back in Hadleigh in the bosom of my family, back to routine once more. Mary's mother had stayed with her while I was away so we took the opportunity of having a night out together while my mother-in-law baby sat. Mary and I went to Southend-on-Sea to see and hear the Tommy Dorsey orchestra with vocalists Helen Forrest and Frank Sinatra Jr. Young Frank looked the image of his father and sang very much in the same style. Helen Forrest was a singer I had admired for a long time. She had sung with all the big American bands including my favourite . . . Harry James. They played all the Tommy Dorsey classics, including 'Tea for Two' and 'On the Sunny Side of the Street.'

I was kept pretty busy at work. As well as *Powertalk*, I produced additional new Ford magazines and brochures such as *Ford Marine Power* and *Ford Construction News*. I issued a string of press releases to the media, gave talks and attended many functions. At that time specialist sports car makers were sprouting like mushrooms. Colin Chapman of Lotus racing car fame had done a deal with Ford to use the Lotus badge on Cosworth/Ford tuned Cortina cars. Colin Chapman himself had started his career by producing the do-it-yourself Lotus Seven car kit complete with Ford engine. The 105E petrol engine which powered the Ford Anglia was adapted for many purposes from cars to boats. Enthusiasts like the four Walklett brothers from Woodbridge in Suffolk began using Ford parts in their Ginetta sports car kits and racing cars, Bob, Ivor, Trevers and Douglas, each specializing in various aspects of car production. I took Ieuan along there once when he and Dorothy visited us in Hadleigh, he was in his element talking to the four brothers and seeing Ginetta cars in the process of being constructed.

One of the most memorable rides I ever had was when I went to the Morgan car works in Malvern. This famous marque had been founded by H. F. S. Morgan, who initially made a name for himself by making the familiar three-wheelers with the engine mounted on the front. Their sports cars are now collectors icons and when I visited them in the sixties they were beginning to increase production gradually. When 'HFS' died, the reins were taken over by his son Peter. Talking to Peter when he was showing me around their workshops, I was struck by the enthusiasm he exuded. Coming as I did, straight from the giant Ford works, the contrast couldn't be greater. Here in Malvern, Morgan were producing cars that were hand built, with wooden chassis and only made to order. He knew all the workforce personally, many of them having been with the company for scores of years. Peter offered to take me out for a spin in one of his Ford powered sports cars, which I eagerly accepted. Not forgetting that he had considerable racing experience including the Le Mans, I nevertheless had a eye opener when we sped around the Malvern hills at a breathtaking speed, cornering on what I thought were two wheels and an elbow, before returning to base and the haven of the factory. What a ride!

Other specialist car makers using Ford power units included TVR, Merlyn and Gilbern, but it was in the marine field that Ford played a major role, of which a lot of people were not aware. The Daily Express International Boat Show was held each year at Earls Court in London. This was the mecca for boating enthusiasts who were able to see the latest products from complete craft to accessories. Ford had a huge input at the show with an exhibition stand displaying a range of engines specially adapted (marinised) for powering boats. These engines were a work of art, some being cutaway to show the moving parts, others polished and chromed to highlight their features. I regularly attended these shows to represent Ford and to liaise with customer manufacturers and the media.

The *Daily Express* were keen supporters of boating and especially power boat racing. Each year they organised the Daily Express

Offshore Powerboat Race from Cowes to Torquay. This race attracted entries from all over the world. Some of the craft were powered by marinised Ford diesel engines and so it was my task to monitor these and feature them in Powertalk. I looked forward to my stay in the 'Imperial' at Torquay. Being organised by the *Daily Express*, the media coverage was extensive making my job a lot easier. In 1962, for example, three boats powered by Ford engines were among the first eight craft to cross the finishing line in the second International Offshore Powerboat Race. Fairey Huntsman and Fairey Huntress craft driven respectively by Charles Currey and Peter Twiss (test pilot and former world air speed record holder), were winners. Of the 42 starters only 18 finished the race.

The petrol engine fitted to Ford Anglia cars was a popular power unit for yachtsmen to use as an auxiliary motor. Edward Delmar-Morgan, a professional electrical engineer and a noted author of books and articles on motor boating and yachting, fitted one of these engines in his yacht *Laura*. When he invited me for a cruise down the English Channel, I jumped at the chance. He had marinised the engine himself with parts supplied by Wortham Blake Ltd, a major company in this field. He kept his yacht at Newhaven and it was a glorious summers day when I arrived at the port for the trip. *Laura* was 35 feet in length, weighed eleven tons, having been built in 1908. We sailed out into the Channel and enjoyed a perfect day's sailing. Edward was quite an interesting individual. He was an acknowledged expert on navigation, a capable ice skater and a Black Belt at judo. Of particular interest to me was the fact that he was a friend of author Arthur Ransome, whose books *Swallows and Amazons* and *Coot Club* had been my favourite reading when I was a boy.

From sea level to one of the highest mountain regions in Britain was another feat I had to accomplish. I discovered that the highest Ford engine to be seen working in the UK was to be found in the Cairngorms in Scotland. Ski-ing was taking off, literally, and Scotland was becoming popular among followers of the sport. A ski lift had been installed at Aviemore and a Ford engine was the power unit operating the lift. It was sited at the top, a couple of thousand feet up the mountain. So, off I trekked to investigate this phenomenon. I left King's Cross railway station with Ford photographer, Ted Hillman, travelling north to Scotland. I had never been to that country before and was very much looking forward to the visit.

Travelling through York, Newcastle-upon-Tyne, Edinburgh and over the Forth Bridge, was a new experience. The winding rail journey (all steam hauled) was wonderful with magnificent scenery. We arrived at Aviemore to find a sleepy little cluster of buildings with a small building which posed as a hotel. The weather wasn't all that bad, a bit cool but dry. The next day we set off for the chair lift which was a goodish walk from the hotel. The lift started from a wooden building and I could see the chairs dangling from the cables which disappeared up the mountain. By now, the wind was beginning to blow a bit and the chap in charge was in two minds whether or not to operate the lift in the prevailing conditions. Eventually he succumbed, and Ted Hillman and myself climbed aboard our individual chairs. Up we went, the chair was swaying in the wind and the ground looked as if it was ten miles down. The slopes were getting whiter and whiter as we ascended, was I glad to get off at the top and stand on terra firma! The snow was lying quite deep but boy was it cold up there! The photographer and me only had our normal town macs on and ordinary shoes and no scarves. We struggled to the hut housing the engine, leaning against the wind as we did so. We took the necessary photos and then beat a hasty retreat back to the lifts before the wind intensified, potentially leaving us stranded on the top of the Cairngorms which rose to over 4,000 feet. That Aviemore Hotel was a real warm haven to descend to on our return to civilisation.

Another large exhibition held annually in London was the International Construction Exhibition held at Crystal Palace on what was later the athletics track. This event covered building and construction machinery from dumpers and rollers to excavators, compressors, concrete mixers and other equipment too numerous to itemise. Ford had a strong presence there as numerous manufacturers featured Ford industrial equipment in their products. The sheer diversity of the types of machinery present never failed to impress me. It was in order to do justice to this that I produced *Ford Industrial Equipment News* which dealt exclusively with these Ford associated products.

A steady stream of folk from Wales came to stay with us in Hadleigh. Arthur and Indeg and my parents often came to see us. Arthur bought a Rover 100 from the dealer Henlys in London. This was delivered to our house in Falbro Crescent, where Arthur duly collected it on a visit. Southend-on-Sea was very near and it was a must for our kinfolk to see the town following it up by a walk along the pier, the longest in the world. One consolation, if anyone got too tired to walk back at least there was a regular train shuttle service on the pier. Everyone enjoyed the view from the end which was always in deep water and a focal point for fishermen.

Looking down from the ruins of Hadleigh Castle, the Thames estuary was clearly visible looking beyond Canvey Island. The Island was at sea level and had a great big defence wall running the length of it to keep the sea out. It was quite pleasant walking along the pathway at the top of the wall, watching the many ships coming and going to London. Hadleigh, Leigh-on-Sea and Westcliffe, were continuous with Southend, it being difficult to know when leaving one and entering another. The main road linking them was dotted with car dealers, I've never seen so many in such a short distance anywhere

Earlier, I described how we crossed the River Severn by ferry and how unpredictable the crossing could be weatherwise. It had been decided that a bridge be constructed to replace the ferry and work started on it during the late fifties and early sixties. Ford equipment was being used to do the job and I drove down to Chepstow to see the construction for myself. On arrival, I was taken by the engineers to see the work in progress. This involved being transferred to the huge pits which would contain the foundations of the high piers which were to support the roadway of the bridge. I watched tons of concrete being poured into the foundations and marvelled at the expertise and work ethos of the men working on the project. Having endured many a ferry crossing, I could not wait to see the day when the bridge would be finished.

Beyond the site of the new bridge to be, was another mammoth building project taking place at Llanwern near Newport, Monmouthshire. To be known as the Spencer Steel Works, this £110 million development was designed to produce 1.4 million tons of steel per annum. Its owners, Richard Thomas & Baldwin Ltd. (RTB), constructed the works on a 2,800-acre marshland site and Queen Elizabeth officially opened it on completion.

Being steeped in the history of iron and steel making in Wales with names like Crawshay, Talbot, Homfray and Guest ringing in my ears, I visited Llanwern with more than usual expectancy. I was not disappointed. The huge complex was mind-boggling. Over 27,000 people were employed and the two blast furnaces each of 30 feet in diameter were the first in Britain to be charged exclusively by automatic means. It was a real eye opener. Plenty of Ford equipment was in use on site, so my visit was very worthwhile.

Working for the Ford Motor Company really was a unique experience. Their products infiltrated a fantastic spectrum of social and economic life. I became involved in projects in the glamorous world of entertainment through the making of films such as *Lawrence of Arabia* starring Peter O'Toole, Alec Guinness, Anthony Quinn and Jack Hawkins and directed by David Lean. This Sam Spiegel production was filmed in Jordon and Spain and the stirring shots of horsemen galloping flat out across the desert were captured by cameras mounted on a special platform called a 'Dolly' which ran on rails and was powered by a Ford V8 engine enabling it to do speeds of up to 30 mph. Another epic production at the time was the James Bond film *From Russia with Love*. With Sean Connery as James Bond, scenes depicting an exciting powerboat chase featured the Fairey Huntsman class powerboats powered by Ford diesel engines, the same type of craft that took part in the Daily Express Offshore Powerboat Race from Cowes to Torquay.

On the family front, Arthur and Indeg became the proud parents of a baby girl they named Catherine. However, eclipsing even that splendid news was the fact that Mary was once more expecting our second child. We were over the moon again, if that was at all possible! Mary's mother was now spending a lot of time with us and she was very welcome. I can safely say that Mary's mother was the best mother-in-law one could wish for. Nothing was too much bother for her and she and I got on like a house on fire. Our friends Vic and Josie living opposite were great and we had our local doctor living just yards away in Falbro Crescent. To add to the mix, Louis Armstrong and his All Stars band came to play in Southend. Knowing my fanaticism for all things jazz and swing, Mary gave me dispensation to allow me to go and see one of my musical idols on my own, as she would have taken up two seats if she had gone!

Off I went to the Southend cinema where Louis Armstrong was appearing and I secured a prime seat in the front row within a couple of feet of the maestro himself. I could feel the spit from his trumpet! When the curtain went up and the band swung into their routine, I could feel the hairs on the back of my neck tingling. There was the great 'Satchmo' right in front of me mopping his brow with his hankie, blasting out the jazz classics that hitherto I had only heard him play on gramophone records. What a thrill, I came out of that cinema with a spring in my step anxious to get home to tell Mary all about it. I certainly had 'Georgia on my Mind.'

During my years with Ford, I had come across several colleagues who had their roots in Wales. Stan Cross, manager of the Assembly Division at Dagenham, Sam Toy, manager of the truck set-up in Slough who years later became Chairman of the Ford Motor Company Ltd (1980-86). Gerry Thomas (Geraint), who was Fleet Sales Manager at Cheapside, London. I discovered that Gerry was related to Mary's uncle Dick Davies, who lived in Llanelli. This

Ford/Welsh connection went right back to the days of Henry Ford. His right-hand man and senior research assistant, Harold Wills, was Welsh and in 1903, designed the now famous Ford logo. Henry himself was an eccentric individual. Born from farming stock he thought history was 'bunk.' He was alleged to have said that you could have any colour Ford car you like, as long as it was black. It was also said that when he made the original Model T car, he would order its components from suppliers to be packed in wooden cases of specified sizes, so that when dismantled, they could be incorporated into the floor assembly of the car, thus saving a lot of cash.

Christmas of 1963 passed and the birth of our second child was imminent. At last, on January 24th 1964, Richard Wynne Harris was born at 61, Falbro Crescent. Our local doctor and midwife delivered him and my word he was a beautiful strapping baby. Mary's mother and I were downstairs when he was born and heard his first cry. What a moment! We both went upstairs to see them and no words can adequately describe the feeling of meeting your son for the very first time. Mary had done a fine job. Our little family was

Wynne and sheep, Brecon Beacons, 1965.

124

now superbly balanced with both a boy and a girl. To quote a TV programme running at the time, 'That was the week that was.'

During the weeks that followed, I went through the motions of going to work. At least I had a foot in two camps, Wynne was eligible to play rugby for England or Wales. What a thought! We did not have a car of our own as I had access to the Ford VIP pool of Zephyrs kept and serviced for media purposes, at the Great West Road depot. These were all automatic gearbox models, the first I had encountered. I used these cars for transport so the need to purchase my own car did not arise. Ford had expanded quite a bit since I joined the company, particularly by building a giant factory at Halewood, Liverpool, to manufacture the Anglia saloon to be followed later by the Escort model. Having sold his Rover, Arthur bought an Anglia and did a fair mileage in it before, in turn, swapping it for a Cortina when that model was introduced. Dagenham was still churning out cars in their thousands. Ford had taken over the Briggs Body Factory which had been producing the Jowett Javelin for the Jowett Company. This more or less finished off Jowett and they never recoverd. The Javelin had been an outstanding car, which, with the Riley models were truly new post war designs. The Javelin had a flat four engine in the tradition of the pre war Jowetts with which I was so familiar. This was the start of the rapid decline of British motor manufacturers with the disappearance of household names. The same thing was happening in the motor cycle world with the invasion of Japanese-made 'bikes. Truly, the beginning of the end for our traditional marques.

While I was enjoying my work, the fact that my family responsibilities were now greater, so I started to look at other opportunities, jobwise, occurring in my line of work. Not long after Wynne was born, advertisements appeared in the media for someone to project the city of Liverpool and establish a public relations policy for the city. At that time, 1964, Liverpool was buzzing and emerging as the place to be. I applied, as did seventy other applicants and in due course received a letter stating I had been short listed and inviting me to attend an interview in Liverpool.

My Mersey Beat

I COULDN'T BELIEVE THAT I WAS on my way to one of the greatest cities in Britain with an outsize chance of getting the appointment. I was due to be interviewed at 2.30 p.m., so I left Hadleigh at the crack of dawn and arrived in Liverpool in plenty of time for me to gather my wits. The interview was to take place in the Municipal Buildings. I arrived and took my place in a waiting room with five other hopefuls. It seemed that the entire Finance and General Purposes Committee of the City Council would be present under the chairmanship of the leader of Liverpool Council. Alderman William (Bill) Sefton. With butterflies in my stomach, I entered a Victorian room with wood panelling everywhere, to be confronted by, what I then thought, a multitude of councillors. I took my place opposite them at the centre of a long table and faced a barrage of questions. The fact that the Ford Halewood plant on Merseyside was such an important asset for the city and my association with such a reputable firm, undoubtedly was to my advantage, I felt.

I was asked what I already knew about Liverpool and what steps I thought necessary to project the area into the future economically and culturally. One question particularly intrigued me. Alderman Sefton asked me what I thought of The Beatles and were they worthy of the city's support? I replied that while their type of music was not my cup of tea, nevertheless, from the publicity point of view they should be supported and utilised to promote Liverpool. After an age of similar questions I was asked to wait until all the interviews had been completed. A couple of hours later I was asked to go back in the room and Alderman Sefton asked me to sit down. He said that the committee had discussed the merits of all the applicants and had decided that I would be offered the appointment and would I accept. In a daze, I said I would and assured the committee that I would endeavour to do my utmost to further the cause of Liverpool.

Not since Ann and Wynne had been born did I feel so light-headed and walking on air. Here I was at the age of 33, given the job of transforming Liverpool's image to the world. A city of three quarters of a million people, Britain's largest exporting port and the third largest city in England after London and Birmingham. I rang Mary with the news and then set off for Aberystwyth as it was now very late into the evening. We decided it would be better for me to stay the night there with my parents and Arthur and go on to Hadleigh in the morning.

When I got back to Falbro Crescent, Mary and I got down to the serious business of planning another move to a new destination with all that entailed, especially selling our existing house and looking for another in Liverpool. At work, I broke the news to my colleagues at the Ford Motor Company which was sad in a way for me as I owed a lot to Ford and the Ford ethos in shaping my attitude to public relations. I would miss friends like John Drumm, Mike Hodgkinson and Vic Jupp all three in later years going their own separate ways, John to Ford Cologne in Germany, Mike to British Leyland and Vic forming his own business. One of my parting gifts from Ford were some of the newly-introduced Premium Bonds which I still have and which have never won me a prize to this day!

We decided that the best way to sell our house was to do it ourselves. My parents came to stay with us and my father made a 'For Sale' sign which he placed in the front garden. I set off for Liverpool in the meantime to take up my post leaving the family to do the necessary as far a selling the property was concerned. The City Council found me 'digs' in the Sefton Park area which was quite comfortable with a clientele consisting mainly of Arabic origin. I must say I had some very interesting conversations with my fellow lodgers as well as eating food which I had never tasted before.

Liverpool's New P.R.O.

Cutting from the Liverpool Echo, 1964.

One of the first things I did was to buy a new car. Using my Ford contacts I bought a brand new Ford Cortina which was a nice shade of blue with a white roof. Now I was fully mobile.

My new office was situated in the main council offices at the Municipal Building in Dale Street. All the main departments were sited here, Town Clerk's, City Treasurer's and the majority of committee rooms. Behind the building was a car-park which had been the site of an adjoining building but which had been bombed to oblivion during the war. On the opposite side were the Education Department Offices and the next block contained the main Post Office which had a flat roof resulting from a landmine slicing off its upper floors during a wartime air raid. It was to this Post Office that the Moore brothers brought their football coupons to be posted by hand when they first started Littlewoods Pools. A hundred yards or so further on was The Cavern about which I will have more to say later.

Liverpool had never had a public relations policy or personnel before, so that I had to set up my department entirely from scratch. What is more, no other comparable city or

Wynne working on the Ford Cortina.

At my desk in the Municipal Buildings, Liverpool.

Attention!

IS ENGLAND READY

PART ONE of an Express inquiry
edited by PATRICK ROBINSON

NEVER before will Britain have known such an invasion of trained observers and commentators. They'll be here to see football's top event, the World Cup. But on what they see of Britain unofficially their judgment of this country will be based. How prepared are we to play hosts to the world only a few months hence? How will the countless visitors be met?—with warm courtesy or cold tea and down-beat hotels? The answer touches much, much more than the world of sport. It will colour the whole "image" of Britain abroad.

Kicking off at

LIVERPOOL

BIGGER. Better. Gayer. Saucier. And generally more riotous than any other city. Well, it would hardly be Liverpool if they were not planning to dress up their City just like that

...ALL IS ONLY A BIT OF THE

VERDICT: Only Liverpool could team up a dance part- service and families escort visitors all over the area. If I were going to choose where was going to watch the World Cup it would undoubtedly be Merseyside.

For e IT IS the and they Football together "anythi exhilara familie hospita busy t langua to pro

THE CITIES—AS A LEAGUE TABLE

EACH WORLD CUP city has been tested on the five vital factors that will spell success or failure in the eyes of the world. Ten points are awarded for each factor. For your at-a-glance rating of them all, look right.

	Accommodation	Catering	Organisation
Liverpool	9	9	8
Manchester	9	9	10
Sunderland	5	6	9
Sheffield	8	8	
Middlesbrough	4	4	
Birmingham	2	4	

Newspaper reports on Liverpool public relations.

SELLING A CITY . . . By JACK HOUSE

"SELLING a city is just the same as selling a commercial product. Whether it's a bar of soap or a city the principles are exactly the same." That's what Lyndon Harris said to me in Liverpool, and Lyndon Harris should know.

Mr Harris is public relations officer for the Corporation of the City of Liverpool. He is getting accustomed to people beating a path to his door, for he has already received callers from London, Birmingham, Newcastle, and Cardiff, all inquiring about the same thing— how to sell a city.

I was his first visitor from Glasgow, but I earnestly hope that I'm not the last. As you may know, Glasgow Corporation are dickering with the idea of appointing a P.R.O. But they don't seem to have anything very clear on their minds. A recent suggestion is that some one should be seconded from St Andrew's House in Edinburgh to look after public relations for Glasgow. In my opinion this would be the kiss of death to the whole idea. I mentioned it to Mr Harris and, though he was too polite to comment, it struck me that he said somewhat.

...ry like Glasgow

Glasgow Town Council should send a deputation to Liverpool to see how this "City Image and Challenge" does too.
Liverpool is like Glasgow in many ways. Its population is under ours. It is also a seaport. Many of its buildings are as Victorian as ours. It has a Protestant-Catholic problem at times. But Liverpool also has a big problem at times.
...what kind of image (if you will pardon that word) is Liverpool presenting to the world? It doesn't pretend to be a "swinging city."

LYNDON HARRIS

Soap or a city.

young fashion artists who were designing with-it clothes at Liverpool College of Art. Now their designs are stopping the traffic outside the Miss Selfridge shops in London and Manchester, and in Lewis's stores throughout the country.

Three Liverpool films

we'd the s able

Y Liver from

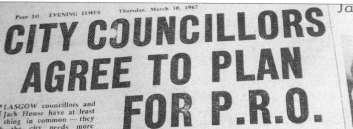

Newspaper reports on Liverpool public relations.

Liverpool recording produced for the 1966 Soccer World Cup.

Liverpool's City magazine, the first of its kind in the UK.

town in Britain had a professional public relations presence either. I decided that I would bring a commercial approach to local government PR utilising all my experience in the industrial field. I was asked to produce a policy document for the city to consider as to how I would recommend this could be achieved. I wrote a comprehensive report which was submitted to the City Council covering my recommendations which included specialised staffing appointments, the production of publicity literature, brochures and the introduction of the UK's first ever local government magazine to be regularly published and distributed world-wide. A new public relations office was to be incorporated in the Municipal Building to which the media and public could access. All departments would be advised to consult me when approached by the media and also when deciding to produce their own publicity material. All press release were to be issued by my office. The format of all advertisements including job adverts were to be approved by me, any direct meetings with the media would be notified to me beforehand in case my presence was deemed necessary. This comprehensive report was placed before the entire Liverpool City Council consisting of 160 councillors and was unanimously approved. It was all systems go!

Back in Hadleigh my father had done a good job in selling our house privately and had found a buyer who could purchase without going through a 'chain.' This meant that I would have to get cracking in finding one in Liverpool pretty quickly. I was advised that the best areas to live were in the south of the city. One of my assistants, Nigel Green, knew a woman who had a house for sale in the Allerton district, so off I went to give it the once over. It was semi detached house in a cul-de-sac with a secondary school and playing field at the bottom of the rear garden. It was immaculate and at the price of £4,500 in 1964, was reasonably priced for this desirable area. Once again, I took the plunge and bought it without Mary having seen it, hoping that she would approve in due course. We packed all our worldly goods and the move was effected from Hadleigh to Liverpool. When Mary saw 42, Chalfont Road, Allerton, Liverpool 18, she was impressed, to my great relief, and we soon settled in. The shops at Allerton Road were within walking distance and again, like in Hadleigh, a doctor had his surgery a few yards down the road.

The PR office soon began to take shape in the Municipal Building. Rooms were adapted to suit my special needs with my private office sited adjacent to the main rooms. Initially, my staff consisted of two senior clerical assistants, three clerical officers and my personal secretary. I soon recruited an additional three journalists and an additional general assistant. I had also obtained council approval for an additional six assistants to man information offices to be sited in various locations in the city.

I will always remember my first sortie into the heart of the city, R. D. Bland, the Baths and Public Laundries Manager and Engineer, asked me to accompany him on a tour of Liverpool's public baths and laundries in some of the deprived areas of the city. When we arrived at the first and we went inside. I could not believe my eyes. It was like stepping back into the world of Charles Dickens. Women with buckets and pans full of washing were literally up to their armpits in hot water, scrubbing away with clouds of steam bellowing from vast boilers it was communal poverty as I imagined it would have looked like in the nineteenth century. What a shock to the system! R. D. Bland was amused by my initial reaction and seemed quite at home carrying out his work. I discovered later that he has been a submarine engineer in the war and relished keeping the boilers, laundries and the maze of pipe work operating efficiently.

The Town Clerk then was Thomas Alker who was nearing retirement age when I was appointed. He was of the old school type of local government official, quiet and unassuming and as long as nobody rocked the boat was easy to get along with. At his stage of career he just wanted a quiet life. In complete contrast, his deputy by the name of Stanley Holmes was aggressive and ambitious. I took a dislike to him as soon as I saw him and felt I could not trust him further than I could throw him. The Assistant Town Clerk in charge of Administration, Ken Brizell, was another smarmy individual and would lick anyone's boots if he thought it would further his cause. He blotted his copybook with me when I was compiling individual annual reports on my staff. He suggested that I should not give my Senior Assistant, Nigel Green, too good a report as he was a Roman Catholic and the possible prospect of him being promoted might not go down too well with the Protestant Party in the city. Needless to say, I regarded Nigel very highly, and I gave him an excellent report and what is more, told him in confidence what Ken Brizell had said.

Liverpool was big business in every sense of the word. The city employed over 40,000 people and was the largest employer on Merseyside. Twenty departments dealt with the entire spectrum of human activity, from education and social services to parks and gardens and the municipal airport at Speke. The City Council owned and administered theatres, conference halls, farms and water undertakings and was the largest landowner in Wales. It was this latter aspect which brought me my first 'exciting' PR episode not long after my arrival in Liverpool. In the ever increasing need and search for water, Liverpool Corporation had flooded the Welsh valley at Tryweryn which was near Bala. The new reservoir named Llyn Celyn has cost Liverpool £20 million to construct and had necessitated the demolition of some twelve farms and the purchase of land of four other farms. This development had raised a tremendous lot of opposition in Wales which manifested itself in demonstrations, meetings and correspondence from the early fifties. The leading Plaid Cymru politician, Gwynfor Evans, went before the entire Liverpool City Council to plead the cause of the opposition to the flooding. This was prior to my arrival, but I remember the Deputy Town Clerk, Stanley Holmes, telling me that Gwynfor Evans' address was so eloquent and persuasive that he almost swayed the councillors to support him. Stanley Holmes said it was one of the most emotional speeches he had ever heard.

To no avail the flooding went ahead and on the 28th October, 1965, the official opening took place at Llyn Celyn with the Lord Mayor of Liverpool, Alderman David Cowley, being present. I will never forget the scene as I accompanied the Lord Mayor. Demonstrators were out in force, shouting and booing and the 'Free Wales Army' were strutting around in their uniforms, the first time to be seen in public. The police were there in large numbers and as the situation began to deteriorate, the Lord Mayor was advised to return to Liverpool while the going was good. I kept a very low profile and was mightily relieved when it was all over. This was a peculiar series of events as far as Liverpool was concerned. Here was a city which had strong Welsh roots including a Welshman, David John Lewis, as Lord Mayor in 1962/63. A large part of the city had been built by Welsh builders and there were strong Welsh communities and religious institutions and churches. In fact, Liverpool was known as, 'the capital of North Wales.' The *Liverpool Daily Post* newspaper had a special North Wales edition. The large stores there such as Lewis' and Owen Owen had special 'Welsh' days for shoppers. Historically, the Welsh settlers in Patagonia had sailed in the middle of the nineteenth century from Liverpool in the ship *Mimosa*. Mary and I attended the centenary of the sailing as guests on board a boat at the

Pierhead. Lunch followed with a sailing down the Mersey and the throwing of mimosa wreaths into the water to commemorate the voyage. Patagonians of Welsh descent had flown over specially for the occasion. The actual plans for the settlement of Patagonia were originally drawn up in a room in Williamson Square not far from my office.

The next task I tackled was to appoint an advertising agency to help me to project Merseyside as a dynamic area to live in or set up in business. I interviewed several top London and Manchester agencies and was impressed by the presentation by Brunning Advertising & Marketing Ltd., who had a strong presence in Liverpool. Their Liverpool team was led by Frank Casey and Tony Jay, assisted by Peter Garner. We drew up a commercial type advertising campaign which had never been seen in local government circles hitherto. By featuring well-known 'Scousers,' I exploited their talents by associating them with projects which were of benefit to the city, in the form of advertisements, which I placed in the national media from the *Financial Times* to the *Radio Times*. I particularly wanted to make use of The Beatles, and I contacted their manager Brian Epstein to ask him if he would be prepared for me to use them in my advertising campaign. He said he was delighted to be able to support his and The Beatles' home town and gave me his full backing. I was the only person who was able to use The Beatles without having to pay them anything! The same thing applied to my use of Cilla Black, who was also managed by Brian Epstein. Cilla was born in Scotland Road and christened Cilla White. Like The Beatles, she was 'discovered' singing in the Cavern by Brian Epstein and had Welsh family connections.

Mary and I had met Brian Epstein when he and us were guests of Hugh Cudlipp, Chairman of Daily Mirror Newspapers, in a 'Daily Mail Dinner to salute the City of Liverpool' held on board *m.v. Aureol* berthed in Liverpool docks. Besides chatting to Brian Epstein and his mother, who was a really nice person, we were entertained by the Band of HM Royal Marines and cabaret with Arthur Worsley,

Lynda Barron (who was very slim then!) and Jimmy Logan. The Prime Minister, Harold Wilson, was there and also the Lord Mayor of Liverpool. Gerald Kaufman, the PM's press secretary, was hovering about and we had a chat with him briefly. Hugh Cudlipp and his brother Percy were both Fleet Street giants and hailed from South Wales. On a more serious note, Mary bought her first Hoover twin tub washing machine from Brian Epstein. He had an electrical/goods shop right by my office. That machine lasted many years and was a different kind of 'spin.'

A major element of my brief was to support the Lord Mayor in his duties. Unlike the administrative staff who were based in the Municipal Buildings, the Lord Mayor operated from the ancient Town Hall which was at the other end of Dale Street. This was an elegant mansion built to the design of George Wood of Bath in 1754. The City Council Chamber occupied the centre of the building and adjacent to this were the state rooms which were reminiscent of the Czar's palaces in St. Petersburg. The Lord Mayor's parlour or lounge/office, was an exquisite room tastefully furnished and very welcoming. A great deal of my time was spent in that building. I liaised closely with the LM's secretary, Cyril Colvin, who was a true gentleman and a real professional.

The basement contained a collection of silver which was quite unique. For decades outgoing Lord Mayors donated a piece of silverware as a matter of custom. This large collection contained some magnificent items from full blown galleons to dinner services and candelabra of all shapes and sizes. I took great pleasure in showing the silver to VIPs visiting the city. Selected pieces would be displayed on the dining tables at official functions held in the Town Hall. I had many late night sessions attending receptions and meetings there. One particular event comes readily to mind. We were holding a reception to honour Sir Laurence Olivier and Geraldine McEwan. As the guests arrived, the Town Hall footman announced their names. Mary and I had just been announced and were standing keeping our wine glasses warm, when 'Larry' and Geraldine entered. In a loud voice to all and sundry, the footman shouted out: "Sir Laurence *Oliver* and Miss Geraldine McEwan!"

It was in the Town Hall that I bumped into my cousin, Roy Jenkins. He was visiting Liverpool officially as Minister of Aviation in Harold Wilson's government. He had been to Speke Airport where he held a press conference and then on to the Town Hall for discussions with the city hierarchy. It was also there that I met Jenny Lee MP, Aneurin Bevan's widow and Roy Kinnear. Many visiting dignitaries stayed at the Adelphi Hotel which was not far from Lime Street railway station. Harold Wilson, who was a local MP for the Huyton district of Liverpool, always stayed there on his visits to his constituency. Once I had to welcome and look after Prime Minister Sir Albert Margai of Sierra Leone and his entourage when he visited the city. He took over most of the Adelphi and we had to treat him with kid gloves. Sierra Leone was one of the main shipping contacts for the Liverpool-based Blue Funnel shipping line. Premier Sir Albert spoke of conditions in his country and told me about the diamond situation there. It seemed you would only have to scrape earth in your back garden to expose diamonds. His ADC was an imposing chap resplendent in military uniform and I was told ready to do the dirty on the Prime Minister if given the opportunity. We steered well clear of him! One of my senior assistants, Norman Parry, who was in his last few years before retiring, was designated to look after the Premier's needs. Unfortunately, he looked after them a bit too well and I found him a bit worse for wear after a hospitality session with some of the Prime Monister's followers. We had to usher him home before anyone twigged the situation and put his pension in jeopardy. Norman never forgot Sir Albert! One thing I can say about the city while I worked there, was the relative harmony and peaceful co-existence between the different ethnic communities. In the past, there had been religious friction between Protestants and Catholics very much as on the larger scale in Northern Ireland, but this did not manifest itself on my watch. The two football clubs, Liverpool and Everton reflected these beliefs with the former mainly backed by Protestants and Everton by Catholics. I was very much involved with the opening of the brand new Catholic Cathedral and the pre publicity arrangements. I had many meetings with Archbishop Beck and his hierarchy and never ceased to be surprised by the abject servitude with which priests and laymen alike displayed in his presence. Even though I had attended St. Brendan's in my Bristol schooldays, this almost grovelling seemed strange to me. The actual opening ceremony was a major event in the history of Liverpool. Nicknamed the 'Mersey Funnel,' because of its conical shape, the guests came from far and wide. There were so many that a lot had to be accommodated in the Philharmonic Hall with pictures of the ceremony relayed to the hall.

This new cathedral was completed when at the same time the massive Anglican Cathedral was also nearing completion. Both cathedrals were sited within a short distance of each other on opposite ends of a street named Hope Street. In typical Liverpool fashion. The Catholic Cathedral was designed by a Protestant and the Anglican Cathedral by a Catholic. The 'Mersey Funnel' looked very stark inside with the use of loads of concrete. The 'lantern' which towered over the centre circular area was a mass of stained glass and at that time the building had more stained glass in it than any other cathedral in the world. In contrast, Liverpool Anglican Cathedral was traditional, being built from sandstone quarried in the area and was one of the two largest cathedrals in the world. I was very impressed when I first went to the top of the building and looked out over Merseyside. It was like looking down from a 'plane and the hills of North Wales and Snowdonia could be seen in the distance on a clear day. A short walk away was sited the first 'drive in' bank to be established on Merseyside. It seemed quite novel that you could just drive in and draw out cash just like a take away, and drive out again. Eventually, a fire destroyed the bank and it was never replaced.

At home things were going along fine. The children and Mary had adjusted to their new surroundings well, in addition to her household chores, Mary played an invaluable role in accompanying me to official functions and similar activities associated with my work. We had one occasion when we were shaken out of our complacency. I had gone to London on council business and was 'phoned by Mary and told that Wynne had got hold of a quantity of car sickness tablets and had eaten them. How many she didn't know. She had contacted the doctor with the result that Wynne had been rushed to hospital in the City Centre for urgent treatment. I caught the next train back to Liverpool and went straight to the hospital. Wynne was standing in a cot looking quite defiant and wanted to go home. The doctors said he had been stomach pumped, but that there was no cause to worry and I could take him home. It was the biggest scare we had experienced to date, what a relief!

As secretary of the United Nations International Co-operation Year Committee in Liverpool and also holding a similar appointment with the Commonwealth Arts Festival, I became very involved as the city became a focal point for links with overseas and drew many visitors to the area. One of the events I organised was the setting off of hundreds of balloons from St. George's Hall with a prize for the finder of the balloon which travelled the furthest away from Liverpool. In addition, I placed special information kiosks at selected points in the city where visitors could obtain data on what was taking place in the world of entertainment and culture. I had become very friendly with Liverpool MP, Bessie Braddock. Bessie was a larger than life character with a heart of gold. A one-time Communist and rebel, she had fought the cause of the poor and deprived all her life. She had been a city councillor prior to entering Parliament and had married John (Jack) Braddock in 1922. He was also a former city councillor and equally rebellious. Jack used to enter the council chamber wearing a red waistcoat and had to be forcefully ejected on several occasion following somewhat heated debates.

Bessie drove a large Rover 75, painted red, and was a familiar sight driving around the city. She used to come into my office most

Fridays for a chat and for me to bring her up to speed on what had been going on in Liverpool during the week, while she was in London. She had a good sense of humour and was a great pal of Ken Dodd and Frankie Vaughan. Every Christmas she sent me a card written personally in red ink. When she heard I was looking for someone to officially open one of the information kiosks she said to me, "I know the very person, my friend Marlene Dietrich." I couldn't believe it, here was this Socialist diehard telling me that one of her best and long-standing friends was the Hollywood megastar Marlene Dietrich! I jumped at the offer and sure as eggs, Bessie came to see me a day or so later and said, "It's all fixed, when do you want her?"

On the day we had agreed, Bessie called for me in her red Rover which she parked outside my office. She opened the rear door for me to get inside and there sitting in the back was Marlene resplendent in her white mac and hat. We introduced ourselves and Bessie drove us across the city. I was struck by Marlene's complexion which was flawless and her complete lack of aloofness. She was easy to talk to and told me she and Bessie had a lot in common, despite appearing to come from two different worlds. She did the necessary at the information kiosk and then Bessie drove us back to my office. The sight of a rotund Bessie Braddock arm in arm with ultra slim, glamorous Marlene Dietrich, is one I will always remember.

Another Merseyside first was the setting up of the first local radio station by the BBC. The BBC felt that following the success of 'pirate' radio stations such as Radio Caroline, it would be a good move to establish a community-type radio station in major cities. Liverpool and Sheffield were the first to be commissioned. A young go-ahead BBC executive named Michael Hancock was given the task of establishing the Liverpool station and he and I collaborated closely in doing this. We became firm friends. This station became known as 'Radio Merseyside' and proved to be a pacesetter in this branch of broadcasting. It was followed in later years by similar stations throughout the UK. It was during Michael's stint at BBC Radio Merseyside that both he and I received invitations to meet

HM Queen Elizabeth at Lord Derby's home, Knowsley Hall, on the fringe of Liverpool. My invitation came as a result of my work with Sir William Mather's 'Operation Springclean Campaign,' which originated in Manchester, with the object of promoting cleanliness and litter clean-up in towns and cities throughout the north-west of England. Michael and I thoroughly enjoyed the experience. I was surprised how young the Queen looked and how she sparkled and laughed quite spontaneously. We attended several functions together, including the Royal Lancashire Show at Blackpool and the Liverpool Show at Wavetree. Later, Michael became a senior executive at BBC Pebble Mill in Birmingham and, in later years, Publicity Director for the JCB Group.

Lord Derby was a prominent figure in Liverpool social circles. As Lord Lieutenant of Lancashire he was responsible for all Royal visits and we conferred on many such visits including those of Princess Alexandra and Princess Margaret. He was a personal friend of the Royal Family and it was said kept a tight reign on Princess Margaret, not standing for any nonsense from her. When Princess Margaret visited the Liverpool Show, I had been using a movie camera and was coming out of the rear of the city's mobile information trailer, when she appeared from a doorway right opposite and there was nobody else about. I raised the camera and looked at her, she smiled and posed with a wave of her hand and so I had an exclusive movie of her. This piece of film is in the City of Liverpool archives.

Soccer and music were the two great 'religions' governing Scousers' lives. The Beatles were at their peak, Gerry and the Pacemakers and Cilla Black were booming and Liverpool and Everton Football Clubs were ruling the roost. A steady stream of personnel visited my office. On one occasion, my secretary Pam ushered two young men in to see me who had come to ask me if the city would be prepared to financially support their new group. Their names were Mike McCartney and Roger McGough. Mike was Beatle Paul McCartney's brother and the group they were forming was called 'The Scaffold.' I told them that it was not our policy to financially back pop groups and I suggested that they asked brother Paul if he could help them out. They later went on to some success with the top of the pops catchy tune 'Lily the Pink.'

Two surprise applicants for jobs in my department were BBC veteran news reader Frank Phillips and Kevin Morgan. My wartime childhood memories of Frank Phillips were strong. His well-known and distinctive voice echoed from countless wireless sets throughout Britain. He had retired from the BBC and fancied doing some public relations work. Having heard of Liverpool's activity in this field he thought he would come and see me. He was not the type of person I was looking for, so sadly, I had to turn him down. Kevin Morgan had just completed a course at Liverpool University and was also looking for a post in public relations. He was Welsh, his brother being John Morgan who fronted many BBC programmes at that time particularly for BBC Wales. Kevin Morgan was unsuccessful on this occasion but went on to pursue a distinguished career in Wales and in later years became a professor in Cardiff.

One of the most moving musical experiences I ever had was when the Welsh National Opera Company came to Liverpool and I showed them around the Town Hall. In one of the main reception rooms, Stanley Holmes, who had now become Town Clerk on Tom Alker's retirement, and I were standing in the centre of the room surrounded by the entire chorus. All of a sudden, they broke into full bodied singing of the 'Nun's Chorus.' I have never ever felt such a sensation, the power and the crescendo was mind-blowing. Both Stanley Holmes and myself were the sole beneficiaries of a full-blooded performance by one of the best operatic choruses to be found anywhere. Truly amazing!

Some of the best champagne I have ever tasted was when the French fleet visited the Port of Liverpool. Six French frigates arrived under the command of Vice-Admiral D'Escabre E. Lahaye, accompanied by French Consul-General M. J. Legram and Captain Chevalier. I was entertained as a guest on the Admiral's ship. The champagne was superb, the best I had hitherto tasted or tasted since.

Ships were constantly paying courtesy visits. Mary and I were guests on the visit of an aircraft carrier which berthed at the Pierhead. We had never been on an aircraft carrier before. The size was awesome and the reception for guests was held in one of the aircraft hangars below decks. To get there we had to stand on the giant deck lifts which were used to convey aircraft from the hangars below to the surface of the deck. We both stood on the lift and descended into the bowels of the ship. The main hangar was like the Albert Hall and was an ideal location to host the reception. After the festivities, we were taken for a tour before disembarking.

On our return home, Mary discovered that a brooch she had been wearing was missing. This brooch had a strong sentimental value as I had given it to he when we got married. It was shaped in the form of three leaves with a central pearl and was a mere two or three inches across. The only thing we could think of was that it must have been lost on the aircraft carrier. The next day, I contacted the captain and told him what I thought had happened and he promised to keep a look out for it. That same afternoon, he came in to my office with the brooch in his hand. He had got the entire ship's crew searching the vessel and they found it lodged between the aircraft lift and the deck.

They say variety is the spice of life. Again, at the Pierhead, I was invited to judge the Del Monte Competition to find the best photogenic baby on the lines of the 'Pears' adverts. This was held on board the Canadian Pacific's liner, *The Empress of Canada*. My fellow judges were Michael Hancock of BBC Radio Merseyside, Geraldo the dance band leader and myself. I was particularly pleased to meet Geraldo as I had grown up listening to his music. One of his female singers, Dorothy Carless, had been a household name in the music business.

While on the subject of music, Tony Jay of Brunnings, like me, was a 'swing' buff. He was no mean performer on the drums. During the war he had even sat in with Bob Crosby (Bing's brother) and the Bob Cats, playing on the drums with them on several sessions.

He and Jan (his wife) accompanied Mary and me on several visits to the Liverpool Philharmonic Hall to see visiting big bands. One of the best was 'Jazz at the Philharmonic' featuring a group of individual musicians from the United States who had got together to perform in Liverpool. They included Dizzy Gillespie – a trumpet player who had a style of his own and played a trumpet of a unique shape – Clark Terry, Coleman Hawkins, Zoot Sims, James Moody and Benny Carter – all on saxophones, Bob Cranshaw on double bass, T-Bone Walker on guitar, Teddy Wilson on piano and Louie Bellson on drums. What a lineup! Teddy Wilson played in the same style as Earl Hines who I had seen with Jack Teagarden in Cardiff when I was a teenager. Wilson had played with Louis Armstrong's orchestra before he joined Benny Goodman. His playing with the Goodman trios and quartets is renowned and his playing in the Goodman recording of 'She's Funny That Way' is a classic. Louie Bellson was one of the top drummers ever to take up drumsticks. Discovered by ace drummer Gene Krupa, he joined Benny Goodman in 1941 and after service in the army during the war, he went from Goodman in 1947, played with the Tommy Dorsey Orchestra before moving on later to play drums for the Harry James Orchestra. Some of my favourite LP records are of Bellson playing with Harry James. Gene Krupa, Louie Bellson and Buddy Rich were, without doubt, the best drummer musicians ever.

Other bands I saw with Mary at the Philharmonic included Duke Ellington's, Count Basie's, and Woody Herman's. I always booked seats in the front row. We were just feet away from the Count and Duke, two of some of the greatest musicians in the history of music. I'll never forget the Woody Herman's 'herd' rendering of 'Danny Boy,' the whole orchestra raising the roof of the Philharmonic Hall in their interpretation of this traditional piece of music. The sweet melodic sound of Johnny Hodges playing his saxophone with the Ellington band was a truly memorable experience, he produced a sound quite unique with a tone I have not heard from any other sax player. If you could apply the term 'genius' then these stalwarts of the swing era certainly deserve to be so called. This music was taking place in the city at a time when rubbish was being pumped out by so called 'bands' who managed to hoodwink the public and manipulate the commercial music world. Many of these were yobs of the first order, taking drugs and leading a life which was morally and spiritually depraved. Unfortunately, this was a trend which has continued to the present day. Let's hope the pendulum will swing the opposite way in the not too distant future restoring the melodius and sophisticated side of the sound of true music.

Near our house just across the road in Mather Avenue, was the Liverpool City Police College where the police horses were stabled. It was a great sight to see the mounted police setting out each Saturday for the ride to Anfield or Goodison Park where they undertook crowd control. It was like seeing a troop of confederate cavalry setting out across the prairie to attack the enemy. On the whole, to be fair, the Liverpool and Everton football fans were rarely any trouble and were some of the best behaved in the UK. The mounted police also carried out their duties at Aintree on race days and especially when the Grand National took place. The major player at Aintree was Mrs Topham. She was a real character, a former chorus girl, she owned the racecourse and was always looking for ways and means of raising capital. She tried her best to get the city to back her and I remember going to see her at the racecourse to discuss the matter with her. She was not too successful in getting City of Liverpool backing as it was a purely commercial undertaking but we did get her as much publicity for the Grand national as was feasible. I featured it in quite a few publications my office produced.

The commercial aspects frequently clashed with municipal interests. Shortly after I arrived in the city I was landed with a tricky situation. Each Christmas time the incumbent Lord Mayor drew upon a charitable fund called the Lord Mayor's Children's Fund, to purchase toys and gifts for poor children in the city. The serving Lord Mayor at the time also owned and ran a toy shop. He gave instructions that all the toys were to be purchased from his shop.

When I got to hear about this I was amazed and promptly had a strong word with the Town Clerk. He immediately called in the Lord mayor and told him that this was not ethical in no uncertain terms, with the result that the toys were purchased from another independent source and what could have been an embarrassing situation duly avoided.

An amusing event occurred involving another former Lord Mayor named Harry Livermore (later Sir Harry). We were both in the back of the mayoral limousine heading for a meeting at Speke Airport when a nearby car backfired, Alderman Livermore flung himself on top of me and we both landed up on the floor of the car, he being convinced that someone was trying to shoot us. He was a prominent solicitor in Liverpool and featured in many notable legal exercises on Merseyside.

Speke Airport was owned and run by the City of Liverpool. Situated at the south east end of the city, it flanked the River Mersey on one side and the vast housing estate of Speke and the giant Ford factory at Halewood on the inland side. Large industrial units on the Speke estate included Dunlop where they manufactured golf balls, Evans Medical and in complete contrast, set in a cluster of trees just a few yards from the runway, Speke Hall. This was a historic Tudor house which attracted countless visitors and was one of the major tourist venues on Merseyside. Standing in its classic wood panelled rooms next to the priest's 'bolt hole,' it was hard to believe that a massive runway capable of taking Jumbo jets was a mere stone's throw away. The airport director named Keith Porter was an extrovert who loved his work. His assistant at the time later went on to take charge of Manchester Airport. One of the hangars contained one of the last Mosquito aircraft to fly with the RAF. This twin engined 'plane was mainly constructed of wood and played a major role in winning the Second World War. Very few of them survived post war. So it was decided that this particular aircraft was worth preserving and made airworthy once more. When the work was completed, a 'maiden' fly past over the city was organised. It was very nostalgic to see the Mosquito flying over Liverpool, its Rolls Royce engines sounding as sweet as ever, and to see its distinctive outline as it dipped its wings over the City Centre. It went on to participate in film making in the years to follow, demonstrating to the world the part it played in winning the war.

It was around the network of roads surrounding the airport and Speke Hall that Mary learned to drive a car. It was a good place to practice and, providing we ducked every time a 'plane came in to land, was an ideal location. She later progressed to Wavetree and Penny Lane and went on to pass her driving test around the Penny Lane area. While on the subject of Penny Lane, the City Council had to regularly replace the name sign as Beatle fans constantly removed them. It cost the city a pretty penny!

It was a bone of contention in Liverpool that the BBC regarded Merseyside as second division as far as broadcasting nationwide was concerned. It was felt that Manchester, the deadly rival, was the BBC favourite and anyone from Liverpool who had to be inter-viewed had to travel to the Manchester studio. The Liverpool BBC set-up consisted of a 'lounge' staffed by a representative who would have been more at home in the diplomatic service in Bombay. As a result of the 'upsurge' of happenings on Merseyside, the powers-that-be at the BBC appointed a young reporter to be based in Liver-pool. He was my fellow Welshman, John Humphrys. I remember John coming into my office to introduce himself. He looked very young (as I suppose I did myself), and we chatted about our home-land. He too, had worked on the *Merthyr Express* and *Western Mail*. When in Merthyr he had lodged at the bottom of town on the Cardiff road. John and I saw each other frequently after our initial meeting and attended various functions. We once went as guests to a reception at the English Electric factory near the 'Z Cars' location. This was a time when the political climate in South Africa was nearing melting point in connection with the apartheid situation. John felt very strongly about this and got quite hot under the collar when John Mansel, English Electric's publicity manager, brought the subject up. Mary and I met John and his wife Edna and their little son Christopher at the opening of the revamped Playhouse Theatre. Edna was a very nice girl and I was surprised to learn in later years that she and John had parted. He was always on the go when he was in Liverpool, and I remember him being called on by the BBC to jet off to Scandinavia on assignments at very short notice.

Among some of the most memorable receptions held at the Town Hall was one which Mary and I attended when we both met Tony Blair's father-in-law, Tony Booth. He was cast in 'Till Death Us Do Part at the time. Seldom does an actor appear to be the same in real life as the part they play. Tony Booth did. He was the Scouser in real life and was not backward in coming forward. While talking to him we were joined by Gerry Marsden of Gerry and the Pacemakers. Gerry was a likeable chap, full of humour and deferential in attitude. Like The Beatles, he was managed by Brian Epstein. Unlike The Beatles, he was a straight, clean living individual and I heard no adverse gossip associated with him. A group we also chatted to were The Spinners. They were individuals who got together on a part-time basis to sing folk music associated with the sea and Liverpool folklore. They were very popular then and I used them quite a bit on subsequent publicity campaigns. While at their peak, they decided to disband and go back to their 'day' jobs, much to the regret of many fans on Merseyside.

One of the most pleasant tasks I was asked to perform was to entertain the world renowned actress Dame Peggy Ashcroft when she visited Liverpool. The star of some fifteen films and having a theatre named after her, Dame Peggy was a giant in the theatrical world. She was particularly keen on seeing the two cathedrals and after taking her to see them and giving her a tour of the city, we spent a pleasant time over a meal talking about everyday topics as well as the theatre. She was a quiet, unassuming woman, very much down to earth in her approach to life.

My first encounter with comedian Ken Dodd was when he rang me up to ask me if I could supply his scriptwriter with snippets on

Liverpool which he could incorporate in his material. His writer duly contacted me and it turned out that his name was Eddie Braben, who had himself been born in Liverpool. Eddie wrote most of the Ken Dodd Shows and went on to write the Morecombe and Wise Shows as well. He was a really talented comedy writer and provided scripts for Ronnie Corbett and even David Frost. When I went to Knotty Ash to see Ken Dodd, I found him to be living in an unpretentious house, a home he had been living in for a great part of his life. His father and brother were in the coal merchant business. His mother was a homely type of lady and every time I visited she would make me a lovely cup of tea. I always timed my visits for the afternoon as Ken worked late in the evenings in theatres and always tried to get home afterwards, with the result that he used to get up late in the morning. I usually met him in his study which was lined from floor to ceiling with every conceivable book on humour that had ever been written. He would enter the room wearing his dressing gown and greet me, "Hello young man from Merthyr Tydfil." Ken was of great help to me and we collaborated on many aspects of furthering the Liverpool cause, as I will describe later.

Working closely with the Brunnings advertising agency, I noticed that Peter Garner, their account executive who visited me on a regular basis, started to come to my office even more frequently. It did not take too long to figure that one out. Pam Stubbs, my secretary, was a very pretty, attractive girl and obviously Peter and Pam were becoming very friendly. Romance was in the air. All of us in the office did our best to nurture the blossoming relationship and so it was inevitable that they ultimately became engaged and in due course married.

An important element of my work was to liaise with local organisations and events. I sat on several committees – Liverpool Christmas Lights Committee, which organised the lighting displays in shopping areas such as Bold Street which was the elite shopping district. I sat on the Executive Committee of the North West Institute of

Public Relations which was chaired by Steve Duncan, one of the founders of NALGO. In fact, a lot of time was taken up by this liaison work. The City of Liverpool financially contributed to the International Eisteddfod at Llangollen and I attended meetings there with Jack Pearson, a well-known Liverpudlian who had his finger in many financial pies. Jack who was a bachelor and accountant living with his sister, used to fly off to Majorca practically every weekend to relax and unwind. I took the Liverpool information trailer to the Welsh National Eisteddfod when it was held in Flint. Visits to the City's Colomendy Farm in North Wales where deprived Merseyside children were taken to enjoy and learn something of the countryside, were frequent. Membership of the Liverpool Press Club was a must as this gave me a unique opportunity to meet journalists and news personnel from the media and to exchange information. One of the visitors to the club while I was present was Ted Heath just before he became Prime Minister. He laughed a bit too much for my liking though!

A favourite trip in Liverpool for me was to drive from the Pierhead along the dock road to Bootle. This took me past the world's largest sugar warehouse, past the row upon row of shipping berths with their multitude of vessels of all shapes and sizes, funnels and masts to be seen every couple of yards. This was the route of the old overhead rail/road which had been demolished before I arrived in the city and which was sorely missed by Scousers. They said it provided a panoramic view of the docks and ships I would have loved to have seen it. We took Barbara Castle along this road when she visited as Minister of Transport in the Wilson government. She was a lively personage, shrewd and a good talker. We entertained her in the Town Hall and she held the guests spellbound with an after dinner speech which was witty and informative. Rumours were circulating at the time, completely without fact, that she was David Lloyd George's illegitimate daughter!

Someone who made a great impression on me and told me a lot about Liverpool was John J. Clarke. He was over ninety years of age when I first met him and he had a legal mind as sharp as a razor. Of Gray's Inn and the Northern Circuit, he was a Barrister-at-Law and a Legal Member of the Town Planning Institute. His book, *Outlines of Central Government*, first published in 1919 with a fourteenth edition in 1965, has been described as 'the aristocrat of the textbook world.' He gave me a copy of this book and wrote the following in it:

> *'To my friend*
> *Lyndon Harris*
> *In remembrance of our associations*
> *relative to my City of Liverpool*
> *From John J. Clarke, July 1965.'*

I spent many an hour in his chambers in Water Street discussing various topics from slave trafficking to politics. He told me he had been in competition with Winston Churchill for a university appointment in his younger days but had not been successful due to pressure from 'obscure' sources. Another fascinating thing he mentioned was that a professor from Liverpool had successfully conducted wireless transmissions from Liverpool University to Princes Park, before Marconi claimed to be the first to discover this invention. It appeared that Marconi was a better publicist with an eye for the commercial market. It was certainly a privilege for me to have met and enjoyed the friendship of John Clarke. He was from the traditional old school of high ethics and moral standing and I'm afraid that politicians and administrators of today fall far behind in comparison with his generation.

The two newspapers serving Merseyside were the *Liverpool Daily Post* and *Liverpool Echo*, the latter being an evening paper. They were published from offices near to my office in the Municipal Buildings. They had virtually the monopoly of the local news and their North Wales edition of the *Daily Post* had and has the biggest circulation in North Wales of any daily newspaper. I got on extremely well with the news editor, George Cregeen, who was an excellent journalist with principles. I cannot say the same for his boss and owner of the two newspapers, a man by the name of Alick Jeans. He was a pig of a man who ran his empire with a rod of iron. He treated staff and others as if they had just crawled out of a piece of cheese. When I visited him on the rare occasions that I had to see him he would be up to his eyes in copy with black ink stained hands. His assistants would be running around him like sheep, afraid to say boo to a goose. Such is the power of the press that he was knighted in 1967.

Undoubtedly, 1966 was the most significant year of my time in Liverpool. Following my initial report to the City Council. My plan to produce films depicting life in the city had been put into motion in 1965 and completed in 1966. A front page write-up in the *Liverpool Echo* on January 18th, 1965, illustrated my plans, it read as follows:

LIVERPOOL MUSIC TO BE FEATURED IN FILM
25,000,000 Will See It In Many Countries

100 YEARS OF HISTORY
By Echo Municipal Correspondent

Liverpool music over the past 100 years is featured in a 15-minute film now nearing completion of which a nine minute edition will be shown to audiences totalling 25,000,000 in cinemas both in this country and abroad.

The film, 'And The World Listened,' has been compiled by A.B.C. Pathe and the Liverpool Corporation Public Relations Department and was described by Alderman William Sefton (Leader of the Council) at a Press conference today.

"It is an attempt to relate the growth of Merseyside to the life of today," said Alderman Sefton. Adding that the film in colour covered local music from sea shanties to the latest in pop.

Sea shanties will be sung by the local group, The Spinners, and other contributions will be by the Royal Liverpool Philharmonic Orchestra, The Beatles, Billy J. Kramer and The Searchers.

The film is costing the Corporation £2,500 only for their 15-minute version, but their associates are arranging for the nine-minute edition to be shown to 11,000,000 people in this country and 14,000,000 abroad.

Merseyside music-making and the Mersey Sound played a very important part in the conference. Alderman Sefton putting forward the view that its insistent 'Thump, thump, thump' was representative of Liverpool's determination once it had started something, to carry it through to the end.

EXCITING PLANS

At the moment, Liverpool's present impact on the world was provided by its music-making, but the city's image would soon be further improved by the bringing into effect of the exciting new plans now in hand.

"There are five different forms of development in Liverpool now maturing, and which are now in the negotiating or drawing board stages," said Alderman Sefton.

"In the next two years the picture will take on a completely new face. People will be talking about Liverpool in the same way as they now talk of Coventry or the Barbican development in London. We shall find a tremendous shift in the attitude of the rest of the world and of the country towards Liverpool. We want pop music to take its place in that image."

Alderman Sefton added that the portrayal of violence in a city almost always occurred concurrently with dockland, and not long ago people seemed to be becoming victims of a national cult of projected violence. That was now changing, but in spite of the image that was being projected of Liverpool as a violent city, he did not think this had ever been the case. It was a city where feelings ran high, but that was because of the cosmopolitan character of its people, among whom despite their partisanships, kinder people could not be found.

SPECIAL TIMES

Dealing with more domestic matters, Alderman Sefton raised the question of monthly Press conferences, which his Public Relations sub-committee had turned down. When told by the majority of those present that they would prefer Press conferences called on special occasions, he agreed that this would be the course to be followed in future.

In addition he would instruct all chief officers to be prepared to answer questions from the Press, either directly or through the Public Relations Officer, and he himself would also be available to answer questions.

Summing up, Alderman Sefton said: "I think the image of Liverpool now is quite a good one. It is because Liverpool is a good city, and it is justified. There is nowhere in the country that has the same type of humour, and I put it down completely to the fact that we have had such a gathering together of different ways of life in one community."

My plans developed quickly after that Press conference. I actually commissioned three films illustrating life in Liverpool. One covering the music and culture aspect as described. Another dealing with the industrial and commercial side of Merseyside and the third covering the local government contribution to life in the city. With an enhanced budget, I gave West of England Film Productions of Bristol and Cinechrome of Bournemouth, the contracts for their productions. I secured the best personnel available to feature in the films. In the cultural film I was fortunate to obtain the services of that fabulous virtuoso violinist, Yehudi Menuhin, who narrated the film and together with his sister did a marvellous job in projecting the culture of Merseyside. For the industrial version, I went to the BBC's *Tomorrow's World* programme's presenter, Raymond Baxter, to front the film. All the Merseyside big guns were featured including English Electric, Dunlop, Ford, Vauxhall, Evans Medical, Tate and Lyle, Blue Funnel Shipping, Canadian Pacific and many more too numerous to mention. Shot in full 'Technicolor,' and after my numerous visits to Bristol and Bournemouth, they were all ready to be shown in early 1966.

The next decision was to establish where to have the film's premiere. The obvious conclusion I came to was London. I put this to the City Council and they gave me the go ahead. To gain the maximum publicity and to be able to draw the nation's trend-setters, newspaper editors, politicians, industrialists and others, a central location in London would be essential. I went for the Hilton Hotel in Park Lane. My assistant Nigel and I went down to London to give the hotel the once over and decided that it would fill the bill nicely. I booked the main ballroom and adjoining areas, together with accommodation for my staff, the Lord Mayor and relevant members of the City Council.

To make the most of the occasion, it was decided to expand the premiere to a 'Liverpool in London' premiere and exhibition combined. I thought it would be a marvellous opportunity while we had a captive audience to expound the attractions of the area in a hands on practical way as well. As a centre piece in the ballroom, we erected a display of Liverpool silverware with selected items from the city collection in the Town Hall. The FA League and Championship Cups which were held by Liverpool and Everton Football Clubs, were also prominently displayed. I had the FA Cup locked behind my desk in my office before I personally took it on the train to London before the premiere. It was lighter than I thought!

We spent ages compiling the guest list. I invited cabinet ministers, editors and journalists. People from the world of entertainment together with members of the diplomatic services of many overseas countries and others of influence were included. I appeared beforehand on the BBC television programme *Look North* and was interviewed by Stuart Hall who questioned me on the cost of the exercise, which I was able to inform him was less than taking a full page advertisement in the *Radio Times*. The premiere turned out to be an outstanding success and an occasion both Mary and I will never forget.

Alderman Sefton introduced the films and after they had been shown the guests mingled in the ballroom sampling their delicacies and drinks. The drinks went down so well that Bessie Braddock came to me to tell me that the Foreign Secretary, Michael Stewart, was feeling a bit worse for wear and thought it advisable that he called it a day. She and I managed to smuggle the Foreign Secretary out of a side door into a car without the many media personnel present twigging what was happening. Others present ranged from comedian Arthur Askey and actress Rita Tushingham to theatrical 'giant' Wee Georgie Wood! No city or town had ever staged an event such as this. The amount of goodwill it generated for the Liverpool cause was immeasurable and the feedback obtained was virtually 100% favourable. If the city had to pay in full for this coverage it would have been a mind blowing figure.

1966 also saw me launch Britain's first ever bi-monthly magazine produced by a local government organisation in this country. This magazine, *Liverpool '66*, published by my office, was intended to blow Liverpool's trumpet at home and abroad. Printed in full colour it was a quality production containing articles by guest writers as well as myself and my staff. Contributors gave their services free for the Liverpool cause, typical of this was *Punch* allowing us to use their cartoons without charge. All members of the City Council received copies as did all consulates and embassies with a bulk order going to the governmental Central Office of Information (COI) for distribution through their outlets overseas. Vince Tillotson who headed the COI in the northwest, was so enthusiastic with what we were doing that he asked me if he could bring Professor Poyares, an advisor to the President of Brazil, to see how I conducted PR in Liverpool. I was able to demonstrate to Professor Poyares our strategy and methods when he came and said he was impressed with what he had seen.

Wee Georgie Wood and James Dunn MP at the Hilton, London.

Liverpool born Arthur Askey held aloft by playwright Alun Owen and comedian Johnny Hackett at the Liverpool night at the Hilton Hotel.

'Miss Liverpool,' Linda Foulder, with the FA and League Championship Cups at the Liverpool Hilton night.

LIVERPOOL
city of change & challenge

Get in on the changes,
get to know the facts, quickly.
Write now to:-
**Lyndon Harris,
City Public Relations Office,
Municipal Buildings,
Dale Street, Liverpool 2.**

Typical publicity material emphasising logo.

Bessie Braddock MP with Jimmy Tarbuck, 'Miss Liverpool' and me at the House of Commons.

Myself and staff with Jimmy Tarbuck at the House of Commons.

Ken Dodd sending off Liverpool '66 *at the Town Hall.*

Press conference at the Charing Cross Hotel with Jimmy Tarbuck.

The launch of *Liverpool '66* was timed to coincide with the first passenger train service to travel the newly electrified railway line from Liverpool Lime Street Station to Euston Station in London. My good friend Bessie Braddock had arranged for me to take a copy of the magazine to Prime Minister Harold Wilson at the House of Commons. One of the original horse-drawn stagecoaches was procured and I had Ken Dodd to sit on this blowing a post horn as it left Liverpool Town Hall en route for Lime Street Station. It was great watching the public thronging the route as Ken and the entourage cantered to the station. I travelled down to London on this first electric service and was met at Euston Station by Jimmy Tarbuck, another proud Scouser, who drove me at breakneck pace through the streets of the Metropolis talking non stop, to a Press conference I had organised at the Charing Cross Hotel. At the hotel we were joined by the reigning 'Miss Liverpool,' Maureen Martin. I explained to the media that this magazine launch was part of the city's drive to tell the world all about Merseyside. When it was over, I got back in Jimmy Tarbuck's Mercedes coupé and he again drove me across London to the House of Commons where we were met by Bessie Braddock and ushered to the Prime Minister's private room in the heart of the complex.

There, we were met by Marcia Williams, Harold Wilson's secretary, who had quite a reputation for looking after his interests and was also a political adviser. Nobody or anything got past her en route to the Prime Minister without her say-so. In later years she became known a Baroness Falkender. Jimmy, Bessie and myself joined Harold Wilson, typically puffing on his pipe, and we had a lengthy chat. Being a Huyton, Liverpool MP, the Prime Minister knew a great deal about the area. He was au fait with developments in the city and kept in close contact with celebrities who could further his own political agenda. While we were talking, Marcia brought us in tea and sandwiches and she struck me as being a very nice, homely person, contrary to the chit chat circulating depicting her as a bit of a dragon. I complimented her on the tea and Wilson remarked that

Stepping out with Jimmy Tarbuck in London.

Lord Mayor of Liverpool launching Liverpool '66.

catering generally in the House of Commons had improved since Bessie had become Chairperson of the Catering Committee. I presented the PM with a copy of *Liverpool '66* and afterwards briefed the media waiting in the House of Commons.

Talking to Jimmy Tarbuck, I mentioned that Frankie Vaughan had done a lot for deprived youngsters in Liverpool and that I had heard that he had helped Jimmy when he was a 'bit of a lad' as a youngster. Frankie was also born in Liverpool, he was born in a poor area and was from a family of Russian Jewish origin. He was originally named Frank Abelson but changed his name when he went into show business. I was on his Christmas card list and was impressed by the charitable work he did in his lifetime. He never forgot his roots.

Introducing a magazine such as *Liverpool' 66* had quite an effect on other local government authorities. It had an instant impact on Liverpool's greatest rival, Manchester. On April 1st, 1966, the *Manchester Evening News & Chronicle* carried the following article:

ON THE TOWN HALL BEAT

Why is Manchester missing the boat?

By OCTAVIUS

Watch out, Manchester! Liverpool is making an all-out attempt to oust you from your position of capital of the North West. Before me lies the first salvo fired by the capital of the Merseyside – a glossy magazine entitled *Liverpool '66*. Enclosed is a message from the Lord Mayor, Alderman David Cowley, who writes: "Liverpool has always been a vigorous city. Now we are really going places and we want the world to know about it. This magazine is our new trumpet and we aim to blow it hard."

Stand and deliver, Ken Dodd at the Town Hall send off.

The magazine, which contains articles on future developments in Liverpool, on art, industry, and the docks, with colour pictures, is published by the city's Public Relations Department and it is intended that it should be a monthly magazine. About £25,000 is to be spent this year on producing it.

Basically, it is aimed at people outside Liverpool and the initial circulation 100,000 copies is being sent to people in key positions in industry, commerce, and education throughout the world.

Says Public Relations Officer Mr Lyndon Harris: "We want to sell Liverpool to the world. We want to dangle a carrot before the eyes of potential industrialists and prove to them that Liverpool is not a decrepit squalid city."

Ken Dodd holding a giant Liverpool '66.

What about it Manchester? You are always shouting about being the second city in importance outside London but what are you doing to prove it in the eyes of the world? Publicity and plenty of it is the only way it can be done. Liverpool realises this and I understand and is planning to spend about £100,000 on publicity during the coming year.

Manchester was not the only authority to show an interest in what I was doing in Liverpool. I was asked to advise places like Sheffield, Glasgow and London Boroughs on ways of establishing PR activities and the number of requests for information increased dramatically.

Typical of this response was a series of articles which appeared in the Glasgow *Evening Times* on Tuesday, March 28th, 1967. The first written by Jack House read as follows:

SELLING A CITY

By Jack House

Soap or a City . . . selling is the same

"Selling a city is just the same as selling a commercial product. Whether it's a bar of soap or a city the principles are exactly the same." That's what Lyndon Harris said to me in Liverpool, and Lyndon Harris should know.

Mr Harris is public relations officer for the Corporation of the City of Liverpool. He is getting accustomed to people beating a path to his door, for he has already received callers from London, Birmingham, Newcastle and Cardiff, all inquiring about the same thing – how to sell a city.

I was his first visitor from Glasgow, but I extremely hope I'm not the last. As you may know, Glasgow Corporation are dickering with the idea of appointing a PRO. But they don't seem to have anything very clear on their minds.

A recent suggestion is that someone should be seconded from St. Andrew's House in Edinburgh to look after public relations for Glasgow. In my opinion this would be the kiss of death to the whole idea. I mentioned this to Mr Harris and, though he was too polite to comment, it struck me that he paled somewhat.

VERY LIKE GLASGOW

Glasgow Town Council should be sending a deputation to Liverpool to see how this 'City of Change and Challenge' does the job. Liverpool is very much like Glasgow in many ways. Its population is just under ours. It is also a seaport. Many of its principal buildings are as Victorian as ours. It has slums. And Liverpool has a Protestant-Catholic set-up which can be a big problem at times.

But what kind of image (if you will pardon that tired old word) is Liverpool presenting to the world today? It doesn't pretend to be a 'swinging city,' which London is in the minds of some American journalists. It presents itself as a vital, new, supremely energetic town. And that isn't just because of The Beatles – though, mind you, they've helped.

Every month 10,000 important people get a beautifully produced magazine entitled *Liverpool '67* (it was *Liverpool '66* last year, of course). Half of these go abroad. The home half go to every MP in this country, the editors of all daily, evening and Sunday newspapers, members of the Institute of Directors, and so on. Among the overseas readers is the Pope.

NO ADVERTISEMENTS

This magazine is free and does not contain a single advertisement. It is up to the standard of the best-produced magazines in this country or the USA. It costs Liverpool Corporation £25,000 a year, and they think it's well worth it.

Not only is it spreading news of the enterprise and events in the city, but it's bringing practical results. The very first number brought two important business inquiries from London on the day the magazine reached there. In a later number there was a feature on six young fashion artists who were designing with-it clothes at Liverpool College of Art. Now their designs are stopping the traffic outside the Miss Selfridge shops in London and Manchester, and in Lewis's stores throughout the country.

THREE LIVERPOOL FILMS

Just under a fortnight ago, Liverpool presented a special evening show in a London hotel. Under the title 'Living City,' they screened three new films about Liverpool, all in colour of course. One was 'Turn of the Tide,' about the emergence of Liverpool as the greatest exporting port in the Commonwealth; then 'Rates for the Job,' on Liverpool's public services; and 'Liverpool Sounding,' the leisure life of a great city.

These three short films cost £8,000. Add to that the cost of the presentation in London, where some of the biggest industries in Liverpool had exhibitions of their work on show.

Mr Harris was quizzed on BBC television about 'Living City.' One of these bright young chaps asked him how much it had cost and was it worth it? "Well," said Lyndon Harris, "It cost £2,000 to put on, and that's what we would have had to pay for a page advertisement in the *Radio Times!*"

At the show in London such noted Liverpudlians were present as Arthur Askey, Jimmy Tarbuck, Rita Tushingham, Norman Vaughan and Wee Georgie Wood.

"Where were Ken Dodd and The Beatles?" I asked. "Oh, for goodness sake," cried Mr Harris, "If we'd had every Liverpudlian who's made good on the stage and screen we wouldn't have been able to get anybody else in."

You'd almost think Lyndon Harris was a Liverpudlian himself, the way he speaks. But not from his accent, which is unmistakably Welsh. He comes, as a matter of fact, from Merthyr Tydfil. He has a staff of ten, shortly to be increased to thirteen. He was a journalist

168

Samples of my Liverpool media
advertisements.

himself for ten years, and three of his staff are journalists. But Lyndon Harris is also a member of the Institute of Public Relations, which takes five years and a couple of examinations to achieve. He was a PRO for Ford's in Dagenham before he went to Liverpool.

Now he is in charge of an operation which costs the city £100,000 a year. That comes to just under a penny on the rates. Before he took over there was only an Information Office (just as we have in Glasgow) and it cost £18,000 a year.

CORPORATION UNAFRAID

You can see that when the new Liverpool slogan was coined, 'City of Change and Challenge,' the corporation were afraid of neither the change or the challenge.'

The second article by Jack House in the Glasgow *Evening Times* continued pressing the Glasgow powers-that-be to follow the Liverpool pattern, with the following article which was published Wednesday, March 29th, 1967:

No Place for Amateurs

Appointing a Public Relations Officer for Glasgow isn't the simple thing it sounds on the surface. That's what I discovered when I went to Liverpool and met Lyndon Harris, the outstanding PRO for any city in Britain.

Already there's a suspicion that a Glasgow PRO would be required to trumpet forth the great achievements of the party in power. That happens to be the Labour Party at the moment, but at the May elections it could easily be the Progressive Party. So I'm not taking sides.

How do they manage in Liverpool, which is so like Glasgow but presents such a better face to the world? They manage by taking public relations seriously, by spending nearly a penny on the rates on this job (£100,000 a year), by appointing a man who knows the job and not a well-meaning amateur from the Civil Service, and by agreeing among themselves that the City of Liverpool is more important than internal politics.

First of all Liverpool City Council established a Public Relations Committee. The Lord Mayor of Liverpool and all the leaders of the city parties sit on it. It meets about once a month to discuss the public relations situation with Lyndon Harris and his colleagues.

ATTACK

"We have a two pronged attack," said Mr Harris to me as we sat in the River Room, an ultra-modern restaurant which looks over the Mersey. (We could have been overlooking the Clyde if our corporation really got down to it.) "We have an internal job," he said, "interpreting local affairs to the ratepayers, and we have also to sell Liverpool outside the city boundary. There are thirty departments in Liverpool Corporation, and any one of them can call on us for help or publicity. We regard the Public Relations Department as a clearing house for news. Any newspaperman can go to a department for his information, or to a councillor, but after two years of this department we find that the press come direct to us. We don't look on our job as trying to conceal things."

I asked him what he did when Liverpool was denigrated as Glasgow is so often on television and in newspapers. "We admit there are things wrong with Liverpool," he said. "We have the same troubles that any big city has. All we do is try to redress the balance – not by denying these things exist, but by trying to give the complete picture. Of course, we have one advantage, and that is that Liverpudlians are very proud of their city. Yes, we have a religious problem here, and what we do is to try and arrange social gatherings for both sides, advise on dates of functions and generally use diplomacy."

What else does a city PRO do? I think the list will surprise the Corporation of Glasgow.

PRESTIGE

First of all, Lyndon Harris saw that Liverpool Corporation bought the franking rights for the whole of the city. That meant that every letter and postcard which leaves Liverpool carries the proud slogan, 'City of Change and Challenge.'

The style and design of civic notepaper and envelopes came under the PRO, and so did newspaper advertising. In the old days each of the 30 departments of the corporation was responsible for its own advertising. Now, the PRO arranges the advertising through a Liverpool firm. It costs £8,000 a year.

"This is part of the prestige of the city," said Lyndon Harris. "It's all wrong if Liverpool's own advertisements have an amateur air." The Public Relations Office have a photographic department which costs £3,500 a year. They employ a press cuttings agency at £1,500 a year. They run exhibitions, mainly in Liverpool and this comes to around £6,000 per annum. In the Walker Art Gallery there is an enormous model showing what the new Liverpool is going to look like. This cost £25,000. It is surrounded by big murals showing how the slums are going to be replaced, and how city traffic is going to be dealt with. There is a bank of telephones, and the theory is that you just lift one and a voice tells you the story of the change and challenge.

171

TOWER

Already the new Liverpool is going up, and there is a great beacon tower, taller than the Blackpool Tower, which will have a restaurant on the top of it. Everything connected with Liverpool comes into the orbit of the Public Relations Office. They are concerned with the cleaning and the flood-lighting of buildings. It cost £25,000 to clean St. George's Hall, the equivalent of our St. Andrew's Hall, if only we still had it!

Already, they have given great publicity to Liverpool's civic airport at Speke. When the new £3 million runway was opened they brought not only the general press but the trade press to Liverpool and took them out to the civic airport on civic buses. They have printed 50,000 guides to Liverpool in four languages. They are redesigning the Liverpool *What's On*, which will cost £3,000 a year. And at the moment they are working on a new industrial guide to Liverpool.

APPROACH

"Local government is big business," explained Lyndon Harris. "Liverpool Corporation has more than 40,000 employees, which makes them the largest employers on Merseyside. So there should be a business approach to everything that Liverpool Corporation may do."

I sincerely trust that Glasgow Corporation will take a tip from Liverpool. Public relations for a great city should not be entrusted to amateurs, no matter how nice the chaps are. Internal politics should be forgotten for the good of the community.

On the home front, Ann had started school at Booker Avenue Primary School, to be followed in due course by Wynne. I bought an HMV stereogram from one of the oldest established music shop in Liverpool – Rushworth & Drapers – and my first stereo record to accompany it was Shirley Bassey singing 'Hey Big Spender.' I also threw discretion to the winds and lashed out on an LP of Count Basie and his Orchestra.

172

There were several pleasant walks near our home. Clarke Gardens, Calderstone Park and Otterspool Promenade readily springing to mind. Otterspool was very unusual. Situated on the bank of the River Mersey it was reclaimed land from the river brought about by the waste and rubbish collected from the city households dumping it into the Mersey and then landscaping it over. A lesson for future generations!

At Christmas and New Year, there were wonderful displays of lights and decorations in the city centre. On every New Year's Eve, all the ships in the docks from Bootle to Garston sounded their sirens in a cacophony of sound which must have deafened anyone in their immediate vicinity.

We made frequent trips by road to see my family in Aberystwyth and Mary's mother in Carmarthen. I knew every manhole cover on that route and every possible pull-in where children could be sick! Mary was not too good a traveller either, but did improve dramatically when she started driving herself. I firmly believe that clutching the driving wheel herself made all the difference.

In 1966, England was given the task of organising the soccer World Cup matches. Liverpool was selected as the venue for the group, quarter finals and semi-final matches. What a fillip for this football mad city! The Public Relations Sub-Committee of the City duly met, the outcome being that they asked me to pull out all the stops to take advantage of the situation for the benefit of Merseyside and to co-operate all I could with the organisers. This was to be the biggest sporting event to have taken place in Britain, attracting record numbers of media personnel from around the world. A World Cup Soccer Liaison Committee was set up in Liverpool and I was appointed to sit on it as the official representative of the City of Liverpool.

My brief was to liaise with the visiting teams, journalists, television and radio personnel. Provide information for the many thousands of supporters from this country and abroad, and to provide multi-language literature which would ensure their stay in Liverpool was memorable. Goodison Park, the home of Everton Football Club, was the ground selected to hold the matches and the participating teams were to be accommodated around the area. The first 'important' business the committee had to tackle was for all its members to visit Burton the tailors to be measured for our official blue World Cup suits, resplendent with the Jules Rimet World Cup Trophy emblazoned on the jacket pocket. The teams playing in Liverpool were to be Brazil, Bulgaria, Hungary and Portugal all in Group 3, and later Portugal v, Korean DPR in the quarter finals and West Germany v. USSR in the semi-finals. Among

Footballing legend Pele in Liverpool for the World Cup.

the players were Pele of Brazil and Eusebio of Portugal. Eusebio went on to become the top scorer in the 1966 World Cup competition.

I was present at the Brazil versus Portugal match at Goodison Park. The atmosphere was electric prior to the kick-off. With both Pele and Eusebio on the pitch, expectations were high. Coming out of the VIP lounge and taking one's seat was pure magic. The green of the turf and the sea of faces all around was awesome. This was the most spectacular and biggest soccer match I had ever attended. Alas, it did not turn out to be a heart-stopper. The Brazilian team was awful and were beaten three goals to one by Portugal. Pele hardly got into the game, which was a big disappointment. On the other hand, Eusebio was brilliant and was one of the best players I had ever watched. Even Billy Wright, the former England International and husband of Joy, one of the Beverley Sisters, remarked in the VIP

Lounge afterwards that the Brazilians had put on a sub-standard show. Nevertheless, I did enjoy it!

We held receptions for all the teams at the Town Hall, where I was delighted to receive a pendant from the Portuguese team manager. We in turn provided gifts for all the teams in the form of plates made specially by Wedgwood with the City of Liverpool coat of arms featured on them. We gave them ties bearing the Liver Bird, a record of Liverpool sounds which we had produced featuring ship's sirens, The Spinners and The Beatles and other sounds associated with Merseyside. I also produced a multi-language World Cup Brochure highlighting the city. The Press Club in Bold Street played an important role for my liaison with the media. Journalists I assisted included Kenneth Wolstenholme, whose comment at the end of the final match went on to become immortal.

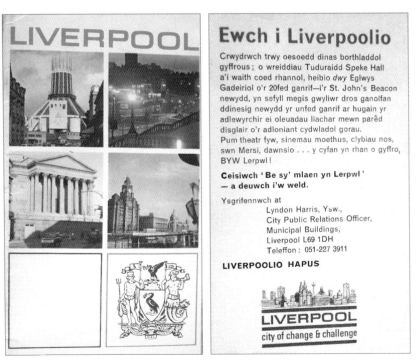

Multi-language brochures produced for World Cup visitors.

As soon as it was announced that England was to host the 1966 Soccer World Cup, the *Daily Express* did an in-depth investigation on how prepared England was to welcome this event. The *Daily Express* featured an inquiry edited by Patrick Robinson which was published on Monday, December 6th, 1965. It read as follows:

Attention!
Is England Ready To Welcome The World?

Never before will Britain have known such an invasion of trained observers and commentators. They'll be here to see football's top event, the World Cup. But on what they see of Britain unofficially their judgement of this country will be based. How prepared are we to play hosts to the world only a few months hence? – with warm courtesy or cold tea and down-beat hotels? The answer touches much, much more than the world of sport. It will colour the whole 'image' of Britain abroad.

Kicking off at
LIVERPOOL

BIGGER. Better. Gayer. Saucier. And generally more riotous than any other city. Well, it would hardly be Liverpool if they were not planning to dress up their City for the World Cup just like that.

Liverpool sees July 1966 as an excuse to stage a fortnight-long Merseyside beano for more than 30,000 foreign visitors watching five matches in Britain's Beat City.

Their 40-page World Cup brochure for visitors, costing nearly £9,000, is stuffed with names like The Black Cat, The Peppermint Lounge, The Iron Door, The Cavern, The Downbeat Club, The Latin Quarter and The Jacaranda.

It tells how to get there. How to get in. Takes you on tour to the cellar clubs where the new Liverpool beat and folk song groups are punching out the music nightly.

Liverpool World Cup organisers have even laid on a dancing partner service for lonely football fans to shake with.

PARTNERS

"All they have to do is ring us from any phone box in the city in any language and our interpreters will call in a partner from a list we have of Littlewood's girls." So said Lyndon Harris, ex-newspaper-man now employed as Liverpool's public relations officer and World Cup spokesman. "There's nothing orthodox about us so half the city may be like a big party. But when they leave Liverpool they are going to know they've been here, believe me. The crowd here are 95 per cent comedians anyway."

Liverpool is probably the best-equipped of all the provincial cities to deal with a foreign arrival of football fans. It is the second largest exporting port in Britain. Its overseas ties are strong. All over the city there are foreign shipping offices from Europe, Africa, South America, and most international shipping lines. The town is geared to the big occasion. They staged the recent Commonwealth Arts Festival like London.

They recently had the largest number of ships ever assembled in a British port – 17 of them representing the Home Fleet, and the city corporation entertained 3,000 naval ratings without a murmur. "We had the dance partner list out for them," said Harris. "We are used to entertaining. Liverpool folk are the most hospitable in Britain. When the World Cup time comes round we will be able to accommodate 66,000 if necessary. No one will be turned away from Merseyside. That I can promise."

"We have even got out a list of 2,000 families prepared to offer foreign visitors hospitality. They will take them for car rides into Wales, to the Lake District or anywhere else they feel like going. As far as we are concerned nothing is too much trouble. We are looking forward to the biggest party atmosphere in Liverpool since the FA Cup was brought here last May, or since The Beatles re-turned in the summer of 1964."

Lyndon Harris is a Welshman from Merthyr Tydfil. He was the Public Relations Officer for Fords in Dagenham before coming to

Liverpool. It has not taken him long to acquire the bouncing Scouse habit of aiming to do everything bigger than everyone else.

BROCHURE

But behind the great plans for a World Cup carnival Liverpool Corporation is intensely aware of the opportunity to sell British. They know the millionaire industrialists from all over the world will be in Britain on 'business trips,' which oddly enough clash with the football. And their Chamber of Commerce is busy producing another fine brochure of what can be bought in Liverpool. They are arranging visits to the factories and everyone in the docks will be showing off their efficiency.

Near Liverpool is the largest car production unit in Europe, Fords at Halewood. There is the Standard Triumph works. Meccano's who are planning a toy trade drive in World Cup week. Dunlops, and English Electric, who make everything from washing machines to turbo-electric plants for dams.

"Liverpool is going to be a trading shop window for the world," said Harris. "We see it as a giant prestige fortnight in which we are going to sell Liverpool."

In the middle of the town they have been given a huge show-room by millionaire John Moores, ex-Everton chairman, to turn into a central information bureau. This will be staffed night and day with interpreters and officials with answers to every question a foreigner could ask. Like Manchester, Liverpool is trying to fix a World Cup inquiry number in every telephone box in the city.

Their brochure is obviously going to be a masterpiece. Fifty thousand will be printed in five languages giving all travel details, hotels, restaurants, clubs, dentists, churches coinage and rates of exchange, with maps giving every detail of the city. And if any foreign fan in Liverpool is taken ill they too will contact his family and take over his welfare.

So far Liverpool looks like spending £20,000 on the World Cup, but it may turn out to be a lot more. The corporation are unlikely to care much what it costs. For the Lord Mayor of Liverpool, Alderman David Cowley, is a rabid Liverpool fan and never misses a

match. His keenness on soccer rather has the effect of getting everyone sparking on the project with an extra fierceness.

EXTENSIONS

Thousands of bedrooms have been collared in a 50-mile radius up
and down that North West coastline by the Liverpool accommodation men. In Southport, New Brighton, and as far up as Blackpool
they have reserved hotels. The transport for fans is being provided
by the corporation, private coaches taking them anywhere they
want to go. "And if a Frenchman or a Brazilian wants to drink wine
till 4 a.m., you can bet your life he won't have any trouble here,"
said Harris. "His biggest worry might be trying to find a way not
to drink wine until four o'clock in the morning."

"We anticipate the magistrates will allow late extensions on the
pub closing times, and there are plenty of good late night clubs in
the city. We have nearly 40 restaurants in the city centre. We have
tried to think of everything. One of the restaurants right in the city
centre has agreed to turn itself into an overseas visitors coffee
lounge and social centre, with the overseas newspapers being
brought in. Next door to the lounge there is a 500-seater restaurant.
And within a short distance of the centre we have four theatres and
almost a dozen cinemas. They'll have plenty to do in Liverpool."

Harris anticipates another invasion of the city by the dozens of
pop groups who have left to find international fame. "Most of them
are Soccer fans so they are bound to all be back for the World Cup."

QUICKEST

"What with all the footballers and The Beatles here together anything might go on. I never thought I'd see a sight like two dozen
football fans swarming all over the Bank of England roof here when
the FA Cup arrived. But when you think about it, the World Cup
is going to be bigger still."

For the visiting journalists Liverpool have laid on the finest
building in the city – the new Mountford Hall, opened this year by
the Prime Minister as the latest addition to the University. It looks
like the UNO building in New York and will house 1,700 overseas

179

journalists. It will be operated 24 hours a day by messengers. And already the direct link lines to other countries are being fitted in by engineers. Liverpool aim to make it the quickest phone service in the World Cup (of course) and outside the centre cars and coaches will be waiting day and night for Pressmen who wish to move about the city.

"I suppose there is a chance we have forgotten something," said Harris. "Just a faint chance. But we have tried not to. And if we have we'll soon put it right."

VERDICT

"Only Liverpool could dream up a dance partner service and families to escort visitors all over the area. If I were going to choose where I was going to watch the World Cup it would undoubtedly be Merseyside."

The *Daily Express* published a 'League table' in the same issue which looked at the salient points necessary to have a successful World Cup in the six venue cities. It read:

Liverpool . . . . 45 points
Manchester . . . . 44 points
Sunderland . . . . 34 points
Sheffield . . . . 30 points
Middlesbrough . . . . 17 points
Birmingham . . . . 14 points

My World Cup suit certainly saw plenty of action during this fortnight which, of course, saw England triumphant. A feat never repeated since! The only other football occasion which came anywhere near it while in Liverpool, was when the city gave the reception in St. George's Hall for the cups-winning Liverpool and Everton teams. They travelled from Speke Airport on open-top buses to a slap-up civic reception with plenty to eat and drink. Mary and I

WORLD CHAMPIONSHIP
JULES RIMET CUP 1966

LUNCHEON
given by The Lord Mayor and
Lady Mayoress of Liverpool
(Alderman and Mrs. Herbert M. Allen)
on the occasion of the Semi-Final of
the World Cup in Liverpool
TOWN HALL . LIVERPOOL
25th JULY, 1966

Special 1966 World Cup banquet menu.

were in the thick of it, rubbing shoulders with the likes of Allan Ball and Bill Shankly and I must say we thoroughly enjoyed our 'sparkling cassata.'

Just after the conclusion of the World Cup, my Uncle Gilbert was taken seriously ill at his home in Ewell, Surrey. This necessitated my mother going from Aberystwyth to look after her brother to be joined later by my father. Sadly, Gilbert died within a few weeks and my parents stayed on at his house to wind up his estate. During this period, Mary, myself and the children, Ann and Wynne, visited Ewell and enjoyed the walks around the Epsom Derby racecourse which was within walking distance. Eventually, my parents returned to Aberystwyth and our link with Ewell was broken.

During the sixties, Liverpool was undergoing a transformation in its infrastructure and general planning. Walter Bor, an architect and the City Planning Officer, had drawn up exciting plans for the city's development like for example, the St. Johns's Market Scheme. sited close to the Municipal Buildings, I could see the progress of this construction by looking out of my office window. It was dominated by a ventilation tower taller then the famous Blackpool Tower. This was designed to extract the fumes, etc., from the shopping precinct and to disperse them high in the air. Incorporated at the top was to be a revolving restaurant. I watched with keen interest the steady rising of this phoenix from the ashes. When finished it completely changed the skyline of the city and became a conspicuous landmark. A lot of the buildings needed their exteriors cleaned and an ambitious

181

programme was undertaken to included the Town Hall, Municipal Buildings and all the Pierhead and Liver Buildings in this major cosmetic operation. When the job was done, these magnificent edifices were transformed from black, dirty structures, to pristine jewels which were a pleasure to look at.

The Ford plant at Halewood was going from strength to strength. The Escort model was coming off the assembly lines non-stop and was proving to be a best seller. I had wind that my old company was about to bring out a stylish new sporty car to be named 'Capri.' I got in touch with my contact at Ford, Brian Morris, and had a preview of the car. I was instantly smitten and arranged to have one of the first to come off the line. My faithful Cortina was put out to pasture and a spanking new red Capri took its place. This car too proved to be a winner and maintained the Ford reputation of producing stylish automobiles. Another former Ford colleague, Tony Spalding. was the PRO for Vauxhall at their Merseyside factory. Many years later, he became the Chairman of the Institute of Public Relations. Tony, Brian and myself used to pull each others legs about the merits or otherwise of Ford versus Vauxhall. Needless to say, I always backed Ford!

Although I was settled in my work in Liverpool, I still felt a pull towards farming and all matters relating to the countryside. Mary had taken to city life extremely well and the children were enjoying school life. On one of our visits to the family in Aberystwyth, I broached the idea that it would be a good idea to see if our old farm Tŷ Coch was still going strong as I had heard that the chap who bought it off us, Fred Jones, was making heavy weather of it. If we could buy it I thought it would be a good investment for the future. My parents were not averse to the idea and Arthur was enthusiastic. He was now Senior Architect at the Ministry of Agriculture in Aberystwyth and so had kept his finger on the agricultural scene, just as I had.

I decided to travel down to Llandeilo to see Fred Jones at Tŷ Coch Farm and sound him out. I duly arrived at Glanyrafonddu Isaf

Farm, parked the car in their yard and walked the mile or so along the farm track to Tŷ Coch. The place had not changed much, apart from an air of neglect with hedges overgrown, typical of a 'dog and stick' type of farming.

It transpired that Fred Jones was very much on his own with only the help of his young daughter, still in school. I managed to convince him that it would be in the interests of him and that of his family if he sold it to us. He agreed, and in July 1967, Tŷ Coch Farm again came into the ownership of Arthur and myself, jointly.

1967 was also the year that only the second woman in history became the Lord Mayor of Liverpool. She was Ethel Wormald, a remarkable woman, very astute and considerate and together with Alderman David Cowley, was a Lord Mayor for whom I had a lot of respect and we worked well together. I remember, on the first occasion we met in 1965 at a reception in the Town Hall, when Mary and I were introduced to her she exclaimed: "My, there's young you both look!" She was keen on all matters dealing with education and in later years a College in Liverpool was named after her. She ultimately became Dame Ethel Wormald. She died in 1993 at the age of 92.

Liverpool '66 had progressed to *'67, '68* and *'69*. Copies were lodged with the British Library and the National Library of Wales. In 1969, I hosted delegations from New Zealand, Germany, the United States and Holland and liaised with Lord Derby over the visits of Princess Alexandra and Princess Margaret. I attended many functions at the Town Hall, including the visits of the Glyndebourne Opera Company and Sadlers Wells – the list went on and on.

Most weekends I tried to get down to the farm to put into operation works which were essential to carry out before anyone could move into the property. Access was only possible through a right-of-way from the main Llandeilo to Talley road through the yard of Glanyrafonddu Isaf. There was a track from the same road nearer the Goitre Farm, which involved going through a ford in the

River Dulais. This could be a bit dicey when it was in full flood. so, a bridge was the first priority. Arthur designed a suitable bridge and my father obtained the necessary steel work consisting of huge RSJs from the steelworks at Trostre, Llanelli, which was in the process of being demolished. Between us, and with a lot of blood, sweat and tears, we completed the job and now had a spanking new bridge which transformed our access to the farm.

On one Saturday, I left Liverpool to travel to Tŷ Coch and had just arrived when the telephone rang. My colleague, Ken Brizell, informed me that something had cropped up in Liverpool which required my personal attention. I put the 'phone down and immediately drove all the way back to Liverpool to deal with the matter. However, we pressed on with the renovations, concentrating next on the house which was in a pretty primitive state. It had no toilet facilities or bathroom and the main bedroom floor was in a perilous condition, very unsafe. Each weekend, my parents and Arthur would drive down from Aberystwyth and Mary, me and the children from Liverpool and all meet up at Tŷ Coch to carry out the demolition and reconstruction work ourselves. It really was a labour of love.

Back to the Land of My Father's

BY CHRISTMAS 1969, THE ALTERATIONS TO Tŷ Coch farmhouse
had been completed and the access road over the new bridge
resurfaced. This enabled my parents to move down from
Aberystwyth and to take up residence. In the meantime, I had been
approached by a firm of head hunters and offered a lucrative post in
Manchester which through one thing and another, I did not take
up. Mary and I had decided that, in view of my father's increasing
years, and the fact that I longed to get back farming, we would leave
Liverpool and return to Llandeilo. I resigned my post with the City
of Liverpool and we moved back to Wales in March 1970, after
successfully completing the sale of our house, again privately.

Before leaving Liverpool, I was given a lead model of a mounted
Liverpool policeman on his horse dressed in full dress regalia, which
was quite unique to that police force. It was hand crafted by Bill
Oakes, who was a director of Cinechrome Films of Bournemouth,
the firm that had made some of the films on Liverpool for me.
It was a hobby he had enjoyed for many years and he was very
talented. So, with eager anticipation and not a little excitement,
Mary, me and the children arrived back at Tŷ Coch Farm.

Ann and Wynne had done well in Booker Avenue School in
Liverpool and, when they started their new school in Llandeilo, they
found that the standard was not as high, with the result that they
had to 'tread water' for a while until their fellow classmates caught
up with them. It was not long before I found that my beloved Ford
Capri was not the most suitable vehicle for traversing farm roads
and so it was with extreme reluctance that I decided to sell it and get
a more practical vehicle. This turned out to be a Volkswagen Beetle
which Ieuan, my brother-in-law, found for us. This was a grand

little car to drive with its rear placed engine and was reminiscent of the old Jowett cars both marques having flat horizontally opposed cylinder engines.

My father had already secured a new Fordson Super Major tractor and a trailer and it was not long before we added to our machinery pool. With 150 acres to play with there was ample scope for a thriving livestock business. I had decided that a beef and pig enterprise would be best suited to this type of farm which was mainly permanent grassland. It was also imperative that it would be farmed organically. Luckily, Fred Jones had not used any fertilizers or pesticides during his tenure, so the 'natural' integrity of the farm had been preserved. Living on a farm, we had to get a dog and of course it had to be a sheep dog. We found a Border Collie puppy on a farm near Llangadog, which we purchased and he soon became an integral part of our family. We named him 'Rover' and for the next ten years he gave us endless service and pleasure. He was black and white with brown on his paws and around his eyes. His particular forte was to sprint at top speed around a circuit embracing the house and garden looking each time as if he was trying to set up a new lap record. What a dog!

The farm buildings were typical Carmarthenshire type with thick stone walls and stone or slated roofs. While they were sufficient for farming methods used 100 years ago, they were completely inadequate for modern day agriculture. We needed an enterprise which would provide quick financial returns. The answer was . . . pigs!

On a site on the eastern side of the yard we levelled off an area where we had constructed a pit silo some years earlier. This would make a perfect location for a piggery with access to the farm road and services, water and electricity. I decided to plough in the finance from the lump sum pension I had received from the City of Liverpool and invest it in a model piggery which we would build ourselves. Arthur drew up the design and with a new concrete mixer on the back of the tractor we set about the 'executive' task of shovelling sand and chippings the good old fashioned way. The building lacked nothing. It was insulated throughout, ceiling, walls and floors. Automatic water nozzles for drinking were installed and a dung channel down the centre which could be cleaned out mechanically. Infra red lamps were incorporated in all the sow's pens and a vermin proof meal house was attached to store foodstuffs and weighing equipment. My father hand made all the wooden doors and sheeted them in metal. The result was a piggery which would stand comparison with the best to be found anywhere.

I had decided that we would again go for the Welsh breed of pigs, so I paid a visit to Messrs Evans, breeders of the 'Goldfoot' herd in Carmarthenshire, and was impressed by the quality of their stock. We bought a number of pedigree gilts and in due course Mr Evans (senior) delivered them to our spanking new piggery. Mr Evans was a well respected member of the farming fraternity, a cattle and pigs judge, he ran a large farming business. When he saw the new piggery he was impressed, and said so.

I take my hat off to anybody breeding pigs. The sows seem hell-bent on squashing their newly-born offspring, and when the piglets are older they seem equally keen on pruning their contemporaries curly tails or taking a chunk out of the nearest ear. One has to be ever vigilant. There can be no doubt that pigs kept outdoors with access to earth and vegetation, thrive better and are healthier than their counterparts who spend their lives in clinically hygiene conditions indoors and never see the light of day.

The pig business thrived for some time and a steady stream of porkers were supplied to the FMC (Fatstock Marketing Corporation). We sold the odd gilt for breeding purposes and the piggery itself lived up to expectations. This was a high input/output business. A conveyor belt of pigs went out one end and an endless convoy of pig food lorries entered on the other. It didn't take long for the penny to drop and for us to realise that this was not really farming but more of a factory operation. One didn't need a farm to keep pigs on this basis. The writing was on the wall, or rather the account books, so it was decided to get shot of the pig enterprise and concentrate on our other livestock aspirations. We sold our entire breedng herd in one fell swoop to a breeder in Maesteg and that was that!

Cattle has always been my first love. Having bred British Friesian and Jersey breeds previously for dairying, the beef world was newish territory, but it was this aspect of livestock husbandry that appealed the most. Travelling down from Liverpool across the Denbigh moors and the Dolgellau area, I had always admired the Welsh Black cattle grazing the fields and hillsides along the way. Their jet black coats against the green backcloth of the grass looked aesthetically appealing. Their reputation for being able to thrive on next to nothing in the hills and their illustrious history as the native Welsh breed, convinced me that it was a breed that was worth considering. It was decided that Welsh Blacks it would be at Tŷ Coch Farm.

The mecca for Welsh Black sales was undoubtedly Dolgellau. My father and myself went along to a sale there in 1970, it was quite an eye opener! It reminded me of a wild west rodeo with cattle everywhere and stockmen hanging on to halters for dear life. I had always had a soft spot for Aberdeen Angus cattle but shied away from buying any in case they wouldn't thrive in a Welsh environment. Imagine my surprise when I came across a Welsh Black bull in one of the pens which looked like an Angus, had no horns and was of superior conformation to most of the horned bulls in the sale. I had a word with his owner who turned out to be from a farm on our doorstep in Llangadog. His name was Mr G. Haffield and the bull's name was 'Twyn Cymro,' bred by Mr Haffield. He told me that there was a strain of naturally polled Welsh Backs which were registered in a separate section of the Welsh Black Herd Book. Having seen the length of the horns on the horned cattle, I thought that this was where the future of the breed may lie. So, without more ado, when 'Cymro' came into the ring, I bid for him and bought him. All we had to do now was to get some female company for him.

During the ensuing months we attended many sales at Dolgellau, Builth Wells and Tregaron, buying heifers in calf, some with horns, some dehorned and others naturally polled. Animals bearing the Gwyn, Gerddi, Gorlech and Doldowlod prefixes were purchased. After visits to the Aberystwyth Plant Breeding Stations's farm at Morfa Bychan, a large number of naturally polled Morfa heifers were secured. I had already become a member of the Welsh Black Cattle Society in 1968 and had registered the prefix of our new herd as 'Tycoch.' We were now up and running!

It was not long before the first calves arrived and what a thrill that was. Calving out in the fields was like going on a safari. The mothers would stroll nonchalantly away before calving, produce the goods, and then proceed to continue grazing as if nothing had happened, leaving me to go out on expedition to try and find the calf. I have spent many an hour on my knees behind a hedge clasping a pair of binoculars trying to see where and when a cow was calving. It is surprising what you do see when you are lying quietly behind a hedge. Rabbits pop out and start playing and occasionally the odd fox scamper past oblivious to the 'odd' human hiding himself. On a nice sunny day it could be quite pleasant, but more often than not it rained!

It was during this period that Mary and me had some news which delighted us. Mary became pregnant and the baby was expected to be born in early 1971. Our twosome was to become a threesome! Mary went in to the West Wales Hospital in Glangwili, Carmarthen, and on April 20th, 1971, David Lyndon Harris was born. I was walking on air when I went to Carmarthen with Ann and Wynne to see him for the first time. Both mother and child looked great and I couldn't wait to get them home to Tŷ Coch.

We worked out our new routine on the farm now we had an extra 'hand,' and my parents played a big role as babysitters and indispensable back-up. My father had not been feeling too well for some months and in 1972 experienced a stroke which deprived him of his speech and paralysed him on one side. He was determined to overcome this and spent hours clenching and unclenching a soft ball in his hand until he regained the complete use of his arm and leg.

While he could not communicate speech-wise, he could however sing, including the words, and in due course he even regained full control of his speech. I never ceased to be amazed at his perseverance and sheer will-power to overcome his illness.

He did a remarkable thing when David was three. We had an open fireplace in the living room in Tŷ Coch and usually had a roaring fire. One day, David was playing in front of it when he stumbled and fell towards the fire. My father who was sitting in an armchair nearby, instinctively grabbed David and saved him from what would have been a horrendous accident. My father had smoked heavily all his life, both cigarettes and later a pipe. When he had his stroke he gave smoking up overnight and never indulged in that life-destroying habit ever again. Today, like myself and Mary, I am thankful that none of our children, their partners or grandchildren have been lured into this filthy addiction. The recent introduction of a smoking ban in public places is one of the best pieces of legislation to emerge from any government. In June 1972, my parents celebrated their Golden Wedding. They were married in Penydarren, Merthyr Tydfil, in 1922.

The next bit of excitement came when I heard the news that my musical idol of many years, American ace trumpet player Harry James and his Orchestra, were to appear in a cinema in Cheltenham. I immediately obtained tickets for Arthur and myself and we duly set off over the border. When we arrived at the cinema we were ushered into the 'best' seats in the front row where we could see the eyeballs of the musicians. Imagine our astonishment when just minutes before the curtain went up, looking around, there was hardly anyone in the audience! A lady sitting next to us on her own, said she couldn't get over it either. Especially as she had see him perform in the Hollywood Bowl in California to a packed multitude. When the curtain did go up and the band struck up, shivers of sheer delight ran up and down my spine. I could not believe that less than a few feet from me was standing a man whose records we had collected right through the war years in St. Albans, and was actually there within touching distance. Harry James looked right at Arthur and me and said that while he was disappointed by the size of the audience, nevertheless, they would play their complete programme just the same as if it had been a full house. The next couple of hours were absolute heaven as Arthur and I bathed in a swelter of big band classics that restored my faith in humanity. Absolute genius!

On the Welsh Black front, I had heard that a woman was breeding naturally polled cattle at her farm in Tregaron. Her name was Miss Frances Evans, she was also a headmistress of the secondary school in Tregaron. I went to see her at her farm, Tyndomen, which was on the Lampeter to Tregaron road. She had an immense knowledge of the breed which she had inherited from her late father, who was a pioneer in the field of naturally polled Welsh Blacks. She showed me around her 'Caron-Llanio' herd which had been founded by her father, Joseph Evans, in 1955.

While we were crossing the farmyard behind the house, I noticed an elderly man building a wall to one of the outbuildings. I thought he was a hired hand employed to do a bit of labouring and was surprised when Miss Evans introduced me to him – it transpired that he was her uncle, William Evans, a retired Harley Street heart specialist! Doctor William Evans and myself were to have many conversations on the subjects of cattle breeding, human genetics and the part food played in human health over the ensuing years. Doctor Evans lived in a bungalow at the entrance to Tyndomen. It was a comfortable, self-contained home and although he lived on his own, he was within easy walking distance of his niece's house. He enjoyed my visits and his hospitality was second to none. I had my fair share of the odd glass or two of wine with him! He had enjoyed a remarkable career. A leading authority on the heart and cardiography, he was an early developer and user of the electrocardiograph instrument which was to revolutionise the treatment of heart disease.

Indeed, if it had not been for Doctor William Evans, the whole course of British political history would have been altered. In 1936,

Lord Dawson, President of the Royal College of Physicians, asked Doctor Evans to examine the Prime Minister, Stanley Baldwin, at Chequers. For some time his health had been under scrutiny and talks of him resigning were in the air. Baldwin's heart was suspect, so Doctor Evans took along a electrocardiogram which he then used on Mr Baldwin. The result was that Doctor Evans' prognosis was that there was nothing wrong with the Prime Minister' heart and that he could carry on as normal. It is known that Baldwin had been under considerable stress following the death of King George V. He has found out that the new King Edward VIII intended to marry divorcee Mrs Simpson and there was a chasm between him an Lord Beaverbrook on what was the best course for the new King. Lord Dawson's part in all this is open to interpretation, for as physician to both King and Baldwin, it does seem he hunted with both the hare and the hounds. Had Baldwin been forced to resign on grounds of ill health, then he would not have been in a position to enforce the King's abdication. It is now history – the King did abdicate – Doctor Evans undoubtedly influenced the course of British history.

We often talked of the effect diet had on human health. Doctor Evans told me that while the food we eat was obviously important, an even more important factor causing heart trouble was not the amount of animal fat that was consumed, but who your father and mother were and what part they and their forebears' state of health played in the nature of their deaths. In other words, genetics was the key. He and his niece used to conduct experiments by measuring the blood pressure, cholesterol and heartbeat of various farm animals, they then put them on an extremely high saturated fat diet. After a period of this feeding the animals were again checked and it was found that the fat diet had no effect whatsoever! My father and Doctor Evans got on well together and he would give my father a thorough examination when we called to see him. It is interesting to note that Doctor William Evans was one of an exclusive elite who allegedly refused an honour.

The resurgence of the Red Kite in Wales was due to the efforts and dedication of Miss Frances Evans. The local authority used part of her land as a dumping ground on Tyndomen for waste products. Here, many Red Kites could be seen feeding in the early seventies. Miss Evans encouraged this, and if it had not been for her the revival of the species would have been almost impossible. Others have claimed to be responsible for saving them from extinction, but I know for a fact that credit for this should go to Miss Evans. It was a glorious sight to see the Red Kites wheeling and soaring above the green fields of Tyndomen.

As 'Twyn Cymro''s daughters started arriving in our herd it was time to purchase another polled bull to continue with the naturally polled factor. Miss Evans had a young bull who looked the part, named 'Caron-Llanio Domeno.' In due course he arrived at Tŷ Coch and proceeded to do his stuff. I continued to visit Tyndomen for years to come, and both Doctor and Miss Evans came to rely on me to advise them on aspects of cattle breeding. Miss Evans never married, I think she was too busy looking after her farming interests and her uncle to contemplate marriage.

As interest in naturally polled Welsh Blacks increased, the Welsh Black Cattle Society formed a special committee to oversee this aspect. Prominent breeders such as Alun Price of Sennybridge and Richard Wheelock of Treowen, Monmouthshire, and myself were appointed to the committee. In 1967, 13 polled bulls and 38 polled females were registered in the Herd Book. Generally speaking, Welsh Black cattle were virtually unknown outside Wales. Even as I write, this is largely the case today. The breed has a keen following within Wales because of its association with things Welsh. British beef breeds have been superseded by continental type cattle in the UK to the detriment of the Shorthorn, Aberdeen Angus, Hereford and others. In 1967, the overall average price of all pedigree Welsh Black cattle at the Society sales was 86 guineas.

Our Welsh Blacks proved to be an interesting proposition. I found that they were late maturers and tended to be on the 'leggy' side. Their temperament was suspect. Placing them in the cattle crush was like a wild west rodeo. One had to be very quick to avoid finishing up losing digits or even the cattle crush itself. On one occasion, we had a young bull in the stable pen which was ready to have a ring placed in his nose. Our local vet arrived to do the job and despite being held by two halters, when the vet went to approach him, the bull went for him and pinned him against the wall. To cap it all, he (the bull, not the vet), then jumped through the open stable window which was quite small and bolted down the field. He would have given Red Rum a good run in the Grand National! The vet, I'm glad to say, lived to enjoy a well earned retirement.

At one stage I thought this wild tendency was due to the polled factor tracing back to its introduction when Galloways were crossed with horned Welsh Blacks. Belted Welsh Blacks can still be seen around the Dolgelli area harking back to their Belted Galloway forebears. However, I found that the horned cattle had the same outlook on life. When they had their horns cut off they behaved identically to their polled counterparts. There was a ready market for the breed. We sold bulls to Beattock in Dumfries, Scotland, and to a farm on the Leeds/Manchester motorway as well as all over Wales. Our bull 'Tycoch Matthew' won at Abergavenny and sold for the top price. He was a stock bull at Lower Cathedine, just outside Brecon, and produced good stock for their herd. Alun Price, Tanyfedw, Sennybridge, bought several heifers to establish his new Welsh Black herd. He was a noted sheep and cattle judge who had officiated at the Royal Welsh Show regularly. Fat cattle then were selling for around £16 to £17 per cwt. However, farming took a severe blow in 1967 with the outbreak of Foot and Mouth and it was a long time before the industry fully recovered.

Coping with outmoded farm buildings was difficult. It was decided that a completely new complex would have to be built. Arthur drew up a design which was submitted to the relevant authorities, this was subsequently approved. It involved the build-

ing of a new silage shed some 100ft long with an adjacent covered
cattle shed which would accommodate the entire herd. A central
feeding passage would enable the stock to be fed from both sides.
Running alongside the covered cattle shed would be incorporated a
race with handling facilities which would allow handling of animals
to be a simple process and almost a one man job. The materials were
ordered and once again Arthur, my father and me set about building
it ourselves. Once more the cement mixer on the back of the tractor
worked overtime and the only bought in service was the supply of
ready mixed concrete for the 'acres' of floor. When it was completed
it looked magnificent. The amount of work we had put into it was
well worth the effort. We had to make quite a lot of hay prior to this
facility and this was a very dicey operation. In 1973, the big meadow
was flooded after torrential rain and all the lying hay was washed
away ending up in Ferryside! Now, we could make ad lib silage and
self feed it to the stock in the winter or cut it mechanically. Sheer
bliss! The redundant piggery was at this time converted into a double
covered yard catering for young stock- heifers and bulls – providing
an architect designed breeding unit which was unsurpassed in South
Wales.

It was while we were carting silage to the new silo that I met up
with my mother's cousin 'Uncle Davey.' I was driving the tractor
with a load of grass in the trailer when rounding a bend in the farm
road I could see a man standing under a tree on the side of the road.
On getting closer I could see it was him, David Schofield Thomas.
He had come from Merthyr to visit us and had spotted me coming
up the road. Uncle Davey had an illustrious career. A marvellous
tenor, he had sung with the D'Oyly Carte Opera Company. When
travelling to America he was accompanied by his friend and fellow
singer, George Sanders, who went on to become a Hollywood star
and who married Zsa Zsa Gabor. Uncle Davey always enjoyed
recounting the time he was one of the judges in a singing talent
show when one of the competitors was Tom Jones. They turned him
down and awarded the accolade to someone else. A marvellous

thing, hindsight! During the war, he served with the rank of captain in ENSA entertaining the armed services. First cousin to my mother and second cousin to my father, he was the heart and soul of any social gathering, a true extrovert for whom I had the highest regard.

1974 was the year that the saddest happening so far in my life occurred. My father had not been enjoying good health for a couple of months. On examination, he was diagnosed to have lung cancer which was too far advanced for an operation and was given but a short time to live. We were devastated. He had been such a strong healthy person all his life and had not even been to hospital for anything. When he was 21 he experienced some toothache and immediately went to the dentist and told him to take every one of his teeth out so that he would never have to experience that pain again. His downfall, was the fact that he smoked heavily all his life and this undoubtedly caused the lung cancer. After being confined to bed for just a week or so, he died on 7th December, 1974, at the age of 74 years.

My father was a home-loving man. He never went to pubs or other anti-social venues. He was deeply interested in politics and like his father before him, had no man-made religious convictions. He was a great pal to Arthur and me and never ever raised a hand or voice to either of us. Married to my mother (who was also his second cousin) for over half a century, he was the bedrock of the family. His sacrifices for his children were immense and his love of farming played a big part in me taking up agriculture in the early years. He loved children and they all worshipped him. A pioneer motorcyclist and motorist from the first world war to the time he died, he took a keen interest in his sons escapades in these fields which, looking back, must have given him nightmares! A brilliant orator, he was a man who could recount a story or happening which would bring it alive. I wouldn't have changed him for the world!

Life goes on and I continued to persevere with breeding Welsh Blacks. Trade was very up and down in the seventies. Economically speaking, these were difficult times. I sold some steers in the mart, two went for £85 each and four for £49 each. A dead loss!

Having travelled through Breconshire and Herefordshire on many occasions both by motor cycle and car, I had often admired the native Hereford cattle to be seen grazing contentedly in the fields. I was not altogether happy with the Welsh Blacks, being disappointed by their disposition, late maturity and limited marketing potential outside Wales. For some years the Hereford had been the supreme beef breed in Britain and together with the Aberdeen Angus, provided the highest quality meat. Hereford cattle could be found all over the world and merited its reputation for providing 'the roast beef of England.'

I started attending the pedigree Hereford sales in Sennybridge and Hereford in 1975, and was very impressed by the standard of the cattle forward at these sales. I decided that an experiment should be conducted whereby part of the farm should retain the Welsh Blacks, the remainder being devoted to carrying Herefords. Comparisons could then be made as to the merits or otherwise of the two breeds under our prevailing conditions. It was decided that only the best Hereford bloodlines would be selected and that the cattle would be purchased privately direct from the herds. The first breeder I visited was Stacey Jones of Sheephouse, Hay-on-Wye. His 'Penatok' herd was world renowned his stock being regarded as the 'Rolls Royce' of the breed. Stacey had taken Sheephouse over after his late brother, Elwyn Jones, whose 'Atok' herd had been equally famous. Stacey had an admirable eye for quality stock. During our trips around the herd in his BMW, we discussed the merits of the breed and I obtained a fascinating insight to what was involved in breeding Herefords.

Stacey Jones was very reluctant to sell any of his females privately. It took a great deal of persuasion on my part to get him to let me have some. The money aspect was not a barrier as far as he was concerned, he genuinely felt that he wanted his animals to go to a home where they would be appreciated and where a similar breeding programme would be undertaken. We negotiated a deal, I selected half a dozen in calf cows and this was the nucleus of our new Hereford herd. I remember asking Stacey at the time where the name 'Atok' originated. Apparently, he and his brother in their school days were boarders at Christ College in Brecon. They slept in a dormitory with beds lettered from A to K, hence Atok, which Elwyn then adopted in later years as his herd prefix. Stacey did not enjoy robust health, he had a metal plate in his head and I am sure that his health influenced his attitude as to what was to become of his cattle. This would also account for his fondness for his tipple. I don't think he ever got over the demise of his outstanding bull, 'Penatok Crusader.' This was a bull for which he had turned down an offer of £35,000. When 'Crusader' was placed in a crush for routine examination, something mechanical went wrong and the bull fell breaking a leg and had to be put down. This was not only a blow for Stacey but also the Hereford breed.

It was at this time (1976), that we experienced the worst drought I can ever remember. It didn't rain from May to September. Travelling across the countryside was like being in Australia, brown, burnt fields everywhere. Cloudless blue sky day after day with streams, ponds and rivers drying up. Our River Dulais running through Tŷ Coch dried up completely a thing I had never seen before or seen since. If it had not been for the deep pools which were there in the tree sheltered parts of the river bed, we would have been in a right pickle with no drinking water for the cattle. David was five at the time and I took him down to the river where we walked along its bed from Pyllaucochion to Llethermawr without seeing a trickle. I said to him: "Remember this Dave, you may never see the river dry like this again in your lifetime."

It didn't take very long for me to see how the two breeds were shaping up on the farm. It was like chalk and cheese. The Herefords were quiet and docile and grazed contentedly, they were easy to handle in the cattle crush and calved easily without disappearing into the 'bush.' You could safely leave a field gate open without them stampeding to escape to far flung destinations. The die was cast. Herefords it was to be. We dispersed the Welsh Blacks without too much difficulty, selling them to herds all over Wales.

As the Hereford cows started to calve it was necessary for me to procure a Hereford bull. One of the oldest established herds in the breed was the 'Haven' herd owned by Edward Lewis, based at The Haven in Herefordshire. I went along to visit him at The Haven and had a good look at their herd. Edward's son, Leslie, had taken over the management of the stock and he and I got on extremely well being of a similar age. Leslie was handicapped in walking due to him having had polio when he was younger. His enthusiasm for his cattle was infectious. He was from a long family line of Hereford breeders and had exported pedigree Herefords all over the world. For administrative and family reasons, they had a herd within the herd which they named 'Havenfield.' Leslie had a young bull which he thought would suit me and which had just won at the Royal Highland Show in Scotland. This bull, 'Havenfield Ranger,' was a real beauty, of superb breeding and marvellous temperament. Needless to say, I bought him and this was the first time I had purchased an animal for a four figure sum! It was now time for me to join the Hereford Herd Book Society (HHBS). Edward Lewis nominated me for membership and so the 'Redhouse' herd of Herefords was born. Redhouse, of course, being the English translation for Tŷ Coch.

More visits to purchase stock followed. I went to W. E. Thorne & Sons' 'Studdolph' herd in Pembrokeshire. Mr Thorne senior had been Chairman of the HHBS. His sons Robert and George were both following in his footsteps. I suspect Robert was named after 'Vern Robert,' probably the most influential Hereford sire ever. In later years, George too became Chairman of the HHBS. I purchased a number of in calf females from them and they turned out to be a very good buy indeed. Further visits to Stacey Jones secured some more Penatok cows. The third herd I went to, also based in Pembrokeshire was the 'Trewarren' herd owned by David Llewellyn.

This too was an old established herd on a farm overlooking the sea near Milford Haven, one of the most beautiful spots to have a farm. Trewarren really was an idyllic place to live and had real character. The herd came up to my expectations and several cows were bought to swell the Redhouse camp.

The breed was starting to expand in West Wales and it was not too long before a group of interested breeders, including myself, decided to form a club to oversee this expansion. An inaugural meeting was held at the Royal Ivy Bush Hotel in Carmarthen on Thursday, 31st March, 1977, which was attended by 37 members of the HHBS. Mr W. E. Thorne of the Studdolph Herd chaired the meeting and the club was formed, to be known as the Dyfed Hereford Breeder's Club. Over the following years, regular Shows and Sales were held at Carmarthen and proved to be popular. I had the privilege of being invited to act as an official judge at some of these events and ultimately became vice chairman of the club.

Meanwhile, our herd was thriving. The calves were of great conformation and one of the bull calves was outstanding. He was from the Penatok Julia family and was sired by 'Free Town Kendal' who was a stock bull in the Haven Herd. This calf I named 'Redhouse Dan.' He was the typical horned Hereford I had always had in mind. When mature, he weighed well over a ton and produced an outstanding crop of calves. I took him for a breed demonstration organised by the Dyfed Hereford Breeder's Club at Carmarthen Livestock Market. He created quite a stir and exploded a few myths about Hereford breeding in Carmarthenshire.

Young David was keenly interested in the animals and accompanied me to the sales helping to groom the stock for shows and sales. Ann had settled down well in Tre-Gib Secondary School in Llandeilo, as had Wynne. By the time he was 12, Wynne had grown to be almost six feet and was head and shoulders above his classmates. He was an exceptionally good rugby player and athlete. He went on to captain the school's first XV and obtained his County Cap and was a final trialist, playing in the centre for Wales Schools

*Wynne, champion Welsh Schools hurdler and record holder
and Triple Jump Champion and record holder.*

XV. Without being too biased as his father, it was only favouritism by certain teacher selectors which prevented him getting his Welsh cap. He went on to become Wales' 80 metres hurdles champion, 80 metres record holder and Wales triple jump champion and record holder. It took many years for his records to be broken. Wynne was a great help on the farm and threw his weight into haymaking with gusto! He could pick up bales with the best of them.

As sure as eggs as we get settled into a farming routine, something crops up to throw a spanner in the works. This time it was in the Hereford world. Some young breeders intent on trying to make a name for themselves had begun introducing polled bulls and converting their herds to entirely naturally polled stock. This was expanding rapidly and it was in my opinion the wrong thing to do.

The polled animals looked inferior to the traditional horned variety, with narrow heads, lack of width along their backs and had legs like beanstalks, long and lanky, looking as if they would fall sideways in a good wind. Worse still, there was no such thing as a 'naturally' polled Hereford. The polled factor had been brought to Britain from the USA and Canada. Herefords had been crossed with Red Polls on farms where the 'breeders' authenticity was to say the least 'suspect.' This polled progeny was introduced over here and hence the establishing of so called pedigree naturally polled herds. The traditional horned Hereford is a creature of beauty and cannot be mistaken. The propaganda selling of the polled variety in the seventies and eighties without a doubt started the decline in the breed. The commercial bread and butter trade of the traditional Hereford was the supply of crossing bulls for the dairy farmer. A Hereford crossed with the predominant Friesian female produced the familiar all black beast with a white face, socks and tail brush. This was an excellent cross combining the fleshing qualities of the Hereford and the growth and milking attribute of the Friesian. This 'split' in the Hereford camp caused confusion in the commercial and pedigree sectors. Undoubtedly, combined with the introduction of the continental breeds with their tasteless lean meat and the endless stream of anti-fat pundits brainwashing, the writing on the wall was plain to see.

Even old established breeders like the Thornes went polled, their Studdolph herd being relegated to the second division by establishing their 'Ashdale' herd of polled Herefords. Many others followed. It was like battering your head against a brick wall to try to convince them that they were going up the wrong path. Talking the situation over with Stacey Jones, he was convinced that this was a 'blip' and remained optimistic to the end of his days that breeders would see the error of their ways and that the traditional horned Hereford would once more regain the mantle of the world's best beef breed. Capt. de Quincey, breeder of the most famous Hereford herd in the breed's annals (the 'Vern'), would have turned in his grave has he been able to see the foot shooting state of his beloved Herefords by breeders who had been hoodwinked.

I put pen to paper in an endeavour to redress the balance and this evoked some interesting responses. One of the leading traditional breeders, Michael Symonds of Llandinabo Court, Hereford, sent me the following letter:

14th May, 1983.

Dear Mr Harris

I much enjoyed your recent article in Farming News, *which I cut out and sent on to my old friend Benny Dent in Australia, who will, I know, be as delighted as I am that someone is standing up for the true Hereford these days, when we see these stupid young men throwing away the legacy of ages. I was going to write to you anyway but, seeing your further letter in the* News *today (afraid I missed the letter which inspired it but can guess the contents which you have answered so well) I felt I must sit down and congratulate you again.*

You mention the naturally polled Hereford, as the breeders like to call them! Of course there is no such thing. At the last Council meeting of the HHBS Council, which I attended as an elected Member – some two years ago now as I am, of course, only an Honorary Member now, which to the present generation appears to be a term of reproach rather than the honour it used to be! – I was delighted to be able to nail the lie that the Polls arose from a genetic sport. It was brought up by John Young, who was President at the time, and he kept talking about the 'purity' of the polls in general and the American/Canadian polls in particular, until I could stand it no longer. So I got up and quoted to the Council the authentic passage in the 1909 Edition of Macdonald & Sinclair, *which gives in black and white the origin of the American polls – from a Red Poll. In the Chicago paper* Breeders' Gazette *in 1894 a Mr C. T. Merder of the Taylor Co., Iowa, tells how through accident he bred a Hereford cow to a Red Poll bull and the resultant bull calf, polled but Hereford marked, was mated subsequently with a similarly bred cross by a Mr Guthrie of Kansas, except that he had used a Polled Durham in place of the Red Poll. It is all fully authenticated and the various stories of the 'genetic sports,' which seem to have occurred with regularity in America though none has ever been seen in either the UK, Argentina, South Africa or Australia, which together breed more than three times the Herefords ever produced in the USA. Always it has been traced back to a Red Poll on the neighbouring ranch and, as I said to Mr Young, the only 'sport' involved was a sporting Red Poll, which jumped the boundary fence.*

Scientifically, of course the 'sport' theory has been disproved over and over again. The blood grouping of the Poll is different from the true Hereford: genetically it should be the same if the 'sport' had occurred. Zoologically too, the eye socket of the poll is akin to that of the Red Poll and entirely different to that of the true Hereford, which could not have occurred in a 'sport.' Anyway, this is now minuted in the Council Minutes and one lie has been nailed.

The long legged craze, which you castigate so beautifully, is just another, typical trans Atlantic fantasy, which they dress up in pseudo-scientific jargon with college professors contributing their own theories about the lean carcase it produces, the extra growth which comes with a long canon bone and similar nonsense, where-as the truth is very different. In June 1979, I had a visit to the Herd by Wayne Haygood, of New Harmony, Indiana, who at that time was President of the American Hereford Association. And Hop Dickenson, whom I have known for years, and who was – and still is – the Secretary of the American Hereford Association. He is a good friend of Tony Morrison and a very sensible, down to earth sort of chap.

I took them down the fields to see my bull LLANDINABO UBIQUE, which was some 11 years old at the time and running with some cows. He went on the scales at approximately 25 cwt at the time; he was probably the longest bull I have ever bred and beautifully balanced. Both Wayne and Hop looked at him, walked round him, talked together and looked again but said nothing. In the meantime the old bull stopped grazing, served a cow and went on grazing again in a way which only the true Hereford does, and my Stockman Bob and I chatted together, waiting to see what our American friends would say. At last I said: "Well, Wayne, what's the verdict? I suppose his legs are too short for you?" His reply was: "With a perfect body like that, who wants long legs? This is the best bull I have ever seen." So I thanked him and said, "Why then do you all go for long legs these days?" – and his reply summed it all up. He said that he knew I had been to America several times and travelled most of the top herds and others so was aware of the standard of the cows, especially the commercial herds in the USA, that they were, for the most part, poor and small. All their feeding and commercial production was now channelled through the feed lot and this required a certain uniformity of the cattle, steers or heifers, being fed. *The only uniformity they could achieve fast from the motley cow herds across the country was that of height.* Hence the emphasis on long legs and long legged bulls were making the money so breeders were selecting for them. It was as simple as that. It did not really matter how poor the resultant crosses were as long as they appeared roughly the same height in the feed lot. The standard ration of corn fed per head per day was up to 45 lbs per head! I said that was unbelievable; our Herefords would blow up and go off their legs if fed half that per day. Corn for them is almost a waste product these days anyway but it does account for the fact that American beef is flavourless, with no marbling and tender because all carcases are chemically 'tenderised' by injection immediately before slaughter.

And this is what our young men here now want to breed here. Hop Dickenson is coming over again in July and is due to come here to see the cattle and lunch at his own request, so I shall look forward to having another talk with him then. I particularly want to find out about the difficulties in calving they are having now with their long legged animals. I believe it is becoming a serious problem, as any extreme is bound to become in livestock breeding. As de Quincey always used to emphasise – Balance is beauty and all living things must be beautiful or they are wrong; it is the breeders duty to try and put it right.

I believe that there are signs that many people are beginning to get worried at the way things are going in the Hereford world and that is the first step to putting things right. So please continue with your good work; it helps to make people think!

Yours sincerely

Michael Symonds

Breeders of all traditional British breeds were under attack at this time. The French Charollais in particular was making strong headway. My articles resulted in a response even from the Aberdeen Angus Society whose Secretary, R. Anderson, wrote to me:

Dear Mr Harris,

Thoroughly enjoyed your article in this week's Farming News.

Yours sincerely
R. Anderson
(Secretary)

The Aberdeen Angus Society.
7th April, 1983.

I received a picture of a historic Hereford bull from H. C. (Benny) Dent in Sydney, Australia. This reproduction picture hitherto unreproduced, was of 'Wellington (4)' of whom a watercolour appears as the first plate in Volume One of the *Hereford Herd Book*, where he is the fourth bull listed. This painting for over a hundred years was hung in Benny Dent's grandfather's dining room at Kings Pyon, Herefordshire. It was inherited with the property from his Aunt Margaret, who was Benjamin Tomkins daughter. 'Wellington (4)' was born in 1808 and was bred by Benjamin Tomkins and sold in October 1815, for £283.10s.0d. He was according to Mr Tomkins: "The best bull and the best stock getter I ever had."

Benny Dent wrote to me:

Congratulations on your advert in the Breed Journal, *and more to the point that you do breed Herefords and not the mongrels now purported to be.*
   I thought you should have a real Tomkins bull, this painting shows over exaggerated reproduction even in those days.
   All the best in 1983 with your REAL HEREFORDS.

H. C. Dent

Young Redhouse Hereford bull and myself at Tŷ Coch.

Herd sire, 'Havenfield Ranger,' Highland Show winner.

Our Hereford herd grazing contently at Tŷ Coch.

Homebred Redhouse Hereford stock.

The Herefords chewing things over.

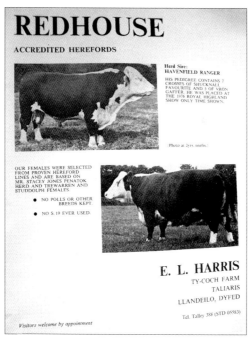

Herd advert in the Hereford Journal.

209

Now that David was growing older, Mary decided that she would resume her career and was successful in obtaining a position with the Civil Service in 1978. She was seconded to the Carmarthen Office of Customs and Excise as PA to the Regional VAT Chief Officer. She worked in the VAT set-up for the next 22 years. The big drawback with farming is that there is never time to take long holidays and this was very much the case as far as we were concerned. We did however, manage a few trips to London. When my cousin Roy Jenkins was made Home Secretary, he asked me to bring Ann and Wynne to see him when we were in London. We went to the Home Office in Whitehall and met him there. This was at a particularly tense time when the IRA was most militant. Security at the Home Office was intense and we had to go through a series of security doors with special codes, which intrigued Ann and Wynne, before we were ushered into Roy's private rooms.

While we were with Roy, I went through the latest findings I had unearthed of our Harris line with him. My quest for digging into the past and finding out what our forebears were like went unabated in the seventies and eighties. In 1982, likewise-minded 'family detectives' got together in Carmarthen to form a society which would help to develop mutual interests in genealogy. As a founder member, I was closely involved in getting the society off the ground and thus was born 'Dyfed Family History Society.' I was asked to handle the public relations and so became the first PRO for the Society. It took off like wildfire once people got to know what the Society was all about. I was invited by Linda Mitchell of the BBC to appear on BBC Radio Wales where I was interviewed at length. Articles appeared such as the following:

Western Mail
Friday, April 30th, 1982.

Finding the roots of family trees

Tracing family trees has become so popular in the past few years that a society has been set up in Dyfed to help people to find their roots.

The inaugural meeting of the Dyfed Family History Society was crowded out a few weeks ago and now local committees are being set up in Carmarthen, Llanelli, Aberystwyth and Haverfordwest. Society spokesman Mr Lyndon Harris said he thought its popularity was due to a natural desire of Welsh people to trace their ancestry.

"The Welsh have a feeling that they want to identify with their past, and with people having more leisure time they want to do more digging into their family tree," he said. The Society will help people trying to trace their forebears. Activities will include visits to places which store archives, discussion groups and seeking advice from experts.

About 120 people attended the first meeting. The Society will hold its annual meeting on Saturday, May 8th, at the Public Library, Carmarthen. How should people anxious to trace their ancestors go about it? "First speak to the older members of the family," said Mr Harris. "Have a long chat and get all the names you can. Once you have got those the next step is to go to the National Library at Aberystwyth where they hold all parish records going back to the 1500s."

"After that you have to trace manorial rolls, county records and old rent books. Some of our members have traced their family back to William the Conqueror. I have gone back as far as the 1600s with my own family and have discovered all sorts of relatives I was unaware of." Mr Harris said that anyone was welcome to join the Society, whether they live in Dyfed or not.

Similarly the *Carmarthen Times* reported:

April 30th, 1982

Families rush to join county 'roots' society

A major 'Roots' society has been formed in Dyfed to help people to trace their family history. And already the Dyfed Family History Society – Cymdeithas Hanes Teuluoedd Dyfed – has a membership of nearly 200.

"I was quite staggered by the organisation and response," said committee member Mr Lyndon Harris of Llandeilo. "About 120 people attended our initial meeting in Carmarthen and membership applications have come in from all over Britain. We have even had someone join from Australia. Tracing family histories has taken off in a big way in recent years and this was borne out by the response to our inaugural meeting."

The Society has been formed to give 'professional' backing to amateur family history researchers. "One of the Society's main instigators was the County Archivist, Miss Mureen Patch," Mr Harris said. "While the Herald of Wales and the National Library of Wales are on our doorstep in Carmarthen and Aberystwyth." All village records are also kept at Aberystwyth and these provide one of the most valuable sources of family information.

The Dyfed Family History Society will operate at two levels – as a County-wide Society and through four local committees based in Carmarthen, Llanelli, Haverfordwest and Aberystwyth. "The Society will effectively operate as a parent body for the local committees," Mr Harris said, "and it will be through the Society that the committees will be able to call on the expertise available to them. It is this availability of expertise which many family researchers lack. Our membership comprises a mixture of people who have been tracing their family trees and others who have yet to start," he said.

Mr Harris continued: "What they all have in common – apart from the desire to trace their family history – is a lack of co-ordination – they have been working individually whereas now they can get together and share their experiences."

The real strength of the Society will come from its ability to help people turn 'rumour' into fact, Mr Harris pointed out. "Most people become interested in their family's through tales told by their elderly relatives," he said. "This 'word of mouth' history is relatively easy to collect but much harder to verify unless one knows where to go for records and information which will bear out this 'spoken history' and put it in to context."

With its membership steadily climbing the Dyfed Family History Society has already set its sights on publishing a quarterly journal.

As well as providing a review of the Society's work and the work of its members, the journal will almost certainly bring to light many 'unknown' historical facts about the three counties which make up Dyfed. But the next step in the Society's development will be a formal one; its first annual meeting at the Library, Carmarthen on May 8th at 2.30 p.m.

From these early beginnings the Society, now in its 25th year, grew and grew, as I put pen to paper, the membership now exceeds 4,500, drawing in 'recruits' from all over the world.

For some time I had been trying to trace the whereabouts of my maternal grandmother's cousins who had emigrated to the USA in the late 1800s. My mother had inherited a bundle of letters which had been written to my grandmother by her first cousin whose married surname was 'Brickner.' They had settled in Ohio and the contents of these letters struck a cord with me as they were so poignant and full of longing for the place of her birth – Merthyr Tydfil. I wrote to local newspapers in Ohio and Pennsylvania seeking information, but without any luck, and had really drawn a blank. Then one day in the early seventies, I received a 'phone call from my old friend Elwyn Bowen in Cefn Coed, Merthyr Tydfil, who told me that an American couple had been visiting the Unitarian, Hen Dŷ Cwrdd (Chapel) in Cefn Coed, he happened by chance to be there and they had asked him if he knew anything about the Rev. David John who was one of the leading Chartists and Unitarians in Merthyr in the mid 1800s, and to whom the lady was related. Elwyn told them he could do better than that and could put them in touch with living descendents of David John, knowing that my mother was the Rev. David John's great-great-granddaughter.

Within hours of hearing from Elwyn, my 'phone again rang and the American lady spoke on the other end. She told me her name and before she could say any more I told her: "I know exactly who you are, you're Bessie Brickner's daughter Violet, my mother's second cousin. I've been trying to track you down for years." There was a dramatic silence and then a voice shaking with emotion said: "I can't believe it, this isn't happening." After a few more exchanges, she asked me if I could go to Merthyr to meet her and her husband and bring my mother along too. My mother and I went to Merthyr the very following day and what a meeting it turned out to be. Violet and Walter Halsey were living in Harrisburg, Pennsylvania. They were over in the UK on holiday and had decided to visit Merthyr to see where Violet's mother had been born before she and her parents emigrated to the USA. Her mother had been born in Vulcan House, Bethesda Street. Violet was quite overcome when I showed her the letters her mother had written to my grandmother. It transpired that she had an older sister, Sarah, who lived with her husband Karl Beckel on a farm in Marion, Ohio. She said she couldn't wait to get back to the States to tell her all about their 'long lost' Welsh family. In the years that followed this historic meeting, we corresponded and met many times of which more anon!

What a momentous year 1985 turned out to be! 'Our little girl,' Ann, married David Evans of Capel Isaac, Llandeilo. The ceremony took place at County Hall, Swansea, and the reception was held at Langland Court, Swansea. They had met in Tre-Gib School where David had been captain of the school's 'first XV' rugby team and later went to college in Liverpool where he obtained his degree and became a chartered surveyor. They set up home in Killay, Swansea, and she could not have picked a nicer husband. Mary and I were delighted to have such a fine son-in-law. I know John and Sheila Evans, David's parents, thought the world of Ann.

In June that year, we had the sad news of cousin David ('Uncle Davy') Schofield Thomas' death in Merthyr. He and my mother had been very close and both he and my parents had been lifelong buddies. Arthur, my mother and me went to his funeral and burial at Cefn Coed Cemetery and afterwards to 14, Well Street, with his son Ronnie and daughters, Christine and Marion. It was an overcast miserable day with a slight drizzle at times, typical funeral weather! As we made our way back to Llandeilo from Merthyr, we were driving past the Llwyn Onn reservoir at Cwmtaff, when on a curve

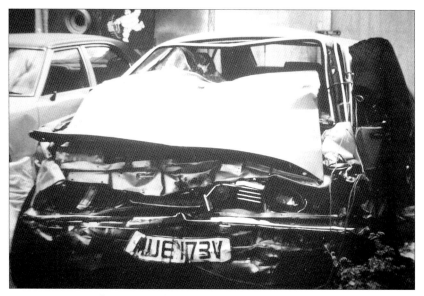

The Princess after the head-on crash near Merthyr.

in the road a Ford Escort car coming towards us at speed, skidded sideways across the road and hit us head on. I instinctively slammed on the brakes but the impact slewed us sideways and the Escort disappeared from my view. I was trapped by my seat belt and couldn't move until a passing motorist who happened to be a nurse on her way to her work in Prince Charles Hospital from her home at Nant Ddu Lodge, cut me free. My mother who had been in the rear had been thrown into the well behind the driving seat and was moaning in some pain. Arthur, in the front passenger seat, had hit the dashboard with some force despite the seat belt, and had damaged his arm. An ambulance arrived on the scene very quickly and my mother, Arthur and me were taken to Prince Charles Hospital. Before I went in the ambulance, I looked around to see where the other car had finished up. To my astonishment I discovered it had completely broken in two, one half near the edge of the reservoir, the other some way down the road towards the Merthyr direction. The driver, I was told later, had been killed outright.

After examinations at the hospital, my mother was found to have broken her femur and also had extensive bruising. Arthur had a sprained wrist and arm bruising and I was lucky, escaping with just a bruised arm. I thanked my lucky stars that I was not a drinker not having touched a drop of alcohol at the funeral, resulting in a clear breathalyzer test. I am positive that our injuries would have been much worse were it not for the fact that I was driving a 2.3 litre Austin Princess which had a massive six cylinder engine mounted transversely across the front, which took the brunt of the impact. The car was completely demolished at the front and a complete write-off. The subsequent inquest exonerated me of any blame.

My mother, who was 84 at the time of the crash, spent the next three months in Prince Charles Hospital. We didn't miss a day in going to visit her and travelled daily to Merthyr from Llandeilo until she was discharged. It amused my mother when she read in the media that 'an elderly lady' had been involved in the crash, as she certainly didn't regard herself as 'elderly' in any shape or form. Ronnie, Margaret his wife and Christine were a tower of strength during this traumatic experience, for which I will be eternally grateful. The accident affected my mother physically for the rest of her life. She was not able to walk without the use of a stick and in later years a walking frame. She had been operated on in hospital and a titanium plate, complete with nuts and bolts, had been fixed to her femur. Mentally, she was not affected in the slightest and she went on to live into her 100th year!

For some years I had been corresponding with relatives in Australia. A lady living in Cranbourne, near Melbourne, had written to the *Merthyr Express* to try and find any relatives in the UK. The secretary of the Merthyr Tydfil Historical Society had seen this and he wrote to me to see if I could help her. It turned out that she was related to my family on my mother's side. I contacted her and we have never looked back since, except in a genealogical way! She was Elwyn Squires and was connected to the Llywelyn line of my maternal grandmother whose grandmother prior to marriage, was

My mother with Stan Thomas (pies) at a Cyfarthfa Castle School Reunion.

Jane Llewelyn of Waunwyllt, Merthyr Tydfil. Jane was descended from a Tomos Llywelyn of Rhigos who was a poet and a puritan as far as his religion was concerned. My grandmother always said that she understood from her family antecedents that Tomos or Thomas translated the bible from English to Welsh but I have yet to pursue this fascinating story. He was born in 1580 so this will require some research.

Jane Llewelyn of Waunwyllt was related to the first Lady Merthyr who was married to Sir William T. Lewis, who subsequently became Lord Merthyr of Sengenydd. Lady Merthyr gave my great-great-grandmother Jane (her cousin), a blue Staffordshire dinner service as a wedding present which has passed down the female line of my family and which is now in my proud possession. Before her marriage, Jane lived in Chapel Row, her husband being Head of the Blacksmiths at Cyfarthfa Iron Works. Living next door was the Parry family of whom the son Joseph went on to become a famous musician noted foe his composition 'Myfanwy.' Joseph used to visit Jane and she would place him on a stool to recite and as a reward would give him a sweet which she kept in the drawer of her Welsh dresser a dresser which again has been passed down through the

217

My mother at Dr. Joseph Parry's house at Chapel Row, Merthyr Tydfil.

Me, mother and Arthur taken at the Osborne Hotel, Swansea.

family and which I also possess. Doctor Joseph Parry's mother hailed from Kidwelly and her cousin, my great-grandmother on my paternal side, lived alongside the Parry family in Chapel Row as well. My great-grandmother was before marriage, Margaret Gravell. She was from Kidwelly also and her father, Daniel (Dan) Gravell, farmed Parc y Mynydd, at Mynydd-y-Garreg, Kidwelly. The history of the Gravell clan is interesting. They are reputed to have come to Kidwelly as part of the Norman influx, primarily to build Kidwelly Castle. They settled permanently in the area and flourished. Looking through contemporary telephone directories, the surname Gravell mainly crops up in the Kidwelly and Carmarthenshire region, very few elsewhere. Some members of the family thinking it would enhance their social status, changed their name to Greville, Grenville and Gravelle, I was told by one who had done so that it 'sounded more posh' than plain Gravell. I was given a pedigree of the family which traced back to Norman times, the surname being spelt then as 'Grevel.' My grandmother used to tell me that all her Gravell menfolk relations were 'big strong men.'

Following on David and Ann's wedding. The wedding of Wynne took place in August, 1987. He had also met his bride, Janet Smith, while they were both at school at Tre-Gib Secondary School, Llandeilo, where Janet was head girl. They had a chapel marriage at Janet's family place of worship at Penygroes, near Ammanford, with the reception afterwards at the Royal Ivy Bush Hotel, Carmarthen. Their honeymoon was spent in Thailand. Both Wynne and Janet had obtained their degrees in London, Mary and I proudly attended Wynne's degree ceremony at Southwark Cathedral where the presentation was conducted by Simon Hughes MP, now Liberal Democrat President.

I was called for jury service during this period, the one and only time to for me to do so. The trial took place at Carmarthen Guildhall and was fascinating, almost up to Rumple of Old Bailey standard. A couple of young men were accused of robbing a petrol filling station at Fforestfach, Swansea, near the Tesco Supermarket. They

Family group including Jackie's family, Arthur, Indeg, Lloyd and Matthew, Wynne, David, Mary and my mother.

wore masks and got away with a substantial amount of cash. The proceedings went on and on, and the deliberations by my fellow jurors even longer, due no doubt, to the tidy expenses accumulating while they pondered. To cut a long story short, while it looked as if the accused had done the robbery, the hard evidence was circumstantial. I held my view that the prosecution was invalid. I was appointed foreman to deliver the jury's verdict of not guilty, which I did.

During the same year (1988), a terrific storm hit the UK which did a tremendous amount of damage to trees, houses and property generally. The winds were of hurricane force and lorries and cars were tossed about like they were Dinky toys. Mary and I drove to London to see Wynne and Janet the day after the storm. Driving over the Cotswolds on the A40 was like something out of a Hollywood blockbuster. Lorries were strewn on their sides and upside down at regular intervals along the road and felled trees and branches were littered everywhere. We eventually arrived at Wynne and Janet's flat which was situated just a few yards from Alexandra Palace, where the first ever television broadcast had taken place pre-war. We took the opportunity during the next few days to visit old haunts and one of the first places we went to was Hadleigh to show Wynne his birthplace. This was the first time we had been back there since leaving for Liverpool in 1964. All the trees and shrubs had matured in Falbro Crescent and it looked completely different. We took Wynne and Janet to Southend and for a walk along the pier which was the longest in the world. Mary and I headed north for St. Albans to try and track down some of my old friends. After a bit of detective work I managed to locate Morris Chalkley my motor cycle 'guru.' He was living with his wife Beryl at Redbourne near St. Albans. He had the surprise of his life when we turned up on his doorstep. I hadn't seen Morris since we left St. Albans some 40 odd years previously. We had a lovely welcome and a pleasant time was had filling in the gaps.

Morris told me where to find my other close friend of 40 years ago – Roger White – he was living in Mount Pleasant Lane, off the Watford Road, within yards of my old school which I had last attended in 1939. Another reunion took place and Roger filled me in on events and people I had known all those years ago. One of these was Joan Cross who had lived next door to me in St. Albans. She too was living in the same area and again, Mary and I went along to see her. She was flabbergasted when she saw me after what must have felt like a lifetime. She had married and was now Joan Signorini and a widow. Her brother Philip, who I had also been close to, was now a Roman Catholic priest at a church in Harrow. After further exploratory forays into the historic streets of St. Albans, which included my one and only ever visit to a Macdonalds! We returned to Llandeilo after the obligatory detour to Harrods!

Education had always been of great interest to me. After all, who could claim to have had more first hand experience of the educational system than me? I was delighted when the opportunity occurred for me to become a governor in the early eighties of Llandeilo County Secondary School – Tre-Gib. I was co-opted as a governor by Carmarthenshire County Council and I served in this capacity for the best part of the next twenty years. This was a school of nearly 1,000 pupils set in a rural area and was the successor of the old grammar school in Llandeilo. Tre-Gib had been built in the grounds of a mansion bearing the same name and a more beautiful location would be hard to find. At the time of my appointment, the outgoing headmaster was Mr Samuel. He had been the head of the old grammar school and had taught Mary a former pupil.

Euros Rees took over the headship and under his stint the school flourished. Euros, who was also an old schoolmate of Mary's, unfortunately suffered heart problems which necessitated him resigning his headship. He never returned to teaching, but I am pleased to say that he recovered remarkably well and continued to lead an active life, particularly in his association with the Glynhir Golf Club. As a stop-gap, Ieuan Jones, the deputy head, took over the mantle until a permanent appointment was made. Ieuan had been in the same form as Arthur's wife, Indeg, in the old grammar school. He had done his teacher training with my old Merthyr friend, Ted Martin, which certainly bears out the saying, "it's a small world." In later years Ieuan became a county councillor and member of the Carmarthen-shire County Council 'Cabinet.'

David's time at Tre-Gib was now coming to an end. He had done well in his exams and had been accepted in Seale Hayne Agricultural College at Plymouth University. The college was situated in Newton Abbott in Devonshire. It was a pleasant campus set on a hill within easy reach of town and the sea, with Exmoor a short distance away. Once more I was renewing my connection with Devon. Journeys over the Severn Bridge down to Newton Abbot via Exeter became regular. Every time we passed Exeter it reminded me of Talley. The bell from ancient Talley Abbey had been taken to Exeter Cathedral in the dim distant past and installed there.

The seventies and eighties had been momentous in the political field. Cousin Roy, part of the 'gang of four,' Roy Jenkins, Shirley Williams, Bill Rodgers and David Owen, had broken from the Labour Party to form the SDP (Social Democratic Party). I was surprised of the move at the time as I thought they would have achieved more by staying in the Labour camp and using their influence to persuade their 'brothers' to follow the democratic line. I was not over partial to Bill Rodgers who I thought was a bit of a drip and told Roy so. Had not Roy been giving an impression of being a claret-loving socialite, he would have fared a lot better in his prospects of becoming leader of the Party and ultimately Prime Minister. With his working Labour credentials, there weren't many who could compete with him. His accent belied this background and as a PR man I was not surprised he suffered for it. Rumours of his associations with American celebrities didn't help either.

However, he did go on to great things becoming Leader of the Liberal Democrats in the House of Lords, President of the European Commission and Chancellor of Oxford University. I remember visiting him at East Hendred where he had his country home and seeing him dashing here and there on University business. He was very fond of his croquet lawns and was also a keen tennis player. His wife Jennifer and I got on well together and she enjoyed showing me the alterations they were making to the house which was then in need of restoration. Roy was an expert on the lives of famous people and wrote many biographies, the best of which was probably that of Winston Churchill. When I used to talk to him about his own and my family tree, he used to be quite reticent which I found disconcerting. Behind the façade of a powerful politician was, I suspect, a 'shy' nature, a man very conscious of his roots and perhaps not coming to terms with his present lifestyle. His mother, Hattie Harris, wore the trousers in the Jenkins household and Roy worshipped her, according to our mutual cousin Marjory in Cefn Coed.

Marjory had kept in close contact with Roy's mother Hattie over the years. Hattie's grandfather, William, my great-grandfather Henry and their brother Thomas, according to Marjory, used to be taken for holidays when they were boys by Eliza Crawshay to her seaside home at Langland, Swansea. Eliza was married to Henry Crawshay of the Cyfarthfa dynasty and he was responsible for the Hirwaun iron works. Eliza before she married Henry was Eliza Harris from Penderyn. Like many women in the Harris clan, she was the dominant force in the marriage which was frowned upon by Henry's father who did everything he could to prevent it. Henry and Eliza had a long and happy marriage and they finished their days on a sumptuous estate in the Forest of Dean, Monmouthshire. The links with the Cyfarthfa Castle branch of the family were not broken. Marjory told me that secret messages used to be taken by the three brothers to Cyfarthfa Castle from Cefn Coed. Thomas, the eldest was the dancing master at the famous ball held in one of the huge buildings at Cyfarthfa Iron Works, a ball which inspired Doctor Joseph Parry at the start of his musical career. Marjory herself had an interesting life, she had been for many years a companion to Lord Merthyr's two spinster aunts who resided at Abergavenny. She too remained a spinster and lived for most of her life in Holford Street in Cefn Coed where she died. She was a refined and stately lady very family orientated and quite independent.

The seventies and eighties were stirring times in the political world. James Callaghan had become Prime Minister who presided over, 'the winter of discontent,' and Margaret Thatcher succeeded him to become the first ever woman British Prime Minister. I had kept my hand in by writing articles and had been approached by the Communication, Advertising and Marketing Foundation (CAM), to assist in raising the standard of professionalism in the communications industry by entering the examinations set by CAM to achieve that goal. I did so and was awarded the Diploma (Dip. CAM). Together with the work of the Institute of Public Relations, this new qualification did much to further educational standards and hence the professional integrity of those in the practice of PR and advertising. I wonder sometimes if the so called 'spin doctors' of today were ever told that ethics is the be all and end all of good PR. If the product is no good, don't sell it! That applies to policy as well as products.

On the farm I was still plodding on endeavouring to earn a crust of bread. While my efforts in the early sixties to convert my compatriots to a more sustainable type of farming by adopting more 'natural' methods, was regarded as bordering on 'cranky,' I kept trying and the following which appeared in the farming press in 1983, typifies my efforts:

IT'S A LOT OF BULL!

What a peculiar business is farming. No other form of employment generates or gives rise to opinions expressed by so many 'experts.' It seems to me that the industry is bombarded by theories designed to make this, the most basic and fundamentally simple following of man, into what is fast becoming a complicated hotch botch of dubious practices.

Take livestock breeding as a prime example. This has become more akin to something out of Mary Quant's world that the sober earthy task it really is. Fashion dictates the ways of cattlemen throughout the world. Fashion pushed by individuals who more often than not have taken to the keeping of animals as a pastime usually financed by funds obtained by manufacturing items like open ended spanners or moth balls. It's probably a toss up whether they go into cattle breeding or become directors of soccer clubs – or both!

Pedigree cattle breeding is in danger of fast becoming a lost art, more's the pity, as the practical eye of the individual who lives with his stock and who has cared for generations of cattle is displaced but the entrepreneur who, because of his lack of the 'touch' and 'eye,' has to resort in sheer frustration to pushing second-rate wares on an unsuspecting public. Nowhere can this be seen more than in the breeding of beef cattle over the last couple of years. Britain, the home of roast beef and quality meat of the most succulent ilk, has been invaded by a variety of breeds which, to say the least, even confuse Mr Heinz!

The funny thing is that some individuals have been duped into thinking that long legged lanky livestock epitomizes perfection when, as any practical chap will know, these awkward looking creatures eat like the proverbial horse, are late maturing – in other words you don't get your money back for years and years – and to cap it all produce meat which is about as appetizing to a hungry navvy as a tin of pilchards. This is the 'can't tell butter from margarine' outlook being foisted on us.

We must not let our native beef breeds fall to the cult of the long legged beast. Surely it is folly to allow what amounts to two hundred years of master breeding of British beef stud stock to go down the drain for what can be no more than a passing fad? Individuals are anxious to make a fast buck by importing stock from our former colonies in order to dilute ours. Colonial stock which may be of doubtful origins inasmuch that some look as if their maternal ancestors were victims of raids by marauding buffaloes in the not too distant past. What is more, these cattle come from farms which are nothing like those to be found here. Farms which have abundant grain for feeding and usually a climate which necessitates housing for long periods. Environmentally, these imported animals are just not suited to grassland dependent holdings.

Yet, hardly a month goes by without hearing of a syndicate or a wealthy businessman who has just paid umpteen thousand dollars for a bull the other side of the Atlantic. A bull whose claim to fame appears to rest on the inability of the average sized human to see over the top of it. This emphasis on height is further pressed home by trimming its tail so short that it looks as if it was bitten off at some early stage of its development. This, I suggest is one of the biggest 'cons' ever perpetrated in beef cattle breeding. Yes, there is a glimmer of light on the horizon. Up and down the country practical livestock men are beginning to question the wisdom of using 'modern' types of breeding bulls. Holstein influence in the dairy industry and the breeding of fine boned Friesians has begun to concentrate the mind wonderfully and it does not take a Russell Grant to forecast the economic implications which will result by using beef bulls of similar conformation.

The writing is on the wall. It is up to the cattlemen to take heed and take advantage of the existence of British beef breeding stock unsullied for generations and which traditionally has proved to be able to deliver the goods at the least cost.

As I have already said, to advocate a simple form of agriculture was to risk being labelled as 'odd.' I had to be careful in the sixties when writing for the *Western Mail* not to alienate the orthodox farming readership by castigating the industry too much. Even today, by advocating organic husbandry one can still come under criticism from sensitive people in the farming world who honestly believe that their intensive methods are the only path to follow if the hungry millions in the world are to get enough to eat. Most things in life are a compromise and a gradual conversion is the obvious route to take. Persuasion by demonstrating that natural farming methods are beneficial health-wise and bank balance-wise is the only way to achieve this goal.

I wrote the following article in the *Western Mail* which appeared on March 2nd, 1961:

Artificial 'aids' leave their marks

By LYNDON HARRIS

Now, more than ever before, unnatural practices in farming are beginning to receive their fair share of publicity through the medium of both the Press and television. No longer are advocates of the 'stop and think first' campaign ridiculed and regarded by all and sundry as unmitigated cranks.

Just look at a random sample at some of the artificial 'aids' in everyday use on the farm – laying batteries, antibiotic feeding of cattle and pigs, artificial insemination, not to mention weed sprays and chemicals used in seed dressings. All these items leave their marks in one form or another on the·pattern of life.

'Industrial' basis

It may be argued that without them, the chances of making money by farming would be slim. Is this in fact the case? Has sufficient thought and research been devoted exclusively to this subject? Is the final result and goal to be reckoned in terms of £.s.d. rather than consideration of factors such as health and the preservation of wild life

To ignore the matter is a sure invitation for trouble. These things have a nasty habit of boomeranging, and once consumer resistance is encountered in respect of a commodity which is of inferior quality as a direct result of one or more of these contemporary practices, then financial repercussions will soon follow in the wake.

One is constantly hearing of bright individuals who boast of the fact that they pursue a farming policy on a purely 'industrial' basis, and proudly announce that they have no time or use for outmoded traditional practices.

Practically every farming conference held nowadays provides a platform for a spate of speakers who wish to spout forth on the virtues of 'progressive management,' and who seem to delight in vying with each other in competition to discover who can frighten the farmer most effectively.

As I see it, the fundamental principles governing agriculture have not altered. It is possible to construct a jet airliner to fly around the world in a few hours, but the day when we will evolve a cow which produces a calf in less than nine months, is far distant.

Better designed

Surely, progress does not mean the contemptuous deliberate transgression of natural laws, but rather the recognition and implemen-

228

tation of contemporary ideas which are in line with, and which are directly complementary to, the fundamental ideal.

Examples springing to mind which illustrate this are modern farm buildings and machinery. Buildings are better designed to perform specific functions today than at any time in our history, resulting in healthier livestock and contented personnel, in turn ensuring greater productivity and profitability.

Twentieth century farm machinery enables us to gather the maximum amount of crops of reasonable quality, with ensuing reduction in the amount of physical discomfort.

Far too many British farms still suffer from a lack of both adequate buildings and the necessary machinery to do a satisfactory job. Greater attention should be devoted to solving this problem, as these two factors play a most, if not the most, important role in influencing the farm income.

It seems farcical to talk of introducing schemes such as calf twinning as standard farming practice, when the stark fact stares us in the face that the percentage of single born calves which die on our farms within a week or so of birth, is estimated to be as much as five per cent.

Drawn attention

A report received recently from Denmark states that in 147 Danish herds no less than 22.5 per cent of the calves died in this initial period. Is this a result of the widespread use of AI (Artificial Insemination), or is it merely inefficient housing, or both?

The BBC has drawn attention to the use of chemical dressing of seed and the effect this had on bird life. Countless birds have eaten this seed and died. Reports from ornithologists and naturalists substantiate this, having come across many dead birds in the course of their work.

I think the BBC also did agriculture a service in showing the excellent farming film on TV recently, depicting methods of manure collection and disposal. This programme was especially interesting in view of the fact that the Cow and Gate farm near Carmarthen was featured demonstrating their unique method of liquid manure irrigation.

This is a truly outstanding example of organic fertilising and an object lesson for the industry. Far too little attention is paid nowadays to the F.Y.M. (Farm Yard Manure), produced on the farm and its value is grossly underestimated. One cow alone produces the equivalent of £8 worth of mineral fertilisers per year, and as I have stated before, in this column, it is a common sight to see manure heaps exposed to the elements on most of our farms, a state of affairs which calls for some official action. What finer lead can the Government give than to introduce a dung stead Subsidy scheme on the same lines as the existing silo subsidy?

Easier distribution

The method adopted by Cow and Gate of mixing the dung and urine of some 5,000 pigs and dairy cattle with water for easier distribution, used to be common practice on many farms in Wales years ago. The familiar 'duck pond' situated near the farm yard can still be seen today. This form of liquid manure was simple and worked well, and farmsteads fortunate to be situated on a steep slope could run the effluent for quite a considerable distance.

When the manure is treated this way and applied to grassland it has been found that the cattle have no objection to grazing the treated grass within a short time of its application and the ensuing balance of grass to clover in the sward is exceptionally good.

Fortunately, there are now a number of highly efficient tractor-mounted liquid manure spreaders on the market which enables farmers on any sized holding to work this system. This is a machine which will pay for itself in more ways than one.

Natural products

It is by adopting methods of this nature whereby natural products are utilised that the hard-pressed small farmer can increase his productivity without a crippling financial outlay.

It is a warped sense of what pays who, which tends to tempt individuals to try and excessively exploit nature. The majority of the ailments afflicting plants and livestock are without doubt exploitation diseases. Short-term measures are expedient for quick profits and any attempt to put a brake on this in the past has had very little effect. 'The wind of change' is rapidly becoming a puff and with a little encouragement will soon become a draught blowing a fresh current of thought through the portals of public opinion.

Since putting these thoughts in writing some forty years ago, things have developed dramatically. Supermarkets dominate the retail trade, farmer's co-ops have dwindled and the extermination of the Milk Marketing Board has left dairy farmers up the river in a boat without a paddle. The public are gradually becoming more aware of the benefit of consuming organic food, and livestock-wise the continental breeds have virtually won, casting our native cattle to rare breeds enclosures. Other results? Today, Foot and Mouth disease is a major problem due to government incompetence. Blue Tongue has entered the British livestock world for the first time. Bovine tuberculosis is rife among dairy herds with a clamour for the execution of the badger, and the meat we buy in the shops is usually tasteless. If anyone feels below par then the standard GP diagnosis is 'a virus' or more fashionable these days, 'an allergy.'

Thus, to hark back to the eighties, the farming scene for me was one of very little cheer. Prices were low, the pedigree horned Hereford was in decline, inflation was causing interest rates to soar and the farming lobby was beginning to lose its clout. Farmers have always been regarded as a lot of well to do, rich individuals, who spend their time fox hunting and attending agricultural shows and marts in their four wheel drive Range Rovers or BMWs. Heavily subsidized, they are regarded by townsfolk as leading an idyllic life. Unfortunately, politicians tend to believe it too and the squeeze has been put on agriculture gradually over the years, largely as a result of ineffective and inadequate communicating by the farming unions in pleading the agricultural cause. The decline continues to the present day. Whereas, forty years ago, practically every farm in Carmarthenshire produced milk, now you would have to travel miles to find one. The large milk processing plants like Whitland and Llangadog

231

and Felinfach have had to close with the resultant loss of large numbers of employees in areas which have no alternative employment prospects.

Beef imports from countries whose hygiene and welfare standards are not a patch on ours have been allowed to flourish unabated, which gives rise to fears that together with the lax immigration controls, they may have led to some of the disease outbreaks experienced in the UK in recent years having been imported too. Nobody in authority will stick their heads above the parapet and take responsibility, it has become the era of 'buck passing.'

As the end of the eighties approached, I decided that another change of my own farming policy was needed. I have already outlined the poor prospects facing the Hereford camp and after a great deal of heart searching and scrutiny of the balance sheets, I decided to sell all my livestock and to concentrate instead on 'dog and stick' farming also known as 'low input, low output' farming. Without more ado I sent the entire herd for slaughter to Craven Arms where I obtained deadweight prices which exceeded their potential breeding value. My beloved bull 'Redhouse Dan' fetched a four-figure sum as meat, which showed what a wonderful carcase he produced. In a way, this was a sad day for both me and the horned Hereford.

From 1988 on, Tŷ Coch was converted to tack sheep in the winter and beef cattle and dairy heifers on rental grazing in the summer. Tegwyn and Mair Davies of Glangwenlais, Cilycwm, brought their cattle to us to graze for very many years until Tegwyn retired. The days of hay and silage making were over for us. The hardest task I now had was to count the stock. Mind you, I have spent ages in a field trying to count animals which are hell bent on moving just as you try to complete the checking process. It doesn't help either when they turn to chase the dog in the middle of the count!

With more time on my hands I kept abreast of the political situation in national politics and local government. For some years I had been pressurizing Merthyr Tydfil County Borough Council to do something about preserving the Grade 2 listed building, Vulcan

Historic Vulcan House, Merthyr, where Chartist Matthew John lived and died. Neglected by Merthyr Borough Council.

House, situated in Bethesda Street, Merthyr. This house and the surrounding grounds was owned by the Council and had been neglected and empty for years. I was particularly concerned as it was the former home of my great-great-grandfather, Matthew John, who was one of the leading Chartists in Merthyr Tydfil in the nineteenth century. He was the last living Merthyr Chartist and he died in Vulcan House in 1888. To date, Merthyr Council has not lifted a finger to preserve this historic building and equally bad, they have disclosed to me under the Freedom of Information Act, that they have not sought financial assistance from any other source. The obvious question is . . . why?

Public Service Calls

ARTHUR WAS APPROACHING RETIREMENT from his post as an architect in the Civil Service and had started work on altering the farm cottage at Tŷ Coch. This involved extensive updating of the existing building which we had used to store cattle feed, and the addition of a completely new wing which had a view across the Towy Valley towards the Black Mountains, a view which would be hard to beat. All the physical building work was undertaken by Arthur from block laying to plumbing and electricity installation. He was ably assisted by his youngest son Lloyd who put his heart and soul into the project. I did my share in digging the foundations with our JCB and David did his stint on the roofing. Arthur compulsively retired at the age of sixty in 1984 and within a short time moved his family from Aberystwyth to the cottage which was renamed 'Oak Cottage.'

With more time on my hands I began to look around to see if I could utilise my media experience in any way. I had been commissioned by BOCM-Pauls cattle feed manufacturers to write promotional literature for them and with other assignments had kept my hand in. There had been some significant developments in the field of local government in Wales by the formation of a new county in 1974 to oversee the old counties of Breconshire, Radnorshire and Montgomeryshire, called Powys. This was the largest geographical county in Wales covering a quarter of the Principality. Just as Liverpool had, Powys was now looking to set up a public relations operation and were actively seeking a suitable professional. I contacted Powys County Council and in October 1988, I attended a meeting in County Hall, Llandrindod Wells where I was interviewed by the Chairman, Chief Executive and other senior councillors. I was given the task and an exciting new prospect opened up for me.

County Hall was a rambling converted hotel harking back to the days when Llandrindod Wells was a Victorian spa town where people from all over Britain came to sample the health giving waters from the springs abounding in the area. The council chamber had been fashioned out of the old pump room where visitors could drink the water which was to say the very least, potent! Across the forecourt were situated the toilets. I was told that one of the most popular pastimes was to clock who could get to the toilets in the shortest possible time after drinking the water! Happy days!

. With its maze of rooms, County Hall took a bit of navigating to find one's way around. I was given a huge room as my office which was deep in the heart of the building. Over at the other end of the building things were not looking so good with the floor being propped up in parts due to the deterioration in the structure. Staff almost needed to wear hard hats to work in that environment! The building was sited in the heart of Llandrindod Wells just a short distance from the lake, quite a beautiful setting. As the County's first ever PRO/Information Officer, it was my brief to draw up a policy document for submission to the Council bearing in mind that a new County Hall was to be built in the near future.

In due course I submitted my proposals which were accepted by the full Council and once again I was in business to market a local government authority. In order to establish a positive identity to which both council employees and the public could relate, I employed a Cardiff graphic studio, Peter Gill Associates, to draw up a suitable logo which reflected the rural nature of Powys and yet was contemporary and easily and instantaneously recognisable. After a great deal of discussion and research, I accepted their design of a Red Kite soaring over the wording 'Powys,' which was in solid green, reflecting the green nature of the Powys countryside. Work on preserving the Red Kite had been pioneered in the County following on Miss Frances Evans' earlier efforts in Tregaron. Powys County Council accepted my recommendation that this should be the County logo and steps were taken to feature it on all appropriate signs in the County, particularly on approach roads to Powys on the

Breconshire, Radnorshire and Montgomeryshire boundaries as well as being featured on all council vehicles.

All advertising by the Powys Council had been haphazard inasmuch as each individual department be it Social Services, Education, Highways, etc; drew up their own designs and wording which did not reflect the status of Powys. I recommended that a professional advertising agency be appointed which would be responsible for drawing up and placing of all advertisements, with me acting as arbiter in case any confusion or dispute arose. This also was approved and I accordingly short-listed several agencies before appointing Mark Williams Associates of Cardiff as the official agency.

Powys stationery was pretty primitive and not compatible with the computer age. I asked Peter Gill Associates to re-design this and they came up with a much improved design incorporating the logo. The office of Chairman was the head of the Powys hierarchy just as a mayor or lord mayor would be the equivalent in town or city. An even more prestigious design of letterhead was produced for this incumbent which reflected the significance of the appointment. The livery of all council lorries, vans and uniforms were included in the make-over and a positive sense of belonging and pride in the job was fostered among the staff and employees generally.

Travelling to my office daily from Llandeilo was to me pleasurable. I love driving and the forty-odd miles to Llandrindod was through some of the most attractive Welsh countryside. Leaving Llandovery and climbing gradually to the Sugar Loaf was like entering another world. The roads were pretty well deserted, especially as I travelled very early in the day, I could vary my route by either going from Beulah to Newbridge-on-Wye, or from Beulah to Builth Wells and then on to Llandrindod. Either way the scenery was ever changing. In the wintertime I sometimes left the office with snow coming down, hardly being able to see the edges of the road around Llanwrtyd Wells and right past the Sugar Loaf, until I came to the road sign 'Carmarthenshire,' immediately the snow ceased and the countryside would be as green as if a line had been drawn at the boundary.

The contrast between Powys County Council and that of my former authority Liverpool City Council struck me immediately. Powys with its 46 councillors was but a minnow. Compared to Liverpool with its 160 councillors. In Powys, the elected members and officials all knew each other and there was a strong feeling of 'togetherness.' The vastness of the county was reflected by its predominance of rural communities in mid and north Powys, contrasting with the more urban belt in the south bordering on the Swansea Valley and eastwards to Merthyr Tydfil and Abergavenny. Whereas, Liverpool Council was run on party political lines as per national politics, Powys Council was made up largely of Independents. These 'Independents,' were in fact very right wing orientated and cast their votes en bloc, albeit individually, very much like 'organised' orthodox political parties.

I had a short period working with the Chief Executive, Mike Greenwood, before he went off to seek fresh pastures in the north of England. He seemed to me to be a very competent official and had good foresight playing a major role in the decision to establish a public relations set-up. He fully backed me in my proposals and I felt I had lost a good ally when he left. In the interim period before his replacement was appointed, Mal Thomas, Assistant Chief Executive, took up the reins. Mal, too, was sympathetic to the PR cause, and he and I worked well together. It turned out that Mal's wife was related by her previous marriage, to Peter Garner of Brunnings Advertising in Liverpool, who had married my former secretary Pam Stubbs! Peter's brother Mike, was an architect in Llandrindod Wells and worked for The National Trust on the restoration of Newton House, the ancient seat of the Dinefwr family at Llandeilo. It truly is a small world!

There was plenty to do in my new post, the only snag being that I pretty well had to do everything myself at first, from issuing press releases, organising visits and meetings and dealing with the public. Publicity for the Cambrian Woolen Mill at Llanwrtyd Wells came under my umbrella. This was a manufacturing outlet run by charitable organisations in conjunction with the Social Services Department of Powys County Council and provided employment for disabled workers. The cloth and allied products produced at the factory/mill, were of the highest quality but the enterprise was always on the financial brink. Mr Potts, the manager, was from the old school of management and while he did his best to remedy the financial aspect, he was fighting a losing battle. I attended many meetings of the Cambrian Board both at Llanwrtyd Wells and County Hall in an effort to redeem the situation. Suffice to say, the Cambrian Mill is still in business today!

1990 was an active year in Powys. It was pretty exciting for Mary and me too. On June 16th, 1990, our daughter Ann gave birth to our first grandchild – Emma Joanne Evans. She was born in Morriston Hospital in Swansea and was absolutely gorgeous! It brought back all the feelings we had when her mother was born in Llandovery. Being a grandparent for the first time is a special emotion and can almost be likened to being born oneself again and embarking on a second lifetime. Ann and David were justifiably very proud parents.

This was also the year that the new County Hall, which had been under construction alongside the existing building, would be completed and officially opened. A new Chief Executive named Alan Barnish commenced his duties in March and I became involved in a series of meetings to plan the official opening of this state of the art new £6,000,000 Powys County Hall. The building was actually finished early in the year and the entire staff moved into the new offices in June. The contrast could not have been greater. Gone were the creaking floors and draughty windows to be replaced by a light airy environment, air conditioned and with a décor which boasted light wooden fittings and an abundance of growing plants on each floor level. Each open plan office was lavishly equipped with computers and the staff and members restaurant was spacious and appetising. As soon as we moved in, the demolition contractors got to work to knock down the old building and in no time at all the site of the old County Hall became part of the car-park.

It was decided that David Hunt MP, Secretary of State for Wales, would be invited to do the honours at the opening. A member of the Royal Family was originally mooted but proved to be unavailable. The Chairman of Powys County Council that year was Councillor Eifion Lewis from Ystradgynlais. He was a real character, a brilliant speaker with a terrific sense of humour, a former mining official and a staunch member of the Labour Party. Eifion and I got on like a house on fire and we spent many a pleasant hour travelling together to meetings and functions and visiting centenarians. On one occasion we went to see a lady in Pantydwr named Mrs E. M. Jones. She was celebrating her 100th birthday and to get to the farm she was living on with her daughter, we had to drive up a farm track in my car, in January, with snow lying on the ground and thick ice on the pools in the road. We managed to get there and when we did the welcome we had from the assembled family was one to remember. The table in the living room was groaning with food of every description and I don't think Eifion, myself or our photographer, Ray Carpenter, ate again for some time. To cap it all, we repeated the exercise again the following year when Maud reached the grand old age of 101. Her mind was as sharp as a tack and her memory of life in Pantydwr and Llanidloes was vivid. I was privileged to visit many 100 year olds during my time in Powys, an experience I would not have missed for all the tea in China.

Peter Wharton, the County Architect, who had designed the new County Hall, was like a hen with her chicks in the run up to the opening. In conjunction with Mark Williams Associates, I produced a lavish booklet describing the building with illustrations and photos which were superb. Each VIP guest at the opening would receive a copy as would the media and a commemorative plaque was ordered for placing on the wall of the council chamber bearing David Hunt's, Peter Wharton's, Eifion Lewis' and others names of those officiating at the ceremony. I had to organise the commissioning and delivery of the plaque and it was almost as bad as coping with an expectant mother. Peter was 'biting his nails' unnecessarily worrying about delivery and what could go wrong on the day.

At my desk in the heart of the new Powys County Hall, Llandrindod Wells (1990).

Secretary of State for Wales, David Hunt MP, opening County Hall.

So, on 27th November, 1990, the new Powys County Hall was opened by the Rt. Hon. David Hunt MP, Secretary of State for Wales. I had arranged for a unique cut glass crystal wine decanter engraved with the Powys Logo and the Secretary of State's name and the date of opening, to be supplied by a master engraver from Builth Wells, named David Williams. The decanter was to be presented to David Hunt before all the assembled guests, by Eifion Lewis (Powys Chairman), on behalf of the people of Powys. I was called upon to introduce the Secretary of State, which I did, to a packed chamber, and Eifion presented him with the decanter following it up with a speech which had David Hunt, the guests and myself rolling in the aisles with laughter. David Hunt said afterwards that he hadn't enjoyed an official function like that for years. Being from Liverpool, he and I knew quite a few mutual acquaintances in the city. The day had been a huge success, nothing had gone wrong and Powys now had an administrative centre which rivalled and I think outshone Cardiff's County Hall.

My workload was steadily increasing week by week. Events requiring media coverage and PR advice were queuing in the pipeline. I sat on the Heart of Wales Executive Committee. This committee was formed to promote the Heart of Wales railway running between Swansea and Shrewsbury. Being one of the few rail lines left in mid Wales and running as it did through some of the most attractive scenery in Wales, it was felt that if it was to avoid the 'Beeching' formula, then it was essential that everything possible should be done to increase the use of the line in order to avoid closure. Stations en route vied with each other for 'best kept station' status, which was a breath of fresh air in these days of overgrown railway lines and unmanned stations.

It was at this time that plans were being laid for the National Eisteddfod of Wales which was to be held in Builth Wells. Also, alongside the canal in Welshpool a museum had been constructed in a former warehouse. The refurbishment had been completed and the opening ceremony took place in May 1990. Powysland Museum became very popular with tourists sited as it was on the canal bank, with barges moored alongside which could be hired for trips down the canal. Restoration of the canal itself was forging ahead full steam and additional yardage was being secured and continues to the present time.

Liaison with industrial concerns and business in Powys was stepped up. One of the more prestigious enterprises in the county was the firm of Laura Ashley. Centred at Carno and Newtown, this business produced high quality fabrics, clothes and soft furnishings, based originally on the designs of the firm's founder, Laura Ashley. It had a world-wide reputation and had outlets in many major towns and cities in the UK. Laura was a Merthyr Tydfil born and bred girl and had attended at the time the same school as Arthur in Merthyr. He remembered her well. After her untimely death, her husband Bernard took over the business and expanded into the hotel world by purchasing the magnificent Llangoed Hall situated between Builth Wells and Brecon. He completely revamped the building, incorporating Laura Ashley products throughout, making it one of the most prestigious hotels in Wales. I attended many meetings and conferences there and found it to be a useful tool in 'selling' the County.

Media interest in what was going on in Powys was growing. Councillors have an inherent mistrust of newspapermen and television reporters, a mistrust which can be minimised by educating them and getting them to meet the media and understanding what is required of them and the appropriate response. To do this, I arranged for the Chairman to hold an informal reception for the media at County Hall so that frank views could be exchanged. Personnel from the *Western Mail, County Times, Mid Wales Journal, Shropshire Star,* BBC (radio and TV), HTV, and national dailies attended and it was voted by them as a huge success. This was the first time such an exercise had been done in Powys and it was to be repeated regularly while I was there. Good relations were established and I was fortunate to be able to call upon the services of an outstanding journalist who wrote for the *County Times* and also contributed to the *Western Mail*. This was John Price from Rhayader, a 'veteran' reporter whose ethics were of the highest standard. John was a tremendous ally and I had the utmost respect for him.

Meanwhile, other great things were stirring in a South Wales valley, at Ebbw Vale. The Garden Festival of Wales was to take place there in 1990 on a site which had previously been a steel works. This Festival was intended to depict and display all that was best in Wales, from the cultural to the industrial, as well as government and local government activities, it was to be a Welsh showpiece. Powys became very involved in this and I was thrown into the deep end to liaise and advise on the contribution the Council could make to the festivities. One of the major players in this Festival was the DBRW (Development Board for Rural Wales), which had its HQ at Ladywell House in Newtown, Powys. The man I had to contact and deal with there was its Chairman, Glyn Davies, who had a farm on the outskirts of Welshpool. Along I trotted to Newtown to see him and duly interviw him. He was a surprising individual and was a fitness fanatic. He'd come into a meeting all hot and bothered having just run a couple of miles around Newtown in his tracksuit. He struck me as being a bit of a bombastic type who didn't suffer fools gladly. He was terse and seemed to lack a sense of humour. However, we got along alright and a plan was hatched whereby the Powys theme would be incorporated in the DBRW exhibit, an exhibit which was costing an arm and a leg. At the preview prior to the official opening, I took the Powys Chairman, County Architect Peter Wharton, and Councillor John Davies in my car to enjoy the lavish hospitality laid on by the DBRW and to see the Powys input on site, which the County Architect's Department had been deeply involved in from the design aspect.

Included among the many visitors to County Hall in 1990, was Barry Jones MP, the Shadow Secretary of State for Wales. In Newtown, the Prince of Wales visited Theatr Hafren and saw for himself the new developments of some cultural aspects of Powys. Following the success of the media reception by the Chairman, I was asked to organise a training session for chairmen of committees on how they should deal with the media. This was to be held at County Hall and all chairmen would be obliged to attend. A firm in Cardiff specialised in this form of training, run by David Parry Jones, former BBC stalwart, and Patrick Hannon also of the BBC, still a regular broadcaster on both radio and TV. They came to see me and we discussed the nitty gritty of the exercise. They asked me to compile a dossier on each chairman outlining where their strengths and weaknesses were, with particular emphasis on the latter. I then produced a list of awkward questions which Patrick would ask them and which were currently contentious, like – "Why close rural schools?"

This media training session went on over a period of one week and was an eye-opener. A couple of the chairmen/women whom I thought would cope admirably were reduced to blithering idiots under questioning, while others shone brilliantly and coped with everything thrown at them. This exposure was very useful for me as it enabled me to cater for future contingencies knowing which councillors would need to be helped when a tricky situation might arise. These interviews were filmed for internal use and when played back to each chairman individually, their reaction was hilarious. It never ceases to surprise me how people clam up when faced with a movie camera or microphone, the most talkative become dumb!

Overshadowing all these events was the birth of our second grandchild, again a baby girl, to Wynne and Janet. Chloe Victoria Harris was born in Morriston Hospital, Swansea, on 28th March, 1991. Chloe too, was a bonny baby and we were all delighted. This was the first granddaughter for Janet's parents, Meryl and Brian Smith. The cameras worked overtime when Mary and I went to see her for the first time. What a joy!

My office was like an open house, anyone wanting advice or a chat would pop in. A frequent visitor was Mrs. Shan Legge-Bourke, High Sheriff of Powys and Lady-in-Waiting to the Princess Royal. She had extensive farming interests at Glanusk near Bwlch, Powys.

New Powys newspaper Powys '90
followed by yearly issues.

She invited me to lunch at Glanusk on one occasion and I was able to learn of her interest in organic farming. She was very attached to the Royal Welsh Show and a very funny lady in the nicest sense. Her daughter 'Tiggy' was once a Royal 'nanny' to Prince Charles' children. Interestingly to me, Shan Legge-Bourke was distantly related to the Crawshay family of Cyfarthfa Castle, Merthyr.

Informing the public was the main thrust of my PR campaign strategy. Just as I had done in Liverpool, I recommended to the Council that the annual report should be produced this time in the form of a tabloid newspaper which, in addition to containing details of the financial position, should also contain articles and illustrations highlighting the authority's services. This was approved and I selected a firm in Haverfordwest to do the printing. Called *Powys '90*, it was published as a 16-page newspaper and was distributed to every household in Powys. It contained the photographs and contact addresses of every councillor. Not a single criticism was made by the public on the expenditure to produce this newspaper. On the contrary, it was hailed as a valuable tool to keep the public informed and even carried council job adverts! Needless to say, the completion and opening of County Hall was prominently featured.

Powys County Council was so pleased with the new County Hall and as it was now more or less 'run in,' it was generally felt that the council tax paying public should have access to the building to see how their hard earned cash was being spent on their behalf. I was asked to come up with some suggestions, the best being that we should have an 'Open Day' and invite all and sundry to come along. Mark Williams Associates and myself got our heads together and we came up with a programme which no other local authority in Wales had attempted up to then or undertaken since.

The Open Day was to be essentially a fun day for all the family. A marquee was erected containing exhibition material showing each of the council departments work. In the large car-park, novelty stalls, roundabouts and musical entertainments were laid on. Vintage cars were on display and the Dyfed/Powys Police organised an exhibition complete with police cars and motor cycles, not to mention the helicopter. The lake in front of County Hall was utilised for a model boat regatta and there were practical demonstrations of fishing there as well. A huge 'Jumping Castle' was featured and the Fire Service displayed their fire engines which proved to be very popular with the young visitors. There was even a steam roller brought in by the Highways Department. Not to be outdone, the County Estates Department exhibited live farm animals, and conducted tours around County Hall took place at regular intervals. The Powys Chairman, Councillor Eifion Lewis, welcomed everyone over the public address system, and balloons were let loose in celebration. The media was there in force and the coverage was beyond expectation. Cynics had said beforehand that it would be a waste of time and that nobody would turn up. Over 30,000 people attended on the day vindicating our efforts and decision to go ahead. A good time was had by all and the message got across in a fun way. Even Mary and my mother went!

At Hay-on-Wye a literary festival was becoming established to be known as the Hay Festival. The town had become a mecca for book lovers with second hand bookshops springing up all over the place. The Festival aimed to attract celebrities in the arts and literary worlds with lectures, exhibitions and readings. Artists, writers and media personalities were invited to take part and people from all over the UK attended. In the initial stages I attended meetings with one of the instigators of the Festival – Peter Florence – to discuss possible ways Powys County Council could assist. Like most things, it always comes down to a question of money, the County's ability to support the Festival financially was strictly limited which did not go down all that well at the time with Peter Florence. However, the Festival did flourish going from strength to strength and today is a roaring success with a world-wide audience.

The Chairman of Powys was increasingly becoming involved in events which came within the sphere of public relations. I was asked to take over the management of the Chairman's diary and to personally advise and accompany the incumbent whenever practicable. This extra work meant that I had to recruit a personal assistant/secretary to enable the extra new PR/Chairman operation to run smoothly. In due course an interview was arranged for a young lady to attend, in County Hall, in June,1991. Sally Williams was interviewed by me and Mal Thomas, Assistant Chief Executive. She was attractive and personable with a good grasp of what PR was all about. Sally had also had a good grounding in politics, her father a solicitor, had been the Conservative MP for Montgomeryshire during the Thatcher era and Sally had even met Mrs Thatcher! Her mother was a former Montgomeryshire beauty queen. I did not hesitate, she was ideal for the post and I offered Sally the job which she accepted. It didn't take her long to settle into the post. Sally liked pigs and had some prime inanimate examples on her desk, bringing a whiff of countryside into County Hall! Her dedication was such that she did not hesitate to travel from her home at Guilsfield an hours drive each way daily. If Sally felt like a break from work she used to fly regularly to Washington DC over a weekend, to see her brother who had a diplomatic post there.

There was increasing talk at this time of local government reorganisation. It was mooted that the existing counties and boroughs in Wales would be abolished and replaced by fewer and larger authorities. Preliminary exploratory meetings were being held throughout Wales to establish the guidelines and method of implementation of this controversial reorganisation proposal. The first meeting I attended was held in County Hall on 26th June, 1991. Little did I know then how involved I would become in this in the years to come.

Ever since I joined Powys I had been pressing the Council to support the Royal Welsh Show in a more tangible form than hitherto. I felt that this agricultural show held on our doorstep in Builth Wells, should be utilised to convey the Powys story and to communicate with our public. With an annual attendance of some 200,000 visitors. It was a 'must' from my point of view. The Council agreed with me and negotiations were opened with the RWAS (Royal Welsh Agricultural Society). Meetings took place with David Walters their Chief Executive and the ball was set in motion. A working committee was established and in due course, I presented my proposals.

My main proposal was that we hire a large marquee, this would house an exhibit from each Powys Council department and these would be placed on 'Nomadic' state of the art exhibition stands. A stage would be incorporated at one end which would feature entertainment such as children face painting, dance and music routines by Powys youth organisations, plus demonstrations by individual departments, like Trading Standards.

A VIP lounge would be incorporated enabling the Chairman and councillors to entertain guests, and the media. Carol Lande, the County Catering Manager, would include a dining area whereby members of the public could relax and obtain refreshments and view the exhibits at the same time, and an information desk would be placed in a prominent position staffed continuously throughout the show opening hours. The green light was given to the plan and it was full speed ahead. The RWAS allocated a prime site for the marquee right behind the main grandstand on one of the best avenues, strategically placed within convenient distance of the toilets!

To draw attention to the Powys Stand I hired a large balloon similar in design to a wartime barrage balloon and had the Powys logo painted on it in large letters. Flying at a couple of hundred feet above the stand, it could be seen for miles as visitors approached the showground and certainly pinpointed the Powys input. Sally and I worked like Trojans prior to the Show liaising with departments, the RWAS, and contractors. As the sole person responsible for the Powys presence, the buck stopped with me. During Show week, I had to be present on the stand by 7.30 a.m. each day to supervise the rising of the balloon which, to comply with the regulations, had to be brought down each night. We even had to get clearance from the RAF in case of low-flying exercises! I was the last to leave after the day's stint, travelling daily from Llandeilo.

Anybody who was anybody visited the Powys exhibit during the five years I was responsible for the County's presence. VIPs from all walks of life were welcomed, ranging from politicians such as Richard Livsey and Jonathan Evans, to Miss Royal Welsh. Even William Hague's mother and father-in-law were guests! Our efforts were highly acclaimed and we had little or no criticism, which speaks volumes bearing in mind that with 46 councillors the chances of someone being awkward would be a certainty, that wasn't the case, it was felt that we had obtained good value for the taxpayer's money.

Regular meetings with David Walters of the RWAS took place throughout the year. In looking at various ways and means of supporting the Society and also to improve facilities for the public on site. We came up with the idea of having a rest area to be constructed in the main avenue running in front of the Powys Stand. It would consist of flower and shrubbery beds to be constructed by County Council gardening experts, and placed on a paved area with the Powys logo set in the form of a mosaic pattern in the centre. The area would be flanked by bench seats which would be of high quality and hand crafted. The scheme was approved and the area which was named 'The Powys Garden,' was completed and officially opened by the Chairman of Powys County Council just prior to the following Royal Welsh Show.

The Chairman had been invited to see the work of the Centre for Alternative Technology which had been established just outside Machynlleth in the County. This was a place where methods of 'eco' friendly practices were examined and pilot schemes made to work. These embraced energy production utilising natural elements such as wind and water. Councillor D. Michael Jones of Cwm Derw, Newtown, and myself went along and were impressed by the work being undertaken there, work which was paving the way for future schemes designed to reduce the risk of 'global warming.' The Centre had become a favourite with Prince Charles who had made several visits. The Centre became another useful tool in my armoury for projecting Powys.

Early in 1992, Sally decided that she would like to move nearer home and the opportunity arose for her to join the journalistic staff of the *County Times* whose editorial office was in Welshpool, right on her doorstep. I was sorry to lose her as she had good writing potential which was borne out and came to fruition when she became Deputy Editor of that newspaper. This meant I had to look for a new man/woman Friday to fill Sally's shoes. After interviewing a raft of applicants, I plumbed for a young woman who had graduated from Pontypridd and who was keen to embark upon a PR career. She was Rachel Howard and she started work with me on 6th May, 1992.

That year saw another historic milestone in my family history. On May 9th, 1992, our first grandson was born to Wynne and Janet. Named Jonathan Rhys James Harris, he was born prematurely at Singleton Hospital, Swansea. The first few weeks of his little life were spent in an incubator and it was a tense time for us all. However, Jonathan was a fighter and pulled through and he has never looked back since, and now, at the age of fifteen, is almost six feet tall and still growing!

Talking of family, an official function I had to attend, with Powys Deputy Chairman at the time, Councillor Dorothy James, was to a lecture being delivered by the guest speaker, Lord Roy Jenkins, at

Official function with Powys Chairman, Mrs Dorothy James.

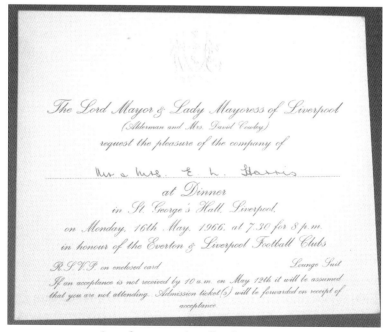

The Lord Mayor & Lady Mayoress of Liverpool
(Alderman and Mrs. David Cowley)
request the pleasure of the company of

Mr & Mrs. E. L. Harris

at Dinner
in St. George's Hall, Liverpool.
on Monday, 16th May, 1966, at 7.30 for 8 p.m.
in honour of the Everton & Liverpool Football Clubs

R.S.V.P. on enclosed card   *Lounge Suit*

If an acceptance is not received by 10 a.m. on May 12th it will be assumed
that you are not attending. Admission ticket(s) will be forwarded on receipt of
acceptance.

One of many similar official invitations.

the Mid Glamorgan Industrial Affairs Centre in Cardiff. He gave a very good talk based on his international experience, particularly his role as President of the European Commission in Brussels. I did not manage to have a chat with him at the time but he did tip me a wink as he walked down the aisle past Councillor James and myself. I explained to her afterwards what the connection was.

Comedian Les Dawson was noted for his cryptic mother-in-law jokes, had he ever known mine he would have been at a loss to find anything derogatory to say about her. Mary lost her mother, Violet Davies, in 1991 having reached the grand age of 90 plus. She was one of the nicest people one could wish to meet and we got on like a house on fire. She loved listening to a good argument, particularly on religion, and was a cook extraordinaire. Of a quiet nature, she was always there for her children and grandchildren and her passing was a real blow. She died suddenly while on a visit to Mary and me at Tŷ Coch Farm. She, too, was Carmarthenshire born and bred, her father having farmed Bryncoch, Ferryside. At the time of writing this, I am looking into her reputed family links with Ivor Novello and General Picton. Her father was related to the noted Anthony brothers of horse racing fame and multi-winners of The Grand National.

It was a shame that she did not live to see our second grandson, Gareth Llyr Evans, who was born on the 10th November, 1992, at Glangwili Hospital, Carmarthen, to Ann and David. We were all thrilled to have a little brother for Emma, and the arrival of Gareth brought our total of grandchildren to four. Two boys and two girls!

The Wales National Eisteddfod was to be held in Powys in 1993. A departure from normal practice was the decision to stage it at the Royal Welsh Showground at Builth Wells. With the permanent buildings on site and good roadways, this was an excellent venue and gave rise to talk of making it a permanent site for the Eisteddfod, thus avoiding its 'Gypsy-like' travelling from one end of the country to the other every year, with the heavy financial burden that moving about entailed. T. A. V. Evans, of Powys Education Authority

David, Ann, Emma and baby Gareth visit me at the Royal Welsh Show.

was closely involved in the planning of the 1993 event and it was not long before the local committee, of which I became a member, was set up. The traditional stones for the Gorsedd Circle were supplied in due course from Vaynor Quarry near Merthyr Tydfil and installed on site in Builth by the Direct Services Department of Powys County Council. The Proclamation Ceremony took place on 4th July, 1992. The next twelve months saw many meetings to thresh out the pros and cons.

While on the subject of meetings, local government reorganisation was beginning to dominate the thoughts and workloads of staff in town halls, county halls and civic centres throughout Wales. In Powys, Chief Executive Alan Barnish was devoting most of his time to ensuring that Powys would not lose out in any possible reorganisation. Lobbying was the order of the day and numerous meetings were laid on with government officials especially the Secretaries of State for Wales, David Hunt, John Redwood and William Hague. Lobbyists were appointed at considerable expense and literature and reports were churned out in quantity. I was asked to support the meetings set up throughout the three counties of Brecon, Radnor and Montgomery, by preparing publicity material and exhibits to persuade the public to support the Powys cause which was one of preserving the status quo. Mal Thomas, the Assistant Chief Executive, did a fantastic job in travelling the length and breadth of Powys giving talks.

I briefed and wrote speech material for individual councillors and even travelled to London to visit lobbyist and political adviser, Douglas Smith, who I had known from my time in Liverpool. Douglas came to Llandrindod Wells to give a presentation to the Chief Executive on his recommendations for getting the message over in Westminster.

Things were hotting up in the campaigning. Montgomeryshire was particularly militant. Their Chairman was constantly sniping at Powys and one or two of their officials were positively vitriolic. Brecon was also opposed to losing its status but Radnor was more sympathetic. The MP for Brecon and Radnor, Jonathan Evans, was uneasy about the situation and in order to allow the public to have a say in the matter and to be able to question him, a special public meeting was held at Powys County Hall, to be addressed by Jonathan. The editor of the *Brecon and Radnor Express*, Mark Williams, rang me to say he could not cover the meeting due to a staff problem and asked me if I would cover it and write the front page lead. I agreed providing he omitted the by line. He in turn agreed and I wrote his front page! Jonathan came in for a sticky time and was relieved when the meeting was over.

Rumours were rife among the staff at County Hall that reorganisation would mean massive job losses and meetings were held and addressed by Alan Barnish to try and allay their fears. The pressure from Montgomery was unrelenting, they even exploited the 'County Feature' when it was their turn to exhibit as the guest county at the

Royal Welsh Show, spewing out propaganda at every opportunity. It really was like a war of attrition.

Life apart from the reorganisation fight went on as usual. Newtown had been experiencing traffic problems in recent years and it had been decided that a second crossing of the River Severn in the town was called for. A new bridge was built and was officially opened by Powys County Council Chairman, Emlyn Kinsey Pugh, on 8th April, 1993. I took Emlyn to the ceremony in my Montego MG, he cut the ribbon, got into my car and we drove over the bridge, the first to do so. During the same month, the new Staylittle Outdoor Centre set in the heart of the mountains near Llanidloes was officially opened by County Councillor Joe Griffiths, of Blaen Hafren. Joe, a former Powys Chairman, had been a Spitfire pilot during the Second World War and had spent some time flying in the far east. He used to vividly recall the thrill he got flying the Spitfire and particularly its ability to climb effortlessly giving a feeling of thrusting power through the back of the pilot's seat as it did so. Joe was one of many octogenarians serving on Powys Council.

Early in 1993, to the surprise of everyone probably bar one, Alan Barnish left Powys County Council. This left a vacuum at a crucial stage in reorganisation negotiations. However, in June 1993, a new Chief Executive was appointed and Neil Pringle stepped into the breech. He was a very different animal to Alan; he gave the impression of being more of an introvert and one to keep things to himself. He soon had to pick up the current situation and he and his wife, who was a qualified nurse, went to live with their children in Cilmery.

The 1993 Royal Welsh Show was an unusual one for me that year inasmuch that the Wales National Eisteddfod was to be held on the showground immediately afterwards. The Show itself went smoothly for us, as usual, but instead of dismantling the Powys Stand when the Show finished, we decided to keep it intact and to use it as our exhibit at the Eisteddfod. This was good PR for the County and provided both the Eisteddfod organisers and us with facilities that were already in place. I manned the Stand in precisely the same way as during the Show. Balloon and all! Looking back, it is amusing now to recall the hospitality that we provided in our VIP lounge. Nobody batted an eyelid when alcoholic drinks were partaken, it was not even mentioned. Nowadays, I believe the 'ban' has been lifted and alcoholic beverages are allowed on the 'Maes.' The Eisteddfod held at Builth was probably one of the best ever. Attendances were excellent, the weather was good and the facilities on the permanent site could not be faulted. It certainly gave the organisers food for thought.

An interesting function took place in 1994 in connection with the Burns Unit at Morriston Hospital, Swansea. It was not long after the special burns facility in Chepstow had been transferred to Morriston Hospital. Ian Govier, the nurse in charge, contacted me and told me that the new Burns Unit had a Powys Ward. In order to provide a light interesting décor, he thought it would be a good idea to line the walls of the ward with framed photographs of Powys scenes. He felt that this would be therapeutic for patients after undergoing serious burns operations and also would help to publicise the County. I thought it an excellent idea and commissioned Powys photographer, Ray Carpenter, to submit samples for approval. I selected a number, he framed them and I arranged for Chairman Michael Jones and myself to go to Swansea for him to present them to the hospital. The ceremony took place with the senior hospital management present together with the Chairman of the Swansea NHS Trust. He, unfortunately, was to be killed in a London train crash in later years.

Meanwhile, Mrs Maud Jones of Henderhiw, Pantydwr, was still going strong and still living at home at the ripe age of 104. Just as we had four years earlier, I again took our Chairman to visit her on her birthday on January 16th, 1995 (birthday 15th). She really was a remarkable lady and still with all her faculties and sense of humour. I must have visited dozens of centenarians during my career but I can safely say that Maud was the most memorable of them all.

Hamish Richards at Powys County Hall with (left to right) – me, County Councillor Joe Griffiths, Hamish, Powys Chairman Marilyn Roberts, Andrew Melding AM.

Local Government guests of Powys Chairman, County Councillor Eifion Lewis, at Llandrindod Wells.

Eluned Morgan MEP talking to Powys Chairman, Michael Jones, and me at Newtown Fire Station.

Chairman Michael and Mrs Jones with my Assistant, Rachel Howard, and me at County Hall.

Journalist John Price and me in deep conversation.

*Surveying the Powys Garden at the Royal Welsh Showground
with David Pitchford, Senior County Architect.*

Overseas educational visitors to Powys County Hall.

*Me keeping an eye on Secretary of State for Wales, William Hague MP,
opening the new Newtown Library.*

Chatting with Lord Wyn Roberts, former Minster of State for Wales.

In November, 1995, the latest Secretary of State for Wales, who had succeeded John Redwood – William Hague MP – paid us a visit at County Hall. We entertained him in the Chairman's private room and I gave him a Powys pen suitably featuring the Powys logo, to add to his collection. He was a very approachable and unassuming individual and we met again at the reopening of the refurbished library at Newtown. By this time the fate of local government in Wales had been sealed. Twenty-two Unitary Authorities were to be established and the changeover was to take place in April 1996. Powys had come out of the mix exceedingly well and would absorb the three existing counties of Breconshire, Radnorshire and Mont-gomeryshire into a brand new Powys County Council. Powys had won!

One of the more pleasing occasions I experienced while at Powys was the reception given by the Chairman of Powys County Council, to Hamish Richards from the International Centre, Cardiff, in July 1995. Accompanied by David Melding (later to become an Assembly Member), he was recognised as an expert in the field of international affairs. Hamish and I went back many years as we were both in the same form in Quakers Yard Grammar School in 1947.

All good things must come to an end, and so it was when April 1996 arrived. Powys County Council ceased to exist and the new 'Unitary' Powys County Council took its place. On the surface, nothing much seemed to have changed, the Powys logo was kept on and all the staff transferred to the new Council, including those of the three former counties. The Chief Executive, Neil Pringle, re-tained his post and a new era dawned. For me the situation was straightforward, I was the first ever County PRO for the old Powys and now I became the first ever County PRO for the new Powys County Council, albeit for a very short time. On June 7th, 1996, I attained the age of 65 and forthwith retired to return to my rural ways.

I had enjoyed the seven years of travelling the road to Llan-drindod Wells daily. The chairmen I had worked with: County

Councillors Lt. Col. J. D. Stephenson, Eifion Lewis, Arthur Smith, Emlyn Kinsey Pugh, Dorothy James, Michael Jones and Marilyn Roberts had been grand people to work for, the exception being Marilyn Roberts who had been a bit of a diva and occasionally devious. The officers on the whole had been a hard-working, friendly bunch, but I had been somewhat disillusioned by the lack of moral standards by some senior personnel. One person behaved like a Mata Hari and climbed the promotion ladder in double quick time. The examples set had been poor and could have graced the pages of the *News of the World*.

It was great being back full-time on the farm once more. It was mid-summer and the countryside was looking beautiful. I did not have to worry about the Royal Welsh Show which was fast approaching, and more time could now be devoted to our children and grandchildren all of whom were growing fast! Mary was still working in the Civil Service keeping the VAT world happy in Carmarthen and our youngest son, David, had graduated with an honours degree from the University of Plymouth's Seale Hayne Agricultural Faculty, at Newton Abbott, Devon, and had obtained a post with the Countryside Council for Wales. Truly, a new era had begun!

Expanding Horizons

PRIOR TO LEAVING POWYS, Mary and I had received an invitation from my mother's cousin Sarah in Ohio, to attend her and her husband Karl's golden wedding anniversary. This also was in June 1996, and with nothing to stop us, we accepted and were soon USA bound.

This was the first time either Mary or myself had been to America. We landed in Newark Airport, New York, in a rainstorm and what followed was a nightmare. Firstly, we had pre-booked a car which, when we went to collect it, the hire firm 'Dollar' had no record of the booking, or so at least the two dimwits at the checkout claimed. Eventually we were given a Dodge Intrepid and as dusk approached we prepared to leave the airport for our Holiday Inn Hotel which was a 'short' distance drive. To my dismay, a glance at the fuel gauge revealed an almost empty petrol tank. I was told that there was a filling station 'just round the corner.' We set off round one corner and another and another, no sign of a filling station! Simultaneously, the heavens opened up and a deluge the like of which I had never experienced, descended upon us. With thunder and lightning and the wipers barely able to cope, now in almost complete darkness, the fuel gauge on zero, and me driving on the right-hand side of the road for the first time ever, we eventually managed to locate a petrol station. We drove in almost delirious with relief only to find that the sole attendant of Asian origin and speaking pigeon English, would not accept a credit card as he did not know how to operate the system. We managed to scrape enough dollars together to buy enough petrol to at least move the fuel gauge needle off zero and enable us to get to our hotel.

The maze of highways around Newark Airport would be difficult to circumnavigate in broad daylight let alone in the dark in a raging storm. We drove up one and down another trying to find the hotel and eventually, many hours after landing, found it and checked in, both of us physically and mentally exhausted from what had been a harrowing experience and a very 'long' day! Incidentally, the hotel was almost in sight of the runway!

We had some time before we had to rendezvous with Sarah's sister, cousin Violet, in Harrisburg, Pennsylvania, prior to driving to Ohio. We decided to travel to see the Niagara Falls, and so the next day, having filled the car to the brim with petrol, we set off north. I was impressed by the countryside as we left Newark, miles upon miles of trees everywhere, quite a surprise as we expected to see bill-boards and diners every few yards. Driving through into Pennsylvania, we passed through towns like Scranton, a town with which I was very familiar with, due to its historic links with South Wales and mining. Many people from my home town of Merthyr Tydfil had gone there seeking work in the nineteenth century.

Driving all day, we at last reached Rochester and the shores of Lake Ontario which to us looked like a vast inland sea, with its sumptuous houses lining its banks and Maple tree orchards. Arriving in Niagara, we checked into our hotel and woke the following morning to what sounded like a continuous roar. Our hotel was close to the falls and the sound of cascading water is what we could hear. Mary and I hurried down with eager anticipation to see for ourselves and what we saw took our breath away. Millions of gallons of water were flowing past at a terrific rate, gurgling and leaping over rocks as it headed to the edge of the waterfall, disappearing over in a frenzy of foam and spray. The drop to the river below was hundreds of feet and a continuous rainbow arched over the tiny boats below carrying sightseers to the foot of the falls. This truly was one of the most spectacular sights to be seen anywhere. It was hard to believe that Charles Blondin had walked across the Niagara Falls in 1859 on a tightrope, and to cap it all also did it on stilts and even later, with a man on his back!

Walking around Goat Island on the American side, was a tranquil experience. The town of Buffalo could be seen in the far distance across the lake and outside a café we were surprised to see a plaque in memory of the visit there of George Thomas, Secretary of State for Wales, and even a Welsh flag in the café itself. We did cross to the Canadian side in a tour bus which proved to be memorable. After a drive through the Canadian countryside, we returned to the US border and our bus was boarded by gun-toting US Customs who wanted to see our visas. Unfortunately, I had left ours in our hotel in Niagara. Mary and I were taken off the bus and marched to the border post, while they contacted the London passport office to check whether we were who we said we were. After confirmation, we had to pay another visa fee before being allowed back on the bus. When we did so, all our fellow American passengers, who had also been held up, cheered as we boarded.

The next stage was to drive down to Harrisburg in Pennsylvania following the Susquehanna River, to meet up with cousin Violet. We broke the journey en route at a place just outside Danville. This town was well-known to me as it was there that my kinsman Doctor Joseph Parry and his family had moved to from Chapel Row in Merthyr Tydfil. Danville had been a prominent iron milling town in the nineteenth century and had attracted a number of iron workers from Cyfarthfa.

We had a superb welcome when we met Violet in Harrisburg, the State Capital. She lived next door to Newt Gringrich's sister. Newt Gringrich was the Speaker of the United States House of Representatives from 1990 to 1995, and was a prominent Republican, he was born in Harrisburg. While there, we visited the State Capital Building and were fortunate to meet the State Governor who showed us around. I asked him if he had heard of Wales and was delighted with his enthusiastic response. The fact that the State was named after a Welshman and that the Declaration of Independence had such a strong Welsh input, was not lost on him.

Our next destination was Marion in Ohio. Violet accompanied Mark, her son, in his car, while her daughter, M'Liss, and her two children came with Mary and me in ours. We drove across the breadth of Pennsylvania, into Ohio, and reached our hotel in Delaware, near Marion, in late evening.

This was real farming country where arable and livestock holdings abounded. After greeting the happy 'golden' couple, Sarah and Karl, on their farm, we all went to the festivities which had been laid on in the local church hall in Marion. What a party that turned out to be! Practically all our American cousins who were descended from Matthew John of Vulcan House, Merthyr, came, from as far apart as Maine and New Mexico. One cousin, David John Jr., had driven across America in his campervan, towing his car behind him. As guests of honour, Mary and I had an unforgettable time which we will always cherish.

Our journey back again, with Violet and Mark in convoy, took us to a fireworks store in Ohio where our relatives wanted to buy fireworks for July 4th. Apparently these stores were not allowed in Pennsylvania, so they took this opportunity to indulge themselves. The place was enormous and packed with 'explosives' from floor to ceiling. Some of the rockets looked as if they had come from Cape Canaveral while the Catherine Wheels could have dwarfed The London Eye! It occurred to us at the time that this was a highly dangerous place to be especially for smokers. Lo and behold, a month or so later, we heard on the news that a fireworks store in Ohio had blown up killing people inside. This was the very place we had visited. We certainly won't go there again in a hurry!

We bade our farewells to Violet and family halfway back to Harrisburg and headed south for Washington DC where we were to meet a cousin on my father's side who lived there, Peggy and her husband Burke. Peg's grandmother and my grandfather Harris were brother and sister. She had emigrated to the USA in the late 1800s. Mary and I stopped at a hotel in Maryland en route, where another adventure befell us. We were having a meal at the hotel in the evening when all of a sudden the fire alarms sounded and the staff ushered us pronto out of the building into the courtyard, for 'safety reasons.' Within minutes the fire brigade arrived with sirens blaring and we anxiously awaited the outcome. It turned out to be a false alarm and we were allowed back in to finish our meal which had by now been ruined. The management couldn't do enough for us and gave us a replacement 'on the house' with their profound apologies, which we gracefully accepted.

Peg and Burke lived in Maryland on the outskirts of Washington and came to collect us the following day and we ended up spending an enjoyable time at their home. This was followed by a tour of Washington which included a visit to a building housing an enormous room called 'The Jesus Room,' so named according to Burke, because when visitors enter the room and see the vastness and height of the columns supporting the ceiling, they exclaim 'Jesus!' This room is where the successful Presidential candidates hold the inaugural ball after being elected President of the United States.

After successfully negotiating the Beltway ring road around Washington, we drove north heading for New York passing through Baltimore, Philadelphia (again associated with Joseph Parry), and on to New Jersey to our original hotel in Newark. The following day was July 4th, Independence Day. We went to Manhattan and walked miles seeing the sights. I particularly wanted to view the Empire State Building, which was the same age as me. Mary and I went to the top and gasped at the view. Normally, I do not like heights but up there looking down at the 'ants' below us, I didn't feel at all nervous and neither did Mary. We could see the twin towers of the Trade Centre clearly. This was a real highlight of our visit to America. Entering the lift for the descent, Mary felt a tap on her shoulder, looking round she saw a huge gorilla who put 'his' arm around her. King Kong had come to life, she survived!

The time for our departure to return to the UK had come. It was with some sadness that we parted with our faithful Dodge Intrepid at Newark Airport. We had driven over 3,500 miles since arriving in the USA (all on the 'wrong' side of the road), without undue mishap.

On the farm things were ticking over satisfactorily. Since 1992, Tŷ Coch had been in the 'Tir Cymen' environmental scheme designed to preserve the countryside and the people earning a living by so doing. We were one of the first farms in Carmarthenshire to enter an agreement with the Countryside Council for Wales, and we embarked on a big hedging and fencing plan to enable the farm to be managed on the correct basis. Fertilizers and pesticides, etc., had never been used and we had been 'organically' minded for years. I therefore decided to join the Soil Association, which is the body responsible for promoting and policing organic production in the UK. Tŷ Coch Farm was granted official Organic Status and licensed in 1997.

At first, livestock from orthodox farms was allowed to graze organically certified land for any length of time. Later, European rules stated that this would only be allowed for a limited period and for a maximum of approximately six months. This meant that if cattle grazed in the summer then sheep would be barred in the winter. The reasons given were cock-eyed, surely, if cattle would not contaminate grass for a given period, then what could be the objection for them to graze for the remaining time? Logically, they should have been banned completely.

This meant that unless we could find organically certified cattle and sheep, our system of summer grazing of cattle and wintering sheep would be unworkable. We managed to keep going along these lines for some time but eventually, having failed to find certified livestock, we had to revert to grazing our organic grass with non organic animals even though we could certify that they came from farms which complied with Soil Association Conditions. Eventually, in 2005, I relinquished our official organic status with the Soil Association and continued to plough our own organic furrow as we had done for the last umpteen years.

My association with Tre-Gib Comprehensive School continued unabated. Glyn Davies, the headteacher, had taken up the reins from deputy Ieuan Jones. Glyn had done a good job; he in turn retired in 1997 and, in April of that year, Julie Griffiths was appointed head. I was one of the members of the committee interviewing her and she appeared to be capable and full of enthusiasm. I worked with her in my capacity as a governor and chairman of the buildings sub-committee for the next eight years. In the latter office, I was witness to the scandalous debacle of the swimming pool at Tre-Gib. This was a pool which had been built from the proceeds of funds raised by the public of Llandeilo and district. After years of use, the fabric of the indoor pool began to deteriorate and restrictions on its use were put in place and eventually it was closed to both the pupils and the general public, who hitherto also had use of the facilities. This meant that children had to be transported to Llandovery or Carmarthen if they wished to learn to swim. A whole generation of pupils were deprived of use of the pool at Tre-Gib.

Responsibility for maintaining the swimming pool had passed to Carmarthenshire County Council. They sent 'experts' to survey the building and they came to the conclusion that it would be too expensive to renovate it and that the best option would be to build a completely new one. Meeting after meeting was called between the school the LEA and the public and county councillors, and it was agreed that wheels would be put in motion to secure funding for a new swimming pool. A public meeting was called which was packed, attended by Carmarthenshire Council officers. Mark James the Chief Executive, categorically told the militant audience that the future of the Tre-Gib pool was safe and that the money would be found to build a new one. Alas, the best laid plans of mice and men, after years of passing the buck, no adequate finance was forthcoming and the whole concept was relegated to the dustbin. As a sop, an all weather running track with associated sports facilities in the grounds of the school were approved. Llandeilo citizens, Tre-Gib pupils, and all and sundry had lost their swimming pool forever.

Just prior to leaving Powys Council, I had swapped my MG Montego which had done sterling service, for a sporty Ford Probe. This was a factory-owned car which had been lightly used for media use. It was purchased from our erstwhile family supplier, C. E. M. Day of Swansea. The Probe was the two litre version and was the first white car I had ever bought. Imported from the USA, it featured the Mazda-based engine and was a real pleasure to drive, economical on petrol and easy to service. Although parts for the car had to be flown from the US, with my Ford contacts this was no problem. Mary also had a new Fiesta, so my old firm was still well supported by the Harris clan. I will always have a soft spot for Ford cars as they continue to provide good value for money and technical specifications which cars costing twice as much fail to match.

Mary and I spent our honeymoon in Paris in 1960, so when the opportunity arose for us both to revisit this romantic city, we jumped at it. In 1997, we went there for a long weekend and to go again after some thirty-seven years was an adventure not to be missed. We travelled by coach from Pont Abraham near Cross Hands and arrived at our hotel in the north of Paris which was next to the old airport. It was a short drive in to the centre of Paris passing en route the new stadium, Stade de France, which was nearing completion. Several years earlier we had celebrated our Silver Wedding at the Caswell Bay Hotel, Swansea. This hotel had one of the best views overlooking Caswell Bay. Unfortunately, in later years it was demolished to make way for a new block of apartments each costing the earth. The passing of this hotel and that of neighbouring Osborne Hotel, without doubt left Swansea the poorer.

We visited all our old haunts in Paris, this time venturing further to visit Versailles. This is a magnificent building but not as imposing as I had been led to expect. In fact both Mary and I were a bit disappointed. Its proximity to housing was a surprise and the length of time one had to queue to get in was enough to put anyone off. A boat trip down the Seine rounded the trip off nicely plus a few skirmishes in the shops to complete the exercise. We drove around the Paris ring road in August, and the following month, September, Princess Diana was killed in one of the very underpasses we had gone through.

This holiday lark was beginning to seem very attractive and so we decided it was about time we visited somewhere warm where we could relax. In late summer of '97, we booked a flight to Majorca flying from Bristol. This was the first shock for me. We had hardly had time to settle down in our seats, before the captain spoke over the intercom: "This is your captain, Pamela McCoy." Mary said the expression on my face was a sight to behold. My jaw dropped and I looked as if I was in a state of shock, which I was! The thought of a woman piloting a plane in which I was a passenger didn't bear thinking about. However, there was nothing I could do about it, as parachutes were not standard issue. To her credit, she did a great job, flying through the night and bringing the plane down to a perfect landing in Palma. We had survived!

Our hotel was sited on the eastern coast of the island at Calas de Majorca. This was a newish town, very compact, with a pleasant beach. As it was a bit remote, we hired a Fiat Punto to transport us around. This was a small car which I thought to be ideal for the narrow roads which had edges over which there were drops of several inches. It was quite usual to see vehicles which had experienced mishaps adorning the sides of the roads. I was told the local police had a strong 'hands on' attitude to careless driving.

So, full of confidence, we set off on our expedition into the hinterland with eager anticipation to explore what Majorca had to offer and my word were we in for a surprise!

We drove north along the coast and followed the shore before heading west towards Alcudia and Port de Pollenca. After a brief stop in Port de Pollenca, we saw a sign pointing to Cap de Formento, which on the road map looked to be the furthest point north on the island. We decided to give it a go and off we drove. What happened next took years off our lives. The road began to rise and get narrower. Bends got more numerous and tighter and we appeared to be on a ridge with a drop of hundreds of feet on each side of the road directly into the sea, without any barriers. Vehicles coming towards us had barely room to pass. With our hearts in our mouths, Mary

271

and I were afraid to look over the edge of the road and my right knee became numb with the force of Mary's grip on it.

Somehow we reached Cap de Formento with its lighthouse, and with the wits scared out of us, we immediately turned around with difficulty in the confined parking area of the lighthouse and re-peated our nightmare journey back to Port de Pollenca. The relief we felt when we eventually reached 'safety,' cannot be described. This was the worst driving experience I had ever encountered and no amount of persuading would ever tempt me to repeat it again.

The rest of our stay in Majorca was very pleasant and helped us to try and put Formento to the back of our minds. A trip on the railway from Palma taking in Valldemossa, Soller and Port de Soller, was memorable. A visit to a nightspot near Palma with entertain-ment by The Drifters was enjoyable, but the jewel of our visit was undoubtedly the trip to the Caves of Drac at Portocristo. This huge limestone cavern with its stalagmites and stalactites and associated caves, was spectacular. With seats arranged in the form of an amphi-theatre in the main cave, facing a lake which was cleverly illuminated to create a mystic atmosphere, together with subtle background music, all combining to produce a dramatic backcloth for a boat silently gliding through the water propelled by a silent boatman, was a moving experience which was quite unique. Dan-yr-Ogof Caves could learn a lot from that complex.

Our hotel was situated overlooking a secluded beach complete with topless sunbathers. The walk from the hotel to the other side of this small resort was along a coastal path which reminded me strongly of the path in Tenby which passed the RNLI Lifeboat Station. At one point along the path (in Majorca not Tenby), could be seen scores of cats of all ages basking in the sun. Although it was September, the weather was glorious with temperatures in the 90s F.

Not long after our return home, my cousin Audrey invited Mary and me together with Arthur and my mother, to meet our mutual cousin from the USA who we had not met before. Related to me on the Harris side, she was staying with Audrey and Peter in Saunders Way, Swansea, and was anxious to meet her Welsh kinsfolk. Molly was from Cleveland, Ohio. She had been trying for years to find her roots in Wales and it was through a letter to the *Merthyr Express* that she was able to find us. Her family name was Eykin and her relatives were the BBC presenters George and Chris Eykin.

The ending of the twentieth century was on us before we realised. The year 2000 was here and we were all that much older. Mary retired on March 5th from her service with HM Customs and Excise. Then, like a bolt out of the blue, on 13th March, 2000, Arthur had a massive heart attack while sleeping, and died. The shock was terrible. He had no warning that there was the remotest possibility of that happening. A non-smoker and drinker, he kept himself fit and looked healthy. Not only a brother, Arthur had been my best pal all my life. We had lived together for most of that time and had gone through events which only he and I had shared. It was a heart-rending act to tell my mother and I will never forget the look on her face when I did so. Life would never be the same again. Of his children, Lloyd took it the hardest, they had been insepar-able, helping his father to revamp The Oak Cottage, and assisting both of us in improving the farm. Arthur was 75 years of age and of course an architect by profession.

Shortly after Arthur's death, Mary and I 'celebrated,' if that was the appropriate word in the circumstances, our 40th wedding anni-versary. We had a quiet get-together with our children and grand-children and hoped that the new millennium would prove to be more peaceful than the last. Just before our anniversary, we attended Lloyd and Sian's wedding which took place on April 1st in Llan-deilo, his father missing it by just a few weeks. We were all adamant that the wedding should go ahead as it was what Arthur would have wished. Afterwards, the newly-wedded couple flew to Mexico for their honeymoon.

This was followed shortly after with the news that Dorothy's husband, Ieuan, had fallen off a wall in Swansea and had been rushed to hospital where he was to spend the next couple of months, before he tragically died on July 7th. Ieuan Gealy was an exceptional man. Not only a brother-in-law, he was a true friend and had one of the most generous and caring personalities of anyone I had ever known. He would help in any way he could, whether it was mending a broken down car or driving miles to accommodate anyone. He never had a bad word to say about anybody and was a devoted father to his children, Mark and Debbie. What Ieuan didn't know about cars and motorbikes wasn't worth knowing. He loved accompanying the High Sheriff of Carmarthenshire and vintage car enthusiast, Johnny Thomas of Nantgaredig, on his London to Brighton veteran car runs. His passing left a hole in the family which could not be plugged.

Running through our bottom fields at Tŷ Coch was a pipeline conveying gas from Swansea to Lampeter. The powers that be decided a bigger pipeline was necessary, and so we were invaded by scores of British Gas officials all anxious to placate us by assurances that everything would be put back in place when the work was completed. We had to have special consideration due to the organic status of the farm. In due course the bulldozers, JCB diggers and associated ironmongery arrived after miles of stock proof fencing along the selected route had been erected. What followed over the next few months was amusing to see but not altogether funny at the time. It was an above average wet summer and at times the pipeline track resembled a motorbike scrambles course, mud everywhere with Land Rovers and trucks sliding and slipping all over the place. I was called upon several times to extricate with our four wheel drive tractor, vehicles which got stuck after the drivers of the 'heavy brigade' had knocked off for the day. To get from one side of the track to the other to allow vehicles and livestock to gain access to fields on either side, a series of temporary gates were installed. Prior to all this, a month or so back, someone had broken into our silage shed where our own JCB was housed and had stolen some crucial hydraulic control valves and a front bucket ram. The police installed a device which would locate any future intruder and which would alert them in the police station.

274

At about two in the morning we were awoken by a 'phone call from the police to say that the alarm had gone off and that they were on their way to us. I dressed, grabbed a torch and went out to the yard and awaited in the best tradition of 'The Bill,' for 'back up' to arrive. We all then crept down to the shed where we could hear scuffling and banging. Imagine our surprise when we flooded the place with light, to see a herd of cows trampling all over the shed and causing havoc. It seems that gates had been left open by the gas workers on our boundary with Glanyrafonddu Isaf, and Geraint Davies's cows had walked along the pipeline and into our shed. Geraint was non too pleased to leave his nice warm bed to have to come and fetch them in the pitch dark.

There was another occasion when the police had to pay us a visit as a result of the alarm going off. That time the culprit was a white barn owl who lived in an adjoining cattle shed. It used to swoop past the alarm when flying out of the shed thus triggering it off. Whoever stole our JCB parts never returned. We had our suspicions as to who it might be, but it would have been very difficult to prove conclusively. The person we thought was the guilty party left the district and we had no further trouble after that.

My clarinet-playing motor cycling pal of my youth in Merthyr Tydfil died in May, 2000. Vernon Bowen went to live in Cheltenham, where he passed away. Vernon had never enjoyed robust health so that the news was no great surprise. He, Ted and myself had been very close in the forties and fifties and though I had not seen him for some considerable time, I did have a long telephone conversation with him just after he came out of a lengthy stay in hospital, and just days before he died. Ted and I travelled to Cheltenham to his funeral and I visited his mother in Dane Street, Merthyr, shortly afterwards.

This was quite a bad period so early into the millennium. Shortly after the National Botanic Garden at Middleton Hall, near Llandeilo, opened, Ann rang us to say her mother-in-law, Sheila Evans, had died suddenly in hospital in Llanelli. Sheila was a lovely person, homely and hard-working. She kept the Post Office in Capel Isaac for many years and was well known. She worshipped her children, David, Ann and Margaret and was so proud of our mutual grandchildren, Emma and Gareth. Our hearts went out to John her husband, she would be sorely missed by all, yet another chapter closes.

At that time the country was in turmoil. The soaring cost of petrol and diesel provoked mass demonstrations by the transport industry. Oil refineries were blockaded by angry lorry drivers throughout the UK. Queues of cars were a common sight at petrol filling stations and as time went by even the pumps went dry. We were fortunate on the farm as the government allowed red agricultural diesel to be used in cars where the normal supply was not available. As most of the price of a gallon of fuel went to the government in tax, the motorist felt hard done by especially as the rest of the world enjoyed much cheaper fuel.

On September 17th, 2000, another milestone in our family history was reached. David brought his girlfriend, Karen Stothard, home to meet us. David had known Karen since college days, as they both had been together at Seale Hayne in Newton Abbott where she also graduated and became a chartered surveyor. Born and bred in Yorkshire, Karen, like David, worked on agricultural affairs, in her case, for the Welsh Assembly Government. I was fascinated to discover that she was related to Charles Dickens and also to another noted author, Monica Dickens, who was a great favourite with my mother. Karen was able to meet my mother and to attend her 99th birthday celebratory dinner held by our family at the Edwinsford Arms in Talley. This was a joyous occasion and it was great to see my mother enjoying being present with her grandchildren and great-grandchildren. It was truly memorable.

My long-standing battle with Merthyr Tydfil County Borough Council on the future of historic Vulcan House continued. My periodic visits to Merthyr revealed the sorry plight of this Grade 2 Listed Building. The roof was getting worse and worse each time

I saw it. Big holes were appearing letting in rain water, and weeds and bushes were growing out of the windows and walls. A really sorry sight! I wrote letters to the *Merthyr Express* and the *Western Mail* which were all published complete with photographs and I wrote by request of the Merthyr Tydfil Historical Society, an article for the *Merthyr Historian*, in which I outlined the historic and cultural history of Vulcan House. I wrote that this was the home of the Merthyr Chartist leader, Matthew John, the last living Merthyr Chartist who died in Vulcan House in 1888. He operated Vulcan Foundry at the rear of the house where he manufactured iron and brass products ranging from water troughs for horses to steam engines and metal patterns and prototypes of all descriptions. Visitors to Pembroke Dock in the nineteenth and twentieth centuries, could see street furniture and horse drinking troughs with the name 'Matthew John, Vulcan Foundry, Merthyr' embossed on them. He renovated the Iron Bridge in Merthyr, one of the oldest iron bridges in the world which was dismantled and allowed to fall to pieces by Merthyr Council over 150 years after is was constructed.

Matthew John was the son of the Rev. David John, a blacksmith by trade, who ultimately became the Unitarian Minister in Merthyr. David John was born in Laugharne, Carmarthenshire, in 1782. Descended from a long line of blacksmiths he set up a smithy in St. Clears and became interested in religion. While there, he met Sarah Russell and married her at Llangan Church near Whitland. Sarah hailed from Kidwelly and was a lot older than him. Like a lot of young hopefuls in West Wales, the attractions of the new iron metropolis of Merthyr Tydfil, drew them there like moths to a candle. David set up his blacksmith shop in Iron Lane, Georgetown, established a schoolroom above it, and became Unitarian Minister for Merthyr. It was here, according to historian Charles Wilkins, that government spies came to see if the Rev. David John was casting bullets for the Chartists. David caught them and threatened to put their heads under his hammer if they didn't clear off. They did! Matthew's brother David John Junior, was a fiery individual and edited the Chartist newspaper *Udgorn Cymru* (Trumpet of Wales). He represented Merthyr and Monmouth at the celebrated Chartist Convention in Manchester in 1840.

Rev. David John was my great-great-great-grandfather; not only was he a man of religion but he was also a brilliant mathematician and keen historian. A tablet on the wall of the now defunct Unitarian Chapel in Thomas Street, Merthyr, reads as follows:

This tablet is dedicated to the Reverend David John
who for thirty years was the faithful and disinterested
Minister of this Chapel in the various relation of husband,
Father and citizen. He left a lasting example of kindness
and integrity his attainments in mathematics and other
branches of knowledge were accurate and extensive
and he was throughout his whole life a zealous reformer
an ardent lover of the truth and an excellent exemplification
of the Christian character, he was born in Laugharne in
Carmarthenshire and died in this parish on 6th January
1853 aged 71 years.

His son Matthew, was buried in the graveyard of the Hen Dŷ Cwrdd Unitarian Chapel in Cefn Coed, where most of the prominent Merthyr Unitarians of the day are to be found buried. The fight to save his old home Vulcan House, is continuing despite the frustrating obstacles. Cadw, the statutory body set up to oversee the preservation of buildings of historic and cultural importance, has been useless in the case of Vulcan House. Their Chief Executive told me that Cadw had no power to make Merthyr Council conform to the Listed Building legislation. The council could do exactly as they wanted with no redress. What a system! As previously stated, I asked Merthyr Council under the Freedom of Information Act, to tell me what steps the Council had taken to obtain financial assistance to renovate Vulcan House? The answer by e-mail came back: none! What pride the elected members have in their cultural heritage!

Despite living in the heart of the country, this didn't prevent me from pursuing my love of jazz and swing. When the Ted Heath Orchestra came to St. David's Hall in Cardiff, I was there. This was not long before Arthur died. We sat in the front of the stalls and wallowed in the big band sound. The band, following Ted Heath's death, was fronted by veteran trombonist Don Lusher, the whole ensemble consisting of members of the original band. To cap it all, Britain's best trumpet player, Kenny Baker, was playing at his very best and Jack Parnell on the drums was doing his stuff. To hear Kenny Baker playing was sheer pleasure. Sitting in the row beside us was Ted Heath's widow, she was thoroughly enjoying herself, and I believe this was the last occasion the band was reunited to play. Every time I used to drive past the bridge in Powys, when I was working there, I thought of Dickie Valentine, who sang with Ted Heath and who was so tragically killed there.

Another visit to Cardiff was to see Lionel Hampton and his Orchestra. Hot from the USA, Hampton was the best jazz xylophonist ever. For years he had played with the Benny Goodman band and was one of the famous Benny Goodman Trio which consisted of Benny himself on clarinet, Lionel Hampton on xylophone and Gene Krupa on drums. When I saw him in Cardiff he was getting on, but still world class.

Talking of world class, a real highlight for me was the visit to the Brangwyn Hall in Swansea to hear Stephane Grappelli play. On this occasion he not only played the violin but also the piano, which I had not heard him play hitherto. People tend to use the word 'genius' for anyone above the norm, but in the case of Grappelli, the word does not do him justice. The tone, dexterity and melody he delivered was sheer heaven. He, too, was 'maturing' but the energy and verve he showed was a lesson to aspiring musicians. They just do not make them like that any more! His erstwhile fellow musician and member of the Hot Club De France, Django Reinhardt, guitarist supreme, could be classed in the same category.

Yet another trip to Swansea was called for when I heard that the world's best drummer and his band were to appear there. I refer to no other than Buddy Rich, who drummed for Harry James before setting up his own big band. The historic head-to-head drumming feat with Gene Krupa was a classic and this record takes a pride of place in my collection. So with great anticipation I landed up in the venue on Kingsway and sat within feet of the great Buddy Rich to hear a couple of hours of breathtaking drum music. I still marvel at the energy level of that man. He must have lost a stone or so during the session and the sweat stood out on his forehead but he did not let up a jot keeping a staccato of drumbeats which transcended 'normal' rhythm. What a night!

The Brangwyn Hall in Swansea was the venue of another pleasurable musical evening when I took Mary, my mother and David, to hear the Syd Lawrence Orchestra in the flesh. Their Glenn Miller renderings were first-class and I can see the surprise on David's face now, when the band started up and the blast of the brass section hit us. The vocalist was Matt Monro, who I thought looked really ill and but a shadow of his former self.

The Harris clan had a new addition in the form of a lovely bouncing baby girl born to nephew Lloyd and Sian, named Tirion. She was born just in time to be included in the 2001 Census taking place that year. On the other end of the scale, my mother was also recorded in the Census, which sadly, proved to be her last. Now in her 100th year, she was in top form until May 2001 but developed pneumonia and died in June. She passed away peacefully with Mary and me each holding her hands. Although named Ann Jane, she was known from birth as 'Nancy.' I owe more to my mother than I can ever express. She worshipped me and would do and did anything she could for Arthur and me. She led an interesting life spanning the whole of the twentieth century (1901-2001). She and my father were inseparable and while in her younger years she was inclined to be shy, from middle age on she became more extrovert and confident. Her appearance when young was striking, her hair was a rich dark red and her love of music played a major role in her life.

An accomplished piano player, my mother passed many a happy hour playing right up to the very end. She was interested in politics and was very close to her grandfather, Alderman David John (grandson of Rev. David John), who was elected to the first ever Merthyr Tydfil Borough Council in 1905 and who served for an unbroken period of eighteen years representing the Cyfarthfa Ward. My mother remembered clearly seeing Keir Hardie with her grandfather, who, while at the time of his election was a Labour councillor, later became disillusioned with Keir Hardie and the Party, becoming an Independent for the rest of his political career on Merthyr Borough Council. He died in 1918.

As a student of family history and genealogy, my pedigree is a little more complicated than the norm. This is because my mother married her second cousin, my father, with the result that I can 'double up' relations on the Harris/Thomas side. My mother's father, William Thomas, through his mother's Harris line, was a first cousin of my father's father, Richard Harris. This meant, for example, Roy Jenkins, Prof. David Brynmor Thomas and lots of cousins were related to both my father and mother. I've spent countless hours explaining this to relatives! Roy used to be intrigued by this.

My mother was in the first intake of pupils into the 'new' Cyfarthfa Castle School in 1912. The Castle had been taken over by the Merthyr Council following the demise of the Crawshay dynasty and converted into a grammar-type school for boys and girls. This was the year the *Titanic* sank. My mother remembered playing music commemorating the *Titanic* sinking, it was a 'top of the pops' of the time. Prior to the 1914/18 Great War, my mother's family spent most of their holidays each year at Llansteffan in Carmarthenshire.

They would travel by train from Merthyr to Ferryside and then cross the Towy on the ferry rowed by members of the local fishing families, particularly the John family, who also manned the Ferryside lifeboat. For years they stayed on The Green at Llansteffan and were very friendly with the Misses John (no relation) who kept the shop there. My mother recalled seeing the trains rolling through Ferryside laden with young men at the outbreak of the 1914 war, setting off to fight in France. Train after train bearing soldiers came through all shouting: "the war will soon be over, we'll be home by Christmas." Another sight which she looked forward to seeing while holidaying in Llansteffan, was to see the steamship *Merthyr* travelling up the Towy to dock in Carmarthen. This was a decent sized ship carrying cargo to the warehouses on Carmarthen Quay. It particularly impressed my mother because of its name.

To think that when she was born the fastest mode of transport on Earth was a horse, there was no radio, TV, planes, cars, washing machines, a health service, income benefits or any other of the so-called 'necessities' of modern-day living. She lived to see all these become commonplace, lived through two world wars and saw man land on the Moon. This was the most inventive and prolific century man had experienced and my mother had witnessed it all. I have many loving memories of her, and her spirit will always be with me.

After my mother's death, things were at a low ebb in our house-hold. After a couple of weeks I decided what was needed was a good holiday for Mary and me. So, we booked a Mediterranean cruise on the best known ocean liner in the world, Cunard's *Queen Elizabeth 2nd* or *QE2*. It was with eager anticipation that we set off for Southampton. As we approached the docks we could see the superstructure of the ship soaring above the surrounding buildings with its gleaming red funnel like a beacon standing out reflecting the sunlight. Arriving at the ship's berth, our car was unloaded by a set of eager beavers who whisked our luggage away, while another annexed the car, not to be seen again until our return.

Entering the *QE2* was like going into the Savoy Hotel. The vast-ness of its interior is the first thing that strikes one, the second being the attentiveness of the cabin staff. Being booked in Grill Class and an outside cabin, no doubt it contributed to their enthusiasm. To the sound of a calypso band, we left Southampton and steamed slowly down the Solent, threading our way through numerous small yachts who were warned of our coming with a booming blast of the ship's siren, this was enough to lift you two feet off the ground when it erupted!

At first, the sea and weather was quite calm and rounding the Isle of Wight was a dawdle. However, the honeymoon was soon to come to an abrupt end, as we entered the Bay of Biscay, the seas became mountainous and the *QE2* began to creak and groan. Mary, by now, began to feel queasy and lay on the bed hoping for the best. The ship was dropping into the troughs with a thud and the waves were crashing over the bows and spraying the deck and bridge. It was very dramatic. Fortunately, none of this had any effect on me and I couldn't wait to go up on deck with my camcorder to capture the fury of the elements. When I arrived there, imagine my surprise when I found that I was the only passenger to be seen, it seemed that the other couple of thousand deemed it prudent to stay below deck. The observation area on the bridge was closed off and there were warning signs displayed. I shot my footage, avoiding the spray and lurches of the ship and returned safely to Mary down below. The conditions were so bad that a large proportion of the crew were indisposed as well, prompting the captain to apologise for the inconvenience and even saying the conditions in the Bay of Biscay were as bad as any he could remember. The captain's reception party was a flop as hardly anyone turned up.

Survive we did, and it was not long before the weather improved considerably. We arrived off the shores of Portugal and steamed up the estuary to the port of Lisbon where we docked almost under the spectacular road bridge across the river which carried road vehicles and trains. Cunard laid on buses to take us around the city of Lisbon, a very clean city with a proud seafaring past. The fact that the language of Brazil is Portuguese bears testimony to their seamanship and exploratory nature.

Our next port of call was Gibraltar. Here, we took a tour around the 'Rock' climbing winding roads until we reached the giant cave deep in the heart of the Rock itself. This was very like the one in Majorca, again with an amphitheatre and tunnels, very impressive! Looking across the Straits, the coast of North Africa was plain to see. The airport looked like a platform in the sea and it was a good thing that aircraft landing there had good brakes or they would end up in the drink. The main road to Spain passed over the runway and every time a plane took off or landed, the road would be closed.

In perfect weather and calm sea, we cruised to Majorca and docked in Palma. Again, we left the ship and did our tour of the city, visiting the cathedral and the castle perched on a hill overlooking Palma, once the abode of the King of Majorca. The heat was terrific, and Mary and I were glad to shelter under the archways surrounding the castle walls. We were quite impressed with Palma, quite historic yet had a good modern shopping atmosphere.

It was a short hop from Majorca to Barcelona our next port of call. The *QE2* docked right near the heart of the city right by the overhead cable car masts. After a whisk around the centre we headed out in our luxury coach passing the big SEAT car factory, aiming for the mountains and the Monastery of Montserrat. This was situated at the end of a narrow road which again wound its way up into the mountains. The view from the Monastery was breathtaking, it nestled under towering rock formations and was a hive of activity, with tourists from everywhere enjoying its tranquillity only broken by the sound of bells ringing at pre-determined intervals.

After a few more shore excursions, we embarked and sailed off to our next destination which was La Coruna in northern Spain, a port which had links with the armada. After seeing the sights in La Coruna we then sailed on to Santanda where Mary and I were impressed by the coastal promenades lined with trees and immaculate gardens full of flowers and flowering shrubs.

As the *QE2* left Santanda, scores of small craft escorted us with their crews waving and cheering, the whole atmosphere being festive, a couple of blasts on the siren in salute was a fitting conclusion to our visit. The next leg of our voyage took us northwards to Bordeaux in France. Due to its size, the *QE2* had to berth some sixty miles from Bordeaux near the mouth of the River Gironde down river from the city. The drive in from the ship took us through acres of vineyards with their immaculate rows of grapevines stretching as far as the eye could see. We did the obligatory stop at a winery and tasted all the local samples. To me, most of it tasted like medicine. I can't stand dry wine, the only type I would drink if so inclined, would be a very sweet white wine. I'm afraid the Rothchilds would be bankrupt if they had to rely on me as a customer. We had a look around Bordeaux and had a nice meal there before heading back to the floating hotel. En route we stopped in Soulac-sur-Mer, a small pretty seaside town not far from our ship. We could see the *QE2* standing out above the dunes as we approached, it was moored at a jetty with hardly any buildings around it and miles from anywhere, it was quite bizarre.

The voyage back to Southampton went smoothly, and apart from the outward bound Biscay episode, the whole cruise had been superb. As for the *QE2*, it was a great ship, the food in the grill restaurant was excellent, the entertainment on board was first-class as our fellow passengers, Esther Rantzen and her daughter, Fiona Bruce, Jim Bowen of 'Bullseye' fame, and many more could confirm. Alas, just like the other famous Cunarder the *Queen Mary*, the *QE2* is to be destined for life as a static hotel in Dubai. What an inglorious end to ship that has crossed the Atlantic umpteen times and played a major role in the Falklands war carrying thousands of troops to fight Argentina.

It was shortly after our return to Llandeilo, that the whole nature of life as we knew it changed for ever. The destruction of the twin towers in New York on 11th September shocked the world. The dramatic sight of the collapse of the building was hard to take in that it was actually happening, it looked like something conjured up for a movie.

Having now been firmly bitten by the cruising bug, we decided to go on a Baltic cruise in 2002. So, in August, we set off for

Harwich to embark on the *Sundream*. While not as big as the *QE2*, nevertheless the ship was large enough to provide first-class facilities and entertainment. Our first port of call was Oslo in Norway. The view from Holmenhollen high above the city looking southwards was spectacular. It was here that the 1952 Winter Olympic Games were held with the ski jump playing a prominent role.

From Olso we steamed on to Stockholm in Sweden reaching the city after passing mile upon mile of islands as the ship sailed up the waterway. Mary and I were very impressed with Stockholm. Like all Scandinavian towns it was spotless and the buildings were immaculate. Their lives seem to be influenced by the sea and water in all its aspects. We visited the Vasa Museum which had been specially built to house a 17th-century ship named *Vasa*. This 64-gun warship sank in 1628 shortly after being launched and after centuries of lying at the bottom was raised and found to be in remarkable condition. Restoration work on it has resulted in a ship which is almost as good as new providing an insight into a period of maritime history quite unique. The enormity of the vessel when standing alongside it hits you and both Mary and myself couldn't take our eyes off it. An interesting snippet we were told was that the Baltic Sea consisted mainly of fresh water which helped to preserve the *Vasa* and also provided drinking water for the area.

Helsinki, which was our next destination was up to our expectations and the tales of the locals taking icy cold dips in the water during the wintertime and transferring to and from hot saunas didn't appeal to us one bit. What did, was the memorial to the Finnish composer, Sibelius, composer of seven symphonies; this consisted of a series of metal tubes of varying lengths joined together and placed in a park on the outskirts of Helsinki.

With the sun beating down out of cloudless skies, we made or way to St. Petersburg in Russia, or as many of my generation knew it, Leningrad. The *Sundream* berthed right in the heart of the city after passing acres of docks and scores of ships in this thriving port. The cruise line organised excursions ashore and we set off to explore the city. What a shock! The buildings were mostly in a bad state of repair and looked neglected and poverty stricken. Grass grew out of pavements and the whole place looked as if it has seen better days, which it had! In complete contrast, the museums and palaces were superb and had been refurbished with no expense spared. I was surprised by the number of canals and waterways to be seen and their width. It was on one of these that I visited the historic battleship *Aurora* which fired the gun which started the Russian revolution in October, 1917. I had always been fascinated with the account of the *Aurora's* participation in the 1917 uprising and to actually stand on the deck with my hand on the gun was a feeling hard to describe, the years seem to roll away and I could almost hear the sounds of revolution reverberating across the city.

In the shopping area of St. Petersburg, I searched in vain for a little old antique shop selling Fabergé Eggs on the cheap but there were certainly plenty of shops selling the popular multi-eggs. We were warned that on no account were we to leave the main body of visitors as beggars in the streets and parks were a hazard and in fact, one of our party off the ship who was confined to a wheelchair, did wander off on his own with a companion and was mugged. Another thing which we noticed was the number of clapped out Lada cars to be seen, it didn't appear that the Russians had such a stringent MOT as we did. Having said that, the city was classical and with a bit of 'tarting' up it could attain its former glory. A drive of some 20 miles out of the city brought us to Catherine's Summer Palace. What a surprise that turned out to be. Talk of opulence, there was enough gold to be seen there to fill all the teeth in the world. It was truly magnificent and the standard of the décor was mind boggling. The Czars certainly knew what they liked and Catherine had impeccable taste. The table bearing china made by Wedgewood which was specially commissioned by Catherine, seemed to be half a mile long.

Leaving the quay at the end of our stay in St. Petersburg, was reminiscent of my time in Liverpool. A Russian army band was playing alongside the ship, their repertoire consisting entirely of Beatle tunes. As we left the berth, strains of 'Penny Lane' and 'Yellow Submarine' were booming out across the water, we could have been on the pier head overlooking the Mersey.

Our next disembarkation was at Tallinn, the capital city of Estonia. A pleasant place, very clean and thriving. Oppressed by the USSR for many years, it was enjoying its freedom and was becoming prosperous which was obvious by the number of BMW and Mercedes cars replacing the former Lada population. We visited the site of the Eurovision Song Contest and the Olympic Swimming Pool before embarking for our longer cruise to Denmark. Passing through the narrow straits between Denmark and Sweden, it was strange to see cars and lorries travelling from one country to the other, approach the centre of the waterway on a motorway, before suddenly disappearing, so it looked, headlong into the sea. It transpired that there was a tunnel hewn out of the rock in the straits which connected the two countries. It was an impressive piece of engineering. I have often thought that something like that could be done to link Scotland to Northern Ireland. When you look at the distance between the two, it seems quite feasible and I am surprised this has not been discussed more. Another of my pet schemes is to link Russia and Alaska with a tunnel under the Bering Strait. This would enable us to drive by road from Wales to South America without leaving the car! Better value for money than sending men to Mars!

Arriving in Copenhagen, the obvious pilgrimage was to see the 'Little Mermaid.' What a letdown! We had a job to see this famous landmark through the throng of people surrounding her. When we did manage to catch a glimpse, it was a bit of a disappointment. I expected to see a larger than life figure, instead here was this tiny statue which you could easily miss if passing by quickly.

A short hop to Holland was next on the agenda. The *Sundream* left the sea and we progressed up a canal linking it to Amsterdam. This journey along the canal was most unusual. Here was this large

'My' Powys logo.

Powys County Hall, Llandrindod Wells.

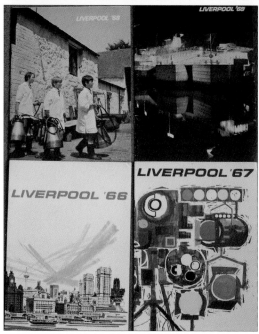

Colourful Liverpool magazine sets the pace.

Ahoy there! Aboard the Queen Mary *at Long Beach, California.*

Mary after our flight over the Grand Canyon.

Relaxing on Fisherman's Wharf, San Francisco, with Alcatraz in the background.

Niagara surging past Mary.

Me, top of the Empire State Building with Twin Towers backcloth.

Outside Raffles Hotel in Singapore.

David, Karen, Mary and Oliver at the Sydney Opera House.

Mary and me in Australia.

Ned Kelly towering over we tourists.

The quaintest pub in Australia!

Mary keeping a straight face outside a 'wonky' pub.

Llandilo in New South Wales, Australia.

Looking out over Hong Kong.

Me against the Vancouver sky-line.

Glorious gardens on Vancouver Island.

Mary at Lake Louise, Canada.

My 1966 Soccer World Cup Liverpool regalia

My 1966 Soccer World Cup Liverpool regalia

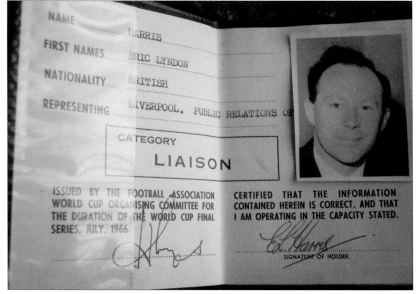

liner travelling through the countryside for miles. From the fields alongside it must have looked as if the ship was passing on dry land. Peering down from the deck it was possible to see everything, cars, tractors cultivating the fields and small ferries crossing the canal at regular intervals. We entered a lock and the whole ship was lifted to the next level for us to continue our journey. Eventually we reached Amsterdam and tied up in the very heart of the city within shouting distance of the railway station.

After a trip around the city, we set off by road to Delft and The Hague in South Holland. At Delft we visited the noted porcelain and pottery factory and saw the famous blue pottery being produced and sold to visitors at astronomical prices. Travelling through The Hague we passed the buildings housing Slobodan Milosovic, the former President of the Republic of Yugoslavia, who was confined there and on trial for atrocities during the Balkan crisis. He died there before the trial ended after suffering a heart attack.

Leaving Holland we headed back to the UK and safely docked at Harwich. The entire cruise had been outstanding. From the time we left to the time we returned, the skies were cloudless, the sun shone nonstop and the sea was like a mill pond. Perfect conditions for a perfect holiday.

In complete contrast to the hot weather experienced on our cruise, the beginning of 2003 proved to be very cold. Hard frosts in January and snow in England were the norm. During this period I had the sad news that Roy (Jenkins) had died. He had not been too well for a long time and his last letters to me had been shakily handwritten. He was 82 when he died and his life had certainly been lived to the full. Despite the high offices he held, he was still Hattie Harris' 'little boy.' His mother worshipped him, and as an only child he was certainly pampered. His accent belied his true nature, both he and Jennifer, who was by now Dame Jennifer, had a long and lasting marriage. The respect in which he was held was demonstrated at his funeral in East Hendred on January 10th, which was attended by world leading figures including Prime Minister

Roy Harris Jenkins,
a heavyweight politician.

Tony Blair, who had the highest regard for Roy. He will be missed on the political front and by all his family. Baron Roy Harris Jenkins of Hillhead of Pontypool in the County of Gwent, did us proud!

One member of the family goes and another arrives. On 27th March, 2003, Lloyd and Sian were blessed with a baby boy, Ioan. Born in Abergavenny, Ioan was another grandson for Arthur and would continue his male Harris line. We were all delighted.

That summer, Mary and I set out on another great adventure, a coast-to-coast railway crossing of the USA. We flew to New York and booked into a hotel close to the famous Carnegie Hall. Standing outside and casting my mind back to 1936, I could imagine the excitement and anticipation of the jazz fans as they entered this hallowed venue to see and hear the renowned Benny Goodman Orchestra concert. It was at this concert that my favourite trumpet player, Harry James, made his mark. Goodman's rendering of 'Sing Sing' was forever etched in the annals of swing music at this epic concert. What I would have given to be there.

In the next couple of days, Mary and I walked the length and breadth of Manhattan visiting the revamped Grand Central Station which was redesigned by a Welsh architect who also designed the new glasshouse at the Wales National Botanic Gardens at Llanarthne, which was recently opened. While on the subject of the Botanic Gardens, Arthur's son-in-law, Neil Vandersteen, made the models for the entrance and the Great Glasshouse at the Wales National Botanic Gardens for his employer, Sir Norman Foster the architect, for whom he heads the model-making team being responsible for projects such as The Reichstag in Berlin, Hong Kong Airport and numerous other constructions throughout the world.

Visiting the site of the 9/11 tragedy was a traumatic experience. It was hard to visualise that this hole in the ground was the base for two gigantic towering skyscrapers, it all looked so peaceful with visitors quietly surveying where the carnage occurred. A cruise down the river helped to cast our sad thoughts aside as we headed up river under the Brooklyn Bridge before heading back to the Statue of Liberty and the shore of Manhattan. Thoughts of the 'Edwards millions' and my grandfather's efforts to claim historic ownership of the Island, were never very far from mind when walking down 5th Avenue or through Central Park.

Our train journey began at Pennsylvania Station for our next stop Washington DC. Once again, thoughts turned to the past. Here we were on this legendry station immortalised by bandleader Glenn Miller with his arrangement of 'Chattanooga Choo Choo' which topped the charts in 1941. We boarded the train, alas not at 'quarter to four' and not on 'Track 29.' We dispensed with 'reading a magazine' and were soon in Baltimore! Prior to leaving the station while we were waiting on the platform, I had an interesting conversation with a Chilean lady who had spent some time in Britain but did not know much about Wales. She knew General Pinochet the notorious former President of Chile and was on her way to the UK in a diplomatic capacity. She thought the General was great and a loyal friend of Mrs Thatcher. By the time we were ready to leave, I had convinced her that Wales was *the* place to visit which she said she would and couldn't wait to see it.

Our Amtrak train via Philadelphia and Baltimore duly arrived in Washington DC and we stayed at an Irish hotel right opposite the station – and what a station! It was huge, with layers of shops and restaurants catering for tastes from all over the world. We saw the US Capitol and the White House. To get to the latter, we had to negotiate yards of hamburger and hotdog stands and kitchens which lined the closed avenues, it was the annual competition and convention for the followers of these delicacies. Mind you, the smell was very appetising!

My cousin Peg had been told that we were coming to Washington so we arranged to meet at the hotel, which we did. Peg and Burke then whisked us off in their car for a grand tour. We went to Georgetown and George Washington's house, had dinner in an exclusive country club and saw parts of Washington which only locals would know about. The following day we visited Arlington Cemetery, burial place of countless American celebrities, politicians and military personnel.

The next leg of our journey was to leave Washington DC on the *Capitol Limited* train for our destination, Chicago. This was a really amusing part of our trip as it involved sleeping overnight on the train. Our exclusive compartment in the day was converted by the conductor into an up and down bunk bed sleeper while we dined in the restaurant car in the evening. Anyone who has not experienced this mode of transport . . . beware! Apart from having to be an accomplished contortionist one has to be on *very* friendly terms with whoever is sharing the facilities or lack of them. The distance from the edge of the beds to the door leading into the corridor leaves about enough room to take a deep breath. On several occasions I had to stick my arm and posterior out of the door to put my pyjamas on and to leave Mary enough room to perform her rituals. We had many a good laugh with our neighbours on the opposite side of the corridor who were undergoing similar acrobatics.

The journey across America from Washington to Chicago via places like Harpers Ferry and Pittsburgh was slow but interesting. Passenger trains in the US have to give way to freight trains which take top priority. This was the case on this leg of the trip and was repeated time after time. Our train was reduced to a crawl for mile after mile while locomotives pulling endless wagons (trucks) rolled by on the fast tracks. As we approached Chicago I couldn't help thinking of my kinsman Henry Harris who travelled from Cefn Coed, Merthyr Tydfil, crossing the Atlantic and going by train and horse-drawn vehicles to attend the World's Fair in Chicago in 1893. They certainly were made of stern stuff in those days!

After a brief sojourn in Chicago we set off again for some more sleeper frolics on the *California Zephyr* heading for Denver, Colorado. At Burlington we crossed the mighty River Mississippi. What a river! It was more like an inland lake even as far north as this and was awesome. Further along the tracks at Omaha we encountered another giant, this time the Missouri. They'd give the Severn and Thames a very big inferiority complex not to mention the Towy and the Taff, what rivers!

Staying at Denver was one of the most enjoyable stops of our epic train journey, The 'mile high city' was bathed in glorious sunshine and the perfume from the tree blossom in the city left a lasting impression with both Mary and me. An exhibition of handcrafted quilts held in the Capitol Building left one marvelling at the expertise and dexterity of the men and women who had so lovingly produced them. The day after our arrival we were due to travel by coach up in to the Rockies but were told it would be delayed an hour or so due to the fact that the snow ploughs hadn't quite cleared the roads of snowdrifts, falls had made them impassable. Bearing in mid that the temperature was 30 degrees centigrade at our hotel in the middle of June, it was hard to believe. Eventually, we set out for the Rocky Mountain National Park via Estes Park, Trail Ridge Road and Grand Lake. We had been warned to take warm clothing and we could see why as the coach wound its way higher and higher with snow piled high on either side. At a stop en route for refreshments and to enable people who were short of breath to recover, a plaque stated that we were over 12,000 feet above sea level and on the highest road in the Rockies.

We departed from Denver by coach to Colorado Springs for a brief stop before continuing to the small town of La Junta. From Colorado Springs we visited The Garden of the Gods Park with its unusual trading post. The giant red rocks situated in the park are truly spectacular and seem to glow when the sun hits them. While Mary and I were admiring them and chatting to each other, a man came up to us and asked us if we were Welsh, we said we were and to our surprise he said that he had lived in Wales some time ago and had managed a Bible shop in The Kingsway, Swansea, before returning to the USA, where he had married and settled down. It really is a small world!

The next stage took us by rail on the *Southwest Chief* for the journey to Flagstaff where we stayed for a few days. Excursion by coach took us in to the blisteringly hot desert to see the geological and historical features along the Navajo Indian Trail. I particularly remember Flagstaff because of a street called Beulah Street. I asked a local if there was any connection with Beulah in Wales, to which he replied that quite a few Welsh people had settled in the area and that a local sheep association had its offices in Beulah Street. From Flagstaff we drove to a town called Williams along the famous Route 66. This town had also been named after a Welsh settler and from here we boarded the a train on the Grand Canyon Railway. This vintage steam train with its restored 1920's coaches staffed by individuals dressed in the period 'western-style' outfits, took us to the South Rim of the Grand Canyon.

To see the Canyon in all its glory we decided to take a flight. Other members of our party were booked in and Mary and I were asked if we would mind joining another group on a another 'plane. We said okay and imagine our surprise when we boarded the twin engined aircraft to discover all our fellow passengers were Japanese!

Undeterred, we settled down for a flight which will be etched in our memory banks for ever. Suddenly, appearing as we flew over the rim, the panorama of the Canyon exceeded our greatest expectations. It simply took our breath away. The immenseness and colouring of the gorge with the Colorado River meandering along its floor was unforgettable. The Grand Canyon is truly one of the great wonders of the world.

After our flight we again boarded the vintage train for our journey back to Williams. En route looking out of the windows we could see cowboys dressed like bandits galloping alongside the train on their horses firing pistols into the air. The train slowed and they then boarded going from carriage to carriage demanding ransom money. One swarthy individual looking very fierce came into our carriage and, to our surprise, asked if any of the passengers were from Wales. We came clean and, dropping his gun, he said his mother was from Ynysybwl and had married an American G.I. during the war and had emigrated to the US where he had been born and lived ever since. Needless to say, Mary and I got off lightly!

Once more we boarded the *Southwest Chief* for the next leg to Los Angeles. On arrival we boarded a coach for our 'hotel' in Long Island which was the original Cunard liner and a boyhood icon for me . . . the *Queen Mary*. I had last seen this magnificent ship over forty years previously when I was working for the Ford Motor Company on a visit to Southampton. Now, used as a hotel, it still looked majestic moored at Long Island and we were about to sample its atmosphere – and what an atmosphere! Our first-class cabin echoed the era of pre-war elegance. Wood panelling and brass permeated the ship and reflected the craftsmanship of British shipbuilders. Standing on the bridge I could imagine the bows ploughing through the Atlantic on its many crossings. I recalled its illustrious war service (1939/45) record, when as a troop ship she carried up to 16,000 soldiers on a single trip from the USA to Britain. The *Queen Mary* was so fast (30 knots) that the German

U-boat submarines could not catch her; Adolf Hitler offered a vast reward and an Iron Cross to any submarine commander who could sink her. He kept his cash and decoration! On one occasion in 1942, the *Queen Mary* was bringing troops to Britain when a light cruiser escorting her crossed her bows, the *Queen Mary* sliced right through the cruiser and was unable to stop to pick up survivors due to her speed and the danger from lurking U-boats, 338 sailors on the cruiser perished.

My stay on the *Queen Mary* was full of nostalgic memories for me. In 1936, the year of her first trans-Atlantic service, my Great Aunt and Uncle Tom and Mary Jane Harris, celebrated their Golden Wedding on the ship as she crossed from the US to England. I stood in the very room where they dined on that auspicious occasion and the vibes I felt were profound. My cousin Crecy had also travelled to America several times in the thirties and always returned with wondrous tales of the ship which, as an eight-year-old, I mopped up, being fascinated by the romanticism of the period. One of my prize possessions was a Dinky Toy model of the *Queen Mary* which I gave to Philip Cross living next door to us in St. Albans, when we moved back in 1946 to Merthyr Tydfil.

Using the ship as our base, we did the usual trips into Los Angeles and the obligatory visits to the film studios. Mary and I were not impressed by LA and it seemed to be populated by people who were to say the least . . . overweight! It was very industrialised and a bit of a sprawl. In due course we transferred from the *Queen Mary* to Los Angeles Union Station to join the *Coast Starlight* for our rail journey, via Santa Barbara, along the Pacific Coast to San Francisco, our ultimate destination in sunny California.

In complete contrast to LA, San Francisco was most impressive and our arrival by coach at night over the Bay Bridge was memorable, with all the lights of the city twinkling from the high-rise buildings. We enjoyed our up and down tour of the city with its cable cars which were heaving with people jammed in like sardines. We celebrated July 4th in San Francisco with a trip to Alcatraz, which appeared to be so peaceful, and it was hard to imagine the conditions that prevailed when the place was going full swing as a prison.

The first sighting of the Golden Gate Bridge was a bit of an anticlimax as I was expecting a mammoth-sized structure which would leave us spellbound – not so, it didn't look as impressive as the Severn Bridge and not half as good as the second Severn Crossing. However, we flew back from San Francisco with warm memories of Macey's and the seals on Fisherman's Wharf, and we did manage to avoid an earthquake!

In the meantime, plans for David and Karen's forthcoming wedding were nearing fruition and on September 6th, 2003, they were married at Machen Church with the reception held at St. Mellons. Yorkshire-born Karen Stothard became Karen Harris. After a wonderful wedding, they honeymooned in Turkey. The last of our brood had fled the nest. It would be interesting to see who would support who when England and Wales clashed at Twickenham or Cardiff!

Another milestone in my life's saga took place in the ensuing year after the wedding. The farm was more or less ticking over on well oiled wheels. Mary and I were not getting any younger and the time was ripe for a move to a more favourable environment. The opportunity arose for us to purchase a bungalow in Llandeilo right next door to Mary's brother and sister-in-law, John and Haulwen. This left our house at Tŷ Coch available for David and Karen, and the move was made. After extensive refurbishment to both house and bungalow, we all settled in to our respective new homes. Our bungalow was only a matter of some five miles from Tŷ Coch Farm so it was comparatively easy for me to travel to supervise operations on the farm. At first, it seemed strange to both Mary and myself to once again have people living all around us. We hadn't had neighbours as such since we were living in Liverpool. It did take some getting used to. It certainly made life easier for Mary with shops within walking distance.

Just before the move from Tŷ Coch, I had my great-grandfather's long case clock repaired. This 'grandfather' clock had never worked in my lifetime. It had been in my grandfather William Thomas's house in Merthyr Tydfil in his front room for years without operating. My mother had inherited it and she told me that she couldn't remember it working from *her* grandfather's time. I happened to be in Brooksbank the jeweller's in Carmarthen one day and I mentioned to Mr Brooksbank the story of the clock. His eyes lit up and he said that he thought he could fix it, clock and watch repairs were his particular speciality. The clock was made by 'Watkins, Merthyr' around 1830 and was an unusual type of clock with its dial set in a round case. Made of mahogany, it was a seven day winding clock which struck the hour. Mr Brooksbank took the clock and in due course returned with a triumphant glint in his eyes and set it up in the hall. It worked beautifully and its striking bell resounded through the house bringing it to life on the hour. My only regret looking back was that my mother dying in her 100th year, never witnessed it working or heard it striking. It now has pride of place in our bungalow and keeps perfect time, it really is a piece of family history come alive.

Following the trauma of moving house, it was decided that we could do with another break in the following year, 2005. We booked for a Mediterranean cruise on the Royal Caribbean's *Legend of the Seas*. This ship was enormous. Sailing from Southampton, we passed the *QE2* which was berthed at the Cunard pier. We were looking down at her as we passed which really brought home the size of our ship. Calling in the old haunts in Portugal and Gibraltar which we had previously visited with the *QE2*, we arrived at the port of Civitavecchia in Italy. This was the nearest port for visiting Rome and it was necessary to take a lengthy coach trip to get there. We arrived in Rome on a blisteringly hot day and made a beeline for the Coliseum. I had always been fascinated by this building since my childhood with its tales of heroism and brutality, particularly concerning our Celtic forebears. Standing inside, I could almost feel the drama and tension of those traumatic events of long ago and thanked my lucky stars that my span on Earth was the present time. On this, my first visit to Rome, I was a little disappointed. I had expected to see a more compact, well defined city, instead finding it to be a bit of a sprawl and very commercial. The Vatican was smaller than I imagined and having queued for ages to get in, found the Sistine Chapel to be heaving with humanity, and despite pleas by the 'minders' for silence, a constant cacophony of voices went unabated.

We then sailed to Villefranche-sur-Mer on the Cote d' Azur and went ashore at Nice. This really did live up to expectations and the run into Monaco/Monte Carlo was impressive. After visiting Grace Kelly's tomb and a quick lap around the Grand Prix circuit, we headed back to the ship having resisted the temptation to break the bank of Monte Carlo at the Casino.

A short hop on the *Legend of the Seas* over to Corsica and we were moored at the capital town of Ajaccio. This was a pleasant place set against a backcloth of jagged mountains and spotlessly clean. The day we arrived the French referendum was taking place on Europe. Everyone was talking politics and I was surprised how well informed the general Corsican public were. Corsica was of course where Napoleon was born, and Mary and I soon found the actual house in which he entered this world. Quite unpretentious, it was in a narrow street not far from where our ship was berthed. We found Corsica to be largely unexploited. The countryside was beautiful and it is only a matter of time before it becomes a major tourist attraction.

At sea once again, we headed for Spain and the city of Barcelona. Here, our ship was able to berth almost in the city centre which was great for shore excursions. Having been there before, it was interesting to see any changes. One thing was guaranteed, its 'new' cathedral would still not have been finished, and it wasn't! Our trip back to the UK went smoothly with a call again in Lisbon en route. Our ship was excellent.

A form of road transport Mary and I have used a lot is by utilising luxury coaches. One of the best holidays we have had was when we travelled to the Italian Dolomites, passing through the Euro Tunnel, crossing France, Switzerland and Austria. From our base near Marmolada and Cavalese, we drove down into the Tirento Valley along a road which caused the hairs on the back of the neck to stand out. At one bend it was like looking down from a 'plane into the valley way down below, with a sheer drop which left nothing to the imagination. Our driver, from Swansea, did a magnificent job in circumnavigating this stretch of road several times during our stay. We visited Lake Garda and Venice. This was our first visit to this renowned city, and we had quite a surprise when we arrived there. Getting off our ferry, it was like arriving in Blackpool. Crowds of people thronged the quays and we had to fight our way to get on a gondola, which we eventually did. The ensuing 'voyage' was enjoyable as we were punted up the Grand Canal, the gondola rocking in the wake of fast craft whizzing by making us hold on to the sides. A chap from Bridgend, who was a 'shipmate' with us in the gondola, put his camera down momentarily and the next minute it had plopped into the water, emulating the *Titanic*.

The other memorable visit to Italy was when we went to stay in Sant Agata on the fringes of Sorrento. From our hotel we had views across the Bay of Naples to Vesuvius. Every morning we woke to the clarion call of a cockerel doing a Pavarotti. Sorrento is a charming town full of character and a place I would go back to again. From there we hydrofoiled to Capri and ascended a precipice by road cut out of the face of the island. Another life-threatening situation! When we got to the top the views were worth the climb. I was particularly keen to see Gracie Fields' old home as I have always been a fan of hers and regard her as one of the world's best singers. I was brought up on 'Sally' and 'Sing as we Go.' Her songwriter and pianist was the talented Welshman, Harry Parr Davies, from Briton Ferry.

After viewing her house, Mary and I sat on a seat watching holi-day-makers walking past. A group came towards us and Mary said, "Isn't that Cecil and Janet?" I looked, and sure as eggs, it was Mary's cousin Cecil and his wife walking towards us. Imagine the surprise and delight when they saw us. They too were on holiday and had no idea we were in the vicinity. To cap it all, they were staying in the next hotel to us in Sant Agata. Cecil was born in Henllan and had a distinguished war career in the RAF. His boyhood pal, also from Henllan, was my former colleague and General Manager of the Ford Motor Company, Sam Rees, whose top of the range Ford car bore the number plate EJ 1.

Trips down the Amalfi Coast by coach and boat were undertaken and the sight of our Italian coach driver negotiating a hairpin bend with no crash barrier and at the same time conducting a con-versation on his mobile 'phone, was very reassuring. The jewel in the crown of our stay was the visit to Pompeii. This did live up to prior expectations and even exceeded them. To see a town frozen in time as a result of the eruption of Vesuvius in AD 79 was an experience. Bodies looking as if they had been sculpted from stone were in dramatic poses and the buildings were in terrific condition and bore testimony to the culture of the Roman Empire. Lead piping in the gardens of Pompeii had been imported from Britain and this probably originated in mid-Wales. Gold from Dolaucothi had certainly found its way to Rome. Carmarthen was a major player in Roman times and of course Roman influence can still be seen throughout Wales and particularly South and West Wales.

Food for Thought

ROM MY CHILDHOOD DAYS I had always thought that life was passing quickly. Today, even more so as one gets older and can see the inevitable approaching. During my short stint in life I have witnessed a decided change in living conditions and attitudes in Britain which has not improved the future outlook for future generations. Undoubtedly, the standard of living has improved beyond belief compared to my parents' time. Good health care, nutrition and employment standards are more or less taken for granted and a get it now and pay later philosophy is the norm. The blot on the horizon, however, is the overcrowding of these small islands which make up the UK. Uncontrolled immigration will be the death knell of British life as we have known it for generations. Non-integration of ethnic groups not able to converse in English and pursuing religious dogma, especially in segregated schools, is storing up trouble and unrest. What is worrying is the fact that open discussion of these topics is regarded as taboo, par-ticularly by the political 'Establishment.' To even mention the name of Enoch Powell is likely to damn one for eternity! Incidentally, Enoch Powell had strong connections with Llandeilo through marriage between his family and that of Llandeilo local veterinary surgeon, Emrys Bowen.

Ever since Adam was a boy, and before, religion has been the catalyst for most of the trouble that has afflicted the world. Organ-ised religious followings have only come into being in comparatively recent times in relation to the physical creation of the planet. Arising from primitive times they were and are a means of keeping people in order and subjugating free thought. You do not have to attend a church, chapel or mosque in order to lead a caring respon-

302

sible life. Commonsense is the best 'religion' anyone can follow. Fear of the unknown is the driving force behind most religious support and it acts as a good insurance policy for getting to the 'next place,' wherever that is.

When asked do I believe in God, I reply it depends what you mean by 'God.' I cannot believe in something I do not know anything about, but it also means I do not disbelieve either – in other words I am an agnostic not an atheist. Furthermore, there is not a living person who can tell us who or what God is. Nobody who has died has ever come back to tell us all what happens after death. The big question is why are we here? Whatever created *everything* does not appear to have done a very good job. People start deteriorating from the minute they are born. Teething problems followed by adolescent ailments, illness, baldness, suicides, murders and all sorts of crimes, 'natural' disasters, global warming afflict us, eventually leading to final cosmic destruction. Every living thing eats each other to survive. Cats pounce on mice, big fish eat little fish, big birds kill little birds, spiders eat flies and, until recent times, man ate man! Just to mention a few. Humans are not superior to animals in the order of things as is borne out by trying to reason with a crocodile if you happen to fall into his watery domain. Not even vegetarians or vegetables can escape this 'eat your neighbour' regime.

Nobody has a clue how *everything* started. There is the 'big bang' theory. Where did the ingredients to cause a 'bang' come from? Who made the ingredients? If there is a 'force' behind it all, and where did it originate and from what? What is 'space?' If 'God' made it, who made 'God?' These are all impossible questions to answer. If we are programmed like a computer, then we will just have to follow the obscure masterplan and have no choice in the matter. The only reasoning which seems clear to me is that if the idea was to make a perfect world, why bother to make it in the first place? Surely *nothing* is perfection in itself! One of the pleasures in life I have is to have a good old exchange of views with Jehovah's Witnesses when they knock on my front door. It never ceases to surprise me how gullible people are, believing implicitly in what they are taught. Still, the whole mystic business keeps scientists, clergymen, researchers and philosophers out of the dole queue!

Looking at matters more down to earth as it were, after many years associated with business and local government, I see the possible break up of the United Kingdom as a real threat. United we stand, divided we fall, is a saying which is relevant to England, Wales, Scotland and Northern Ireland, and the devolution process could be the thin edge of the wedge. As a keen genealogist, the population of theses islands are a mixed bag of breeding anyhow, which has produced a strong 'native' population as a result of this hybrid vigour. Talking shops resulting from devolution and 'jobs for the boys' are the most significant outcomes of the devolution process, plus countless millions spent on building new glass and concrete monoliths at a cost always exceeding their original estimates.

Farming has been let down badly. Who would have guessed that the British Government would be responsible for letting Foot and Mouth Disease loose on the countryside without adequate compensation? Agriculture is of no consequence nowadays with supermarkets holding the reins – woe betide if the UK ever finds that it runs short of food due to external happenings or even a balance of payments problem. Nothing grows in a concrete jungle. Farming gets a bad Press. I've long thought that agricultural shows tend to show farming in a poor light, as they depict country folk as having a whale of a time eating burgers and ice-cream, watching individuals trotting round a ring clutching a horse and wearing a bowler hat (not the horse!). Rows of gleaming cars in the car-parks alongside add to the false air of prosperity and opulence. Shows should concentrate more on the economic situations confronting the industry, concentrating rather less on the doubtful and opinionated 'beauty' aspects of cattle and horse exhibiting and highlighting yokels climbing up greasy poles.

On the home front, 2005 ended with an event which brightened up our lives when Karen gave birth to our youngest grandchild at

Glangwili Hospital in Carmarthen. Born on September 11th, David and Karen named him Oliver Rhys Harris. 'Ollie' has since transformed all our lives and our baby-sitting days commenced all over again.

Mary and I had visited Canada briefly when we first visited the Niagara Falls. We decided we would like to see more of that country and so we set off in 2006 to see both east and west of that vast country. We flew to Toronto with Air Canada and stayed in the centre of the city not far from the CN Tower. One of the first things we did was to go to the top of this edifice and what a view we saw from the observation area. I even persuaded Mary to stand on the glass floor panel, looking down for all of one second! We found Toronto to be a beautiful city, clean with marvellous walks in the parkland alongside Lake Ontario.

We had links with the area, as some years previously we had acted as hosts to some young rugby players from Markham, Toronto, who had come to Llandeilo to play against Tre-Gib County Secondary School. From Toronto, we went by train to Montreal our next stop. I found Montreal to be more commercial than Toronto and bustling. The French element was surprisingly strong and you could almost think you were in Paris. We visited Quebec, another French stronghold. Quebec was a delightful city full of character and history. We absorbed the stories of the storming of the city by the British in the past and admired the picturesque buildings alongside the St. Lawrence Seaway.

From Montreal we flew right across Canada to Calgary in Alberta. A coach tour around the town took in the site of the famous 'Stampede,' and a trip to Fort Calgary was an experience not to be missed. It was at Fort Calgary that the noted Canadian Mounted Police was established. The 'Mounties' museum contained a lot of artefacts relating to the period, including the names of some Welsh immigrants who had joined up and subsequently received land as payment and settled in Canada to farm. From Calgary we drove by coach to our next stop, Banff, set in the heart of the Rocky Mountains. This was Canada as I imagined it to be, spectacular scenery with snow-capped mountains all around. We were warned not to wander too far off the beaten tracks for fear of bears, but for the entire time we were in Canada we did not see a single such animal. Cable car rides to the upper reaches of the mountains revealed breathtaking scenery and the highlight was our visit to Lake Louise which was frozen solid. The backcloth of snow-covered jagged glaciers and mountains was out of this world, needless to say the cameras worked overtime.

The next stage took our coach through the Rocky Mountain National Park to Kelowna in British Columbia. This town on the edge of a huge lake some eighty miles long, was an extemely busy place with a strong commercial background. After a short stay here, we drove on down to Vancouver passing through small towns and large horticultural units. We skirted round Vancouver aiming for the ferry terminal for us to embark on our visit to Vancouver Island. The biggest surprise we had in Canada was the antagonism felt by Canadians against Americans. They hardly had a good word to say for them. It stemmed from the old settler days when the border between Canada and the USA was being drawn up. It appears the Americans tried to 'pinch' more land than they were entitled, even today, this dictated the route of the ship as it zigzagged a dog leg route to avoid crossing into US territorial waters and causing friction between the two countries.

Arriving at Victoria we were struck by the beauty of the Island and the fabulous houses to be seen everywhere. Victoria itself is a thriving dynamic place with a booming tourist industry. The waterfront was like Clapham Junction with ships and yachts coming and going and seaplanes taking off and landing every few minutes. Live entertainment was everywhere and the atmosphere was one of relaxation and also pleasurable activity, the place reeked of class. On a guided tour of Victoria, our tour manager told us that when Vancouver Island was first settled, Welshmen came there to see if it was feasible to set up a Welsh settlement. For one reason or another, this did not materialise. What a superb new 'Little Wales' this would have been. It would have knocked spots off Patagonia!

A visit both Mary and I will always remember was seeing the Butchart Gardens just outside Victoria. Developed from a limestone quarry by Jennie Butchart in the early 1900s, the displays of flowers, shrubs and trees were breathtaking, one mass of glorious colours. The sunken garden and the rose areas were laden with perfume and the pathways and rest areas were tastefully designed and immaculate. It all started as a hobby by Jennie and grew and grew like 'Topsy.' Our 'voyage' back to Vancouver, passing pretty little islands en route, went without any interference from American warships, and we set out to explore this noted city.

Throughout British Columbia I was amazed to see so many Union Jacks flying. They were depicted on buses, advertisements and in house gardens. Vancouver was no exception. We even saw cricket matches in progress in Stanley Park and the feeling of Britishness was everywhere, despite the display of Totem Poles in the Park. The name Vancouver itself was derived from Captain George Vancouver, a British naval officer who died in England comparatively unknown in the 1700s. It was not a city I would rave about and would not wish to go out of my way to visit again. So, we bade a fond farewell to Canada and flew back again by Air Canada to the UK. This airline left a lot to be desired and was quite the worst I have ever flown with, its incompetence had to be seen to be believed, but that's another story. At least we arrived home safe and sound.

Life on the farm at Tŷ Coch continued as before. The grazing of cattle in the summer and sheep in the winter ensured a fairly hassle free existence. With more time on one's hands, thoughts turn to more exploratory excursions overseas while factors such as one's health and inclinations allow us to withstand the trials and tribulations of travel. Motoring has always, and still does, play a major role in my life. Shortly after moving to our new bungalow, I sold the Ford Probe and purchased a two litre turbocharged diesel Rover 75. I had long admired the 75 and having had Rover cars previously, I fancied this latest product to roll off the Rover lines. Unfortunately, at this time the Rover Car Company went bust and the entire marque was sold to the Chinese. This did not deter me and in fact helped me to get a better deal on the purchase of my 75. A deal I have not regretted. The Rover is a delight to drive, rides smoothly and has all the power and economy of fuel anyone could wish for. Jeremy Clarkson and his team did their level best to run down British cars and succeeded, in my opinion, in bringing about the demise of Rover. 'Top Gear' does nothing to improve family motoring, concentrating as it does on cars that are little more than Formula One substitutes, they do not have to get out of first gear to achieve the lawful maximum speed of 60 mph on ordinary roads and 70 mph on dual carriageways and motorways. They are priced at figures which would buy a country estate. What a farce!

At the same time Mary changed her faithful Fiesta for a Ford Ka. What a little stunner this car has proved to be. With a wheel in each corner it holds the road like glue and can be parked on a postage stamp. Everything is round on it, including the instruments and the contours of the bodywork and it is an extremely easy car to clean. It does a sterling job in travelling over farm roads and has a good ground clearance. The Ka easily outshines the old Mini and, I think, will go down in the annals of motoring history as one of the most successful cars ever produced.

One place we could not get to by car was Australia. Some years ago, Karen's grandfather and grandmother had emigrated from Yorkshire to Australia where they had set up home near Sydney, in the Blue Mountains. Grandfather Stothard was to celebrate his 90th birthday in 2007 and Karen thought it would be opportune to take his new great-grandson, Ollie, to see him and her grandmother. Mary and I thought that this would be a good opportunity for us to visit Australia at the same time, we going our separate way to cover most of Australia and then rendezvousing with David and Karen and Ollie in Sydney later.

We didn't fancy flying straight down under in one go, so we arranged for a stopover in Singapore on the way out. We flew with Qantas and duly arrived at Singapore Airport after a ten hour flight.

Boy, what an airport! This was the best we had ever seen, spacious and the décor was fabulous with flowering shrubs, gleaming marble and landscaped to perfection. Everywhere was spotless, you could almost eat off the floor. The staff were friendly and courteous and we had a quick, smooth easy passage with our baggage. Our car drive to our hotel was along avenues of trees and banks of flowers everywhere. What a wonderful first impression of Singapore for a pair of seasoned travellers.

Our hotel was situated in the heart of Singapore within a stone's throw of the famous Raffles Hotel. Sir Thomas Stanford Raffles, who put Singapore on the map in 1819, left a lasting impression, his name cropping up everywhere from streets to parks and build-ings. A short walk from the hotel was Fort Canning Park where Raffles' house was sited. This park was in an elevated position with good views across the hinterland. Mary and I spent several hours sitting under the trees there listening to the breeze stirring the chimes hanging from branches. Singapore's Masonic Lodge was on the edge of the park and heading the list of prominent Freemasons who attended was Sir Thomas himself!

A cable car ride over to the neighbouring island of Sentosa pro-vided a panoramic aerial view of Singapore, and the island proved to be a great attraction for tourists. Dolphin demonstrations were the norm and a wonderful 'Underwater World' teeming with all kinds and species of fish was a highlight. An illuminated 'fountain' display in the night rounded off an enjoyable visit to Sentosa. A boat trip passed the giant lion perpetually spouting water from its mouth was interesting, the lion being synonymous with the name Singapore which means in Indian, 'home of the Lion' or 'Lion City.' It seems early settlers thought they saw a lion when they arrived, but some believe they were mistaken and in fact saw a Tiger; however, 'Lion' won the day. The Indian influence is strong – many from that country were brought to work there by the British and even today, it is popular with Indians as the route from India is well blessed by convenient and regular air schedules.

When I lived in St. Albans during the 39/45 war, I was very aware of the Japanese conquest of Singapore. The dramatic surrender of the British forces was etched on my mind and the sinking of our battleships in that area was a blow to our pride. Pictures of the surrender which took place at Raffles Hotel to a gloating Japanese military were hard to swallow. It was therefore a must for me to visit this historic site to see where all this took place. It was with a strong sense of history that Mary and I walked through the entrance to Raffles Hotel into the tree-lined courtyard and then to the main building. After indulging in a delicious tea, we walked around taking in the atmosphere, reminders of the war were everywhere. The redeeming factor in all this was, of course, that the Japanese lost the war and their forces in that region themselves surrendered to the British, in of all places, Raffles Hotel. If only those walls could talk!

After visiting a pewter workshop and some of the very tasteful art galleries to be found in this spotless city, free from crime and which has a no tipping policy, be it taxi drivers or waiters, we bade Singapore farewell and made for its fabulous airport for the next stage of our journey to Australia. We would certainly visit Singapore again should the opportunity ever arise. Despite the heat, we did not encounter a single fly during our stay! Nor did we encounter any lions or tigers!

Our arrival in Perth in Western Australia was in glorious weather with wall-to-wall blue sky and sunshine. The city is pretty big and miles from any other similar place. Its surrounded by nothing, especially when going inland, and it is a thriving bustling city. The view from Kings Park is spectacular, looking down on the city with the boats passing below on the Swan River. It was in Kings Park that we had our first brief glimpse of a kangaroo which disappeared in a blink of an eye. Perhaps it was the appearance of two policemen riding bicycles which startled it.

This was our first visit to Australia and on our coach trip to Fremantle we had a good opportunity to see Perth's suburbia and all that lay between it and Fremantle. Having been a fan of 'Neighbours' since it was first screened on TV, I was surprised to see how close together the houses were and the absence of swimming pools. Having nearly cooked in the heat on a quick visit to the beach we struck up a conversation with a coach driver. It turned out that he did his driving job part time in addition to running a small farm. When he discovered my connection with farming he couldn't stop talking. The gist of his drift was that livestock farming was difficult around the Perth area and that prices for stock were at rock bottom plus having scarce water resources which made life very difficult. We returned to Perth by boat travelling up the Swan River. This was a very pleasant cruise and we were able to see the luxury homes lining the river. They did have swimming pools!

From Perth we flew inland right across the Australian interior to Ayres Rock passing over mile upon mile of scrubland and rock outcrops. The 'airport' at Ayres Rock was more or less a hangar and a runway in the middle of nowhere. Prior to our arrival there had been a scare of an outbreak of Legionnaires' disease of which we were not made aware until after we had left. A trip to the Olgas, a nearby range of 28 spectacular rock domes followed before we went to see Ayres Rock at sunset. This gigantic Aboriginal shrine is a sandstone rock two miles long, 1,000 ft high and six miles around the base. As the sun sets, the light effect is unusual. However, we were foiled as a constant drizzle marred the scene and the sun was hidden. Not to worry, the sunrise was reputed to be even more wondrous, and so at the crack of dawn Mary and I set out for the Rock with cameras at the ready. It was still cloudy and sunrise was fast approaching. We, in common with all the other onlookers, were about to give it up as a bad job when, suddenly, the clouds parted and the sun shone through for a matter of two or three minutes at the most. The Rock lit up as if it was glowing and I captured it on digital for posterity. What a relief!

A coach ride of over 200 miles across the outback to Alice Springs was next on the agenda. We travelled for miles on the Trans Australia Highway which went from Adelaide to Darwin, without passing a single vehicle. This really was the back of beyond. Occasionally we passed a 'farm,' usually about the size of Powys, but for most of the journey we were on our own. Not the place for a fanbelt to go! Alice Springs was to be our base for a few days and it was quite a distinctive and colourful town. We were now in the very geographical centre of Australia and the heart of the Aboriginal community.

Attending demonstrations of their culture, including the blowing of the didgeridoo, reminded me of Rolf Harris. The Aborigine is a remarkable individual with a unique culture with an appreciation of visual art based on the colours and topography of the Australian environment. They are also a sensitive people. We were advised not to take photographs of them face to face as they could be 'difficult.' The future development of Alice Springs is restricted by the fact that the town is surrounded by Aboriginal land which does not allow expansion, hence property such as housing tends to be expensive. In addition, a strong US military presence plays an important role in the prosperity of the town.

An unusual location we visited was the Flying Doctor Base which was the nerve centre for a medical help service covering a mind-boggling area. It made the UK look like a postage stamp. It was here also in Alice Springs that the 'School of the Air' education of children by means of wireless was operated. Children in outback farms and outposts were able to access education by this means and the examination results were said to be outstanding. I used to think Rhandirmwyn was remote, not any more! They were talking in terms of hundreds of miles in Alice Springs and accepted it as normal. We visited the MacDonnell range of mountains to see the Standley Chasm where we saw our first wallabies close to in the wild. A final call at the 'Old Telegraph Station' from which the town sprang and which is preserved like a time capsule, completed our stay which had been very enjoyable and informative.

From Alice Springs in the Northern Territory, we flew to Cairns in North Queensland. Again flying for hours over largely uninhabited terrain. It began getting greener as we approached Cairns Airport.

Cairns is a prosperous coastal city which gets its fair share of tourists. Our hotel, close to the beach, was spacious and as such places in the tropical regions are planned; our rooms were huge and fitted out with copious ceiling cooling fans. We were warned to be careful about going on the beach or promenade during the night or early morning as crocodiles sometimes liked to emerge from the sea and take a stroll along the beach.

Mary and I boarded our coach for an expedition into the rainforests of the Daintree National Park and travelled on the Skyrail Rainforest Cableway from Caravonica to Kuranda. This cableway carried us high above the rainforest for nearly five miles, and what a view we had. The undulating tree canopy could be seen as far as the eye could see, one mass of green. We passed over the Barron Falls, a gushing, cascading river with foaming rapids way below us. We reached Kuranda, a small town full of character and quaint shops. We were advised to try some ice-cream from a mobile stall in the side street. This stall was owned and manned by an ex-merchant navy man and the ice-cream was made by his wife and was reputed to taste heavenly. We found the stall and bought some. While being served the owner said, "You're from Wales?" I affirmed and he proceeded to tell us that in his sea-going days he had shipped in and out of Swansea and had lived there for several years before returning to his native Australia. He said he intended selling ice-cream for a few more years before retiring and letting his wife take over.

It was while we were in northern Queensland that we visited the really classy small town of Port Douglas. The type of craft in the marina there indicated the prosperity of this area. With its tasteful shopping arcades and sumptuous houses this was quite the most impressive tourist destination Mary and I had seen so far on this trip. Port Douglas is situated about 70km north of Cairns and achieved some notoriety for being the place where Steve Irwin, known as 'Crocodile Hunter,' met his death at Batt Reef off Port Douglas in September, 2006, after being stung by a Stingray. US President Bill Clinton and his wife Hilary chose Port Douglas as the only place to have a vacation when on their tour of Australia in 1996.

Cairns is the popular departure point for visits to the Great Barrier Reef. A fast boat trip soon brought us to Green Island situated on the Reef. With its sandy coves and superb walks this was an idyllic spot with plenty of trees and as its name implies, an abundance of greenery. Feeding the crocodiles in their special enclosure was an educational experience and we were thankful for the stout fences between them and us. Our trip on to the Great Barrier Reef from the island was almost even more spine chilling. The youngster piloting our glass-bottomed boat was so busy giving a running commentary as we headed out over the Reef, that he didn't see a large mooring post sticking out of the sea, and we collided with it, damaging the boat and throwing everybody into confusion. Luckily, nobody was injured and we were able to proceed to view the coral and sea life through the glass bottom.

While on the subject of crocodiles, when in Daintree we went on a special excursion on the river which was reputed to be one of the most heavily stocked crocodile rivers in Australia. We cruised for a considerable distance up and down to no avail, we did not see a single croc! The river warden said that this was most unusual and that they must have all been snoozing on the riverbed. He did go on to say that if one of us fell in he could guarantee that we would soon see a very lively specimen. We had also been warned to apply plenty of fly repellent while in the region, but to our surprise, we hardly saw a fly during the whole time we were in Australia, nor a snake or a spider!

On our next flight we headed south for the city of Sydney with eager anticipation. Our hotel was within short walking distance of the Sydney Harbour Bridge and our first glimpse of this famous landmark, together with the Opera House, was quite a thrill. A tour around Sydney by coach took in most of the city including a stop at Bondi Beach. What an anticlimax that proved to be. We were expecting a huge sweep of sandy beach with surf as high as Blackpool Tower and bronzed lifeguards patrolling the beach. Not a bit of it. Instead, we found a very ordinary looking beach set in a built-up housing area, which Rest Bay in Porthcawl would run rings around. Botany Bay was another nonevent. In fact, the locals did not regard it as of much significance and did not have the same romantic historical association with it as I did, having been brought up on Chartist folklore and the transporting of John Frost and other leading militant Welsh Chartists in the nineteenth century.

David, Karen and our grandson Oliver had also booked into our hotel and we had a splendid reunion in the hotel foyer. David had hired a car and acted as our 'chauffeur' for our stay in Sydney. Visits to the Harbour Bridge and the Opera House followed and a boat trip to Manley was reminiscent of crossing the Bay of Biscay on the QE2, the ferry boat rocked and rolled like nobody's business and Karen was quite glad to reach terra firma. I was kept busy walking Ollie up and down the steps of the Opera House! He walked miles in Sydney. A pleasant memory is of us all drinking coffee on the harbour quayside watching the ferries come and go nonstop.

Karen's grandfather was celebrating his 90th birthday and we all drove out to the Blue Mountains outside Sydney to see both him and Karen's grandmother. On the way to Penrith, David deviated from the route to show us a small place in which he thought we might be interested. Imagine our delight and surprise when the name of the district appeared. None other than 'LLANDILO.' Spelt the old way. This spelling can still be seen on the wall of the old Post Office in Llandeilo today. We went on to meet Karen's grandparents at a country club for lunch and had a pleasant time. I was most interested to hear Karen's grandmother talking about her cousin Monica Dickens and her forebear, Charles. The view over the 'Three Sisters' in the Blue Mountains was spectacular, you can see for miles to the distant horizon with its namesake blue haze.

The time came for us to leave David and family in Sydney for the next stage of our trip. This was a coach drive to Canberra, the country's capital city. En route we stopped for lunch at a sheep shearing station which also laid on a sheep shearing demonstration.

This was quite amusing as the 'expert' shearer succeeded in 'nicking' each sheep he handled and had a dog which was a bit too enthusiastic, scattering the flock left right and centre. He should come to Wales to see how to do the job properly.

Canberra is a beautifully landscaped city with some magnificent buildings. The seat of Australian Government, the Government Building, is an architectural gem and we enjoyed exploring its interior. I have always been interested in Australian political history especially as one of its illustrious Prime Ministers was a Welshman . . . William Morris Hughes, known as 'Billy' Hughes. His photograph and data were prominently featured in Government House, especially as he still remains the longest serving member of the Australian Parliament (51 years). Born in 1862, his father was from Holyhead and his mother from Llansantffraid in Montgomeryshire, Powys, both were Welsh speakers. After his mother died, Billy Hughes went to live with his mother's relatives in Llansantffraid becoming quite a fluent Welsh speaker and later emigrated to Australia in 1884. He died in 1952.

The Welsh/Australian political tradition is still being maintained. Julia Gillard, born and bred in Barry, South Wales, became Deputy Prime Minister of Australia on December 3rd, 2007. She emigrated with her parents to Australia in the 1960s and ultimately became a trade union lawyer, spending most of her adult life in Melbourne. She is reputed to be a 'lively' 46-year-old red-head, who does not suffer fools gladly.

The 1939/45 war is not forgotten by Australians. The Australian War Memorial Museum in Canberra is a 'must' visit for anyone going to that city. With its exhibits of war memorabilia which include a complete Lancaster bomber and a Mosquito fighter as well as Japanese 'planes and even a Japanese submarine, this museum keeps alive the sacrifices Australians made during the conflict. It was a revelation to see the number of schoolchildren visiting it and attending the sounding of 'The Last Post' by the bugler at predetermined regular times.

Travelling from Sydney to Canberra and continuing towards Melbourne, the sight of parched brown countryside was a sight to behold. It had not rained for months, years in some parts, and cattle were being fed on supplementary bought in feed which economically could not be sustainable. What the future holds for Australian agriculture without adequate water supplies I shudder to think. It was remarkable to see huge herds of Angus cattle doing as well as they looked to be doing in the circumstances and says much for the versatility of British breeds of cattle. The shortage of water will be the Achilles heel of future Australian prosperity.

About midway on the main Sydney to Melbourne highway, we entered a township in the heart of the countryside and could not believe our eyes. Right in the middle of the town named Holbrook was a full blown 90 metres long submarine surrounded by flower beds.

Apparently, the town had close connections with the navy and submarines and was named after a 1914/18 war hero submariner, Lieutenant Norman Holbrook, who was awarded the VC in the Turkish campaign. When the submarine *HMAS Otway* was decommissioned in 1968 it was offered to the town of Holbrook by the Australian Navy. The cost of moving it inland was prohibitive for the town and the widow of Lieutenant Holbrook came to the rescue – Gundula Holbrook donated a six figure sum to facilitate the move. This was completed in 1995.

With an overnight stay at the town of Albury, which straddled the New South Wales/Victoria boundary, we were amused by the good natured banter between the inhabitants of these two states. The New South Wales folk called the Victorians 'cowboys,' a nickname which hived back to olden times when there was intense rivalry between them. A rivalry which was reflected in the interstate railway, each having a different gauge terminating at Albury Railway Station, necessitating passenger changing trains for through journeys, a state of affairs which still exists!

In my youth, I loved reading stories of the Aussie folk hero, Ned Kelly. On a par with Robin Hood and Twm Shôn Catti, Ned's story was larger than life and I looked forward to visiting his past haunts. I was not disappointed. On our continued drive from Albury to Melbourne we came to the small town of Glenrowan. This was Ned Kelly's home and the scene of his last stand with the law in 1880. Born in 1865 and supposedly hanged in 1880, Ned Kelly 'lives' on in Glenrowan. A whopping great statue six metres high of him clad in his iron mask and armed, hits you in the eye when you enter the main street. A museum and shops selling Kelly memorabilia dominates this small town. Even now, almost 100 years after his death, some maintain that he was not actually hanged in Melbourne Jail in 1880, but did a deal with his jailers who were sympathetic to him, and ex-convicts themselves and allegedly letting him go free. Nobody saw him dead and no one has ever seen his grave or knows where he was buried. It was said that his last words before being 'hanged' were 'such is life.' Hence the saying which is commonplace today.

Glenrowan is about 200 miles from Melbourne and driving down there was a continuation of the drought conditions we had seen in NSW. Melbourne is a large city with strong sporting connections. This was the place I has been looking forward to visiting for a very long time in order to meet my relative, Elwyn Squires. Elwyn's folk, the Llewelyn family, had emigrated from Merthyr Tydfil in the 1800s and settled in Victoria. She was related to me through my great-great-grandmother, Jane Davies, née Llewelyn, of Waunwyllt, Merthyr Tydfil. Elwyn's son Raymond had visited us at Tŷ Coch some years back, as had her daughter-in-law, Bindi, formerly married to Stewart, Elwyn's other son.

We had a marvellous welcome from Elwyn and the family. She drove Mary and me around Melbourne including a splendid meal at the Melbourne Casino and entertained us royally at her home in Cranbourne a little way out of the city. She and her husband Laurie ran a truck recovery and haulage business and her close relatives farmed extensively in the area on a large scale. We visited one of the farms which was right on the coast in the direction of Phillip Island; here too, the pasture was parched and brown. With names like

Bronwen and Owen in her family, there was no doubting their Welsh origin.

It was with some sadness that we bade Elwyn and Australia farewell when we boarded our long flight to Hong Kong via Sydney. It had been a trip of a lifetime and one Mary and I would not have missed for anything. It had come up to and exceeded expectations but is not the place to go to just for a weekend. Weatherwise, it had been perfect, though the locals would have preferred a deluge lasting months. Such is life!

Our arrival in Hong Kong was quite dramatic. As we approached the airport we descended from a brilliant blue sky to become shrouded in a murky smog which thickened as we approached the runway. It was so thick that at point of touchdown we could not even see the wings of our aircraft. Eventually, it did lift enough for us to see our surroundings en route to our hotel in Kowloon.

A regular shuttle service from the hotel to the ferry terminals enabled us to see this bustling place. At the terminal, was one of the best shopping precincts one would ever wish to see. Tastefully designed, this high-class shopping mecca boasted outlets of most of the world's designer labels and was spotless. We toured most of Hong Kong travelling by coach through the tunnels linking Hong Kong Island. An interesting feature of these tunnels was that the structure itself was suspended above the seabed in free water, due to the depth of the sea, a marvellous piece of engineering. On one occasion, Mary and I were sitting near the seafront when a group of students approached us and said they were doing a project on tourism in Hong Kong, and asked us for our opinion as obvious visitors followed by a request for them to be photographed with us, which we gladly did. Funnily enough, exactly the same thing happened over at Repulse Bay, this time a younger set of schoolgirls neatly dressed in school uniform, asked if they too could be photographed with us. Such is fame!

One of the best places to view Hong Kong is Victoria Park which is a high vantage point above the. Metropolis. The day we went there it was quite cool and looking down we could see the sky-scrapers looming out of the low cloud and mist. Walking the streets the air was not that good either and it was quite common to see locals wearing face masks to protect themselves. A trip to Aberdeen, home to a thriving community of people living in a variety of junks, sampans and boats followed, and we cruised among them enabling us to see a traditional way of Chinese life, which the locals told us, was declining rapidly due to increasing prosperity, enabling them to secure property on dry land. A highlight of our visit was the dinner we had in the revolving restaurant in what was the tallest building in Hong Kong. Looking out at the twinkling lights was like being in fairyland and this experience was repeated when we took a night-time boat trip around the harbour.

Arriving back safely in the UK, flying with Qantas, we had travelled with this airline on nine individual flights embracing Singapore, Australia and Hong Kong. Their service was excellent with no delays and punctual arrivals, all contributing to the making of a fantastic holiday.

What of the future? Any more exciting trips in the pipeline one may ask? None at the time of writing this. The year 2008 is now with us. Mary and I look forward to enjoying the experience of seeing our grandchildren blossom forth. What the future holds for them and the rest of mankind is unpredictable. I can only hope that the sole 'religion' which matters, namely commonsense, will prevail. Good public relations is the key to a harmonious lifestyle whatever one's colour or creed, be it institutional or personal. One thing I have learned in this life is the predictability of the unpredictable in mankind. Finally, I again quote Ned Kelly, who summed it all up in his famous last words . . . "Such is life."